Tulane Studies in Political Science

VOLUME XIV

College and University Government

A Handbook of Principle and Practice

by

HENRY L. MASON

TULANE UNIVERSITY

NEW ORLEANS

1972

*This volume may be purchased for $ 4.00, plus postage,
from the Department of Political Science,
Tulane University, New Orleans, Louisiana 70118.*

ISBN 90 247 1195 9

Distributed by
The American Association of
University Professors
with the support of
The Esso Education Foundation

PRINTED IN THE NETHERLANDS

TABLE OF CONTENTS

Acknowledgments   VII

Introduction   IX

CHAPTER 1. PRINCIPLES OF COLLEGE AND UNIVERSITY
GOVERNMENT: A GUIDE THROUGH SOME RECENT
LITERATURE   I

A. The University as a Decision-Making Milieu   I
   1. Non-Hierarchical Organization   I
   2. "Collegialization" of Decision-Making   4
   3. An Untenable Dichotomy: Academic vs. Financial
      Affairs   7
   4. The Culture of the University and University Govern-
      ment   8
   5. Structural Patterns for Government Among Inter-
      dependent Components   12
   6. Ambiguities of University Government   17
   7. The Faculty's Status: Professionals or Employees?   19

B. The Board of Trustees – the Reality of Limited
   Power vs. the Myth of Unlimited Sovereignty   25

C. The Administration – Relationships to the Academic Process   33
   1. The Need for the Administrative Component   33
   2. What Role for the President?   36
   3. Administrative Organization   41

D. The Administration-Faculty Relationship   44
   1. Shared Authority   44
   2. Irritants Between Administration and Faculty   47

E. Faculty Participation in University Government   55
   1. Faculty Participation as a Right and Duty   55
   2. Conditions for Faculty Participation   56
   3. Faculty Reluctance   57
   4. Levels of Faculty Participation   62
   5. Improved Structures for Faculty Participation   65
   6. Roles for the AAUP Chapter   67

F. University Senates 70
 1. Size and Composition 71
 2. The Importance of Administration Membership 73
 3. The Weakness of Senates 75

G. The Department – Core Unit of the Faculty 77

H. Student Participation in Government 81
 1. Reasons for Student Participation 81
 2. Principles and Basic Restrictions 83
 3. Levels of Student Participation 86

CHAPTER 2. PROVISIONS FOR COLLEGE AND UNIVERSITY
GOVERNMENT: A GUIDE THROUGH SOME RECENT CON-
STITUTIONAL DOCUMENTS 91

I. THE FOUR COMPONENTS AND THEIR RELATIONSHIP 91

A. The Board 91
 1. Composition and Overall Organization 91
 2. General Authority 94

B. The Administration 95
 1. Composition and Overall Organization 95
 2. General Authority 97

C. The Faculty 99
 1. Composition and Overall Organization 99
 2. General Authority 101

D. The Students 106

II. STRUCTURES 109

A. System-Level Structures 109
 1. A State College System 110
 2. A State University System in the West 111
 3. A City University System 111
 4. A State University System in the East 112
 5. A Community College System 113
 6. Coordinating Mechanisms 114

B. The General Faculty Assembly 115
 1. Functions 115
 2. Membership 119
 3. Officers 120
 4. Procedures 121
 5. Committees 123

C. The Senate   128
1. Functions   128
2. Membership   135
3. Officers   142
4. Procedures   144
5. Committees   149

D. The College Faculty Assembly   159
1. Functions   159
2. Membership, Officers, Procedures and Committees   161
3. The Graduate Faculty   163

E. The Department   164
1. Functions   164
2. Membership and Officers   165
3. Procedures and Committees   169

F. Constitutional Documents   171
1. Adoption   171
2. Amendment   172

CHAPTER 3. SUGGESTED CONSTITUTIONAL PROVISIONS   175

APPENDICES   200
A. Statement on Government of Colleges and Universities (AAUP)   200
B. Table 1, Report of the Survey Subcommittee of Committee T (AAUP)   211
C. Draft Statement on Student Participation in College and University Government (AAUP)   212
D. Constitution and By-Laws for the Faculty of the Graduate School (Tulane University)   218

Bibliographical References   226

Index of Names   229

Index of Subjects   231

ACKNOWLEDGMENTS

I owe a great debt of gratitude to numerous persons. Louis Joughin of the Washington office of the AAUP generously shared with me his extensive knowledge, his acute sense of academic values and traditions, and his long experience with the AAUP's involvements in problems of university government. Ralph Brown of Yale University, Addison Hickman of Southern Illinois University, and Bert Davis and Larry Poston of the AAUP's Washington office also helped me most significantly with their comments. I appreciate their assistance even more because I am only too aware how much of a burden of duties they were carrying as they undertook the additional one of reading my manuscript. For their sake I wish that this handbook could have made a more original contribution than is indicated by its present scope. Although all of the above persons were either officials or national officers of the AAUP, my book is in no way AAUP-sponsored or AAUP-approved. As a member of its Committee T on College and University Government and as a past member of its national Council, I have of course absorbed many of the Association's doctrines and prejudices, yet the positions taken here are entirely my own and do not reflect in any way an official or unofficial stand of the AAUP.

Valuable assistance was also rendered to me at Tulane University. My colleague Richard P. Adams provided expert advice on all kinds of matters; another colleague, Robert S. Robins, made several useful comments on the manuscript. Gabriele von Massenbach (the present Mrs. Roland Timmerman) was an intelligent, hard-working research assistant whose good judgment showed on many occasions. Last, but not least, the secretarial staff of the department of Political Science – Mrs. Lorena Hawkins, Mrs. Mary Lou Ford, and Mrs. Norma Reed – was as reliable and cooperative as always. Mrs. Reed also assisted with the index.

The financial assistance for this study came mainly from the Esso Education Foundation, through funds administered by the AAUP. Additional assistance was provided by the AAUP (with General Secretary Bert Davis and his staff providing innumerable services) and Tulane University. Again, neither the Esso Education Foundation, nor the AAUP or Tulane, is in any way responsible for what is entirely a private effort on my part.

INTRODUCTION

This handbook is intended to be of assistance to those members of academic institutions who are devising a system of government for their colleges or universities, or applying and adapting a system adopted previously. The advice provided here is conventional in the sense that it is based on the kinds of principles and constitutional arrangements which have been put forward in the United States at least since World War II, with due regard for improvements and innovations of the last few years. No attempt is made to change the basic explicit or implicit patterns of academic government in a direction which would result in altogether novel, unconventional models. There may be a place for the construction of such "revolutionary" models, but not in this handbook. Thus, there are only sporadic references to collective bargaining as a form of, or part of, university government. Faculties in the United States have yet to accumulate meaningful experience in this sphere, and it is certainly too early to predict how conventional models of university government will be adapted to widespread use of collective bargaining in academe. Maybe, in the not too distant future, two handbooks will be required, one for the conventional models and one for collective bargaining. Even less allowance is made for various "student power" models which may be emerging on several campuses in the United States.[1] The model presented here suggests considerable participation and influence by students at various levels of academic government, but it also reflects the centrality of the administration and faculty as chief academic decision-makers of the university. Obviously, the conventional model of this handbook cannot provide responses to various kinds of physical force techniques on the part of "student power" activists striking in the utterly helpless milieu of the campus – particularly not if the appli-

[1] "Student power" is more in evidence at numerous Western European and Japanese universities. For example, with respect to Germany, note the account by a sociologist: J. Habermas, *Protestbewegung und Hochschulreform* (Frankfurt am Main: Suhrkamp Verlag, 1969); also, the reports and analyses edited by a historian: E. Nolte, *Deutsche Universitäten 1969* (Marburg, 1970).

cation of such techniques in the university is intended to hit at a "sick" off-campus society. The present author is convinced that academic institutions in the United States are not operating on the brink of a revolutionary situation; if they were, the writing of this handbook would be useless.

The first chapter surveys contemporary writings which provide an insight into basic assumptions and principles of university government. The relevant literature is not extensive, but it does provide a reasonably cohesive picture; surprisingly, perhaps, all kinds of authors display much agreement on fundamental principles supported by the American Association of University Professors.

The second chapter describes a variety of constitutional provisions selected from a sample of some one hundred colleges and universities. This sample was obtained without the slightest pretense at scientific rigor. The analyzed constitutions are recent, and they represent a wide spectrum of types of academic institutions; frequently they were selected because they seemed to reflect, more or less fully, the practices favored by the AAUP. In view of the rapidly changing constitutional scene in many institutions, a constitutional provision cited here may be out of date by the time the handbook appears in print. However, the purpose of the constitutional survey is to illustrate and assist comparison rather than to pinpoint the constitutional realities at a particular institution. Of course, written constitutions cannot reveal the realities of governmental practice. The best constitution may go to waste in an institution whose actual system of government is backward and dysfunctional to academic purposes. Inversely, a primitive, confused constitutional document may not hinder the academic flourishing of another college or university.

Unfortunately, the scope of this handbook did not permit scientific investigation into the conceptual or decision-making reality at academic institutions. The literature in political science or sociology hardly contains substantial studies of the actual processes of government in universities. Professor Gladys Kammerer devoted the Presidential Address at the 1968 Annual Meeting of the Southern Political Science Association to a fervent lament about the failure of political scientists to study "our own political behavior as faculty members within the university context," although the "whole world of campus politics is right at our doors quite literally for systematic study by the political scientist." Yet, "nowhere can one find any study in depth of university faculty senates, bases of representation of colleges in senates, typical cleavages and the kinds of issues which causes cleavages, university faculty committee structures, and behavior within committees" – nor, for example, "any real structural-functional analysis of the university presidency" or "an intellectually respectable analysis of a dean's roles." As Logan Wilson remarked in 1969, "if anybody has ever made a really thoroughgoing empirical study of how decisions are now arrived at on a single American college or university campus, I am unaware of it." [2] Fortunately, the first such studies did appear in 1970. Under the auspices of the Center for Research and Development in Higher Education at Berkeley, three intensive case studies of academic government were undertaken – at Fresno State College, the Twin Cities campus of the University of Minnesota, and the University of California at Berkeley. Moreover, a comparative monograph by T. R. McConnell and Kenneth Mortimer, based on the three case studies, was published in 1971.[3] Some day political scientists or sociologists may produce sophisticated scholarly insights into academic government; perhaps, future versions of this handbook will reflect this urgently needed work.

The "Suggested Constitutional Provisions" which constitute the third chapter do not represent a systematic analysis of policy preferences as molded into "model" constitutional codes. Instead, they constitute a kind of basic amalgam of the principles expressed in the first chapter and the provisions analyzed in the second chapter, by a faculty member who has been a fascinated participant in many areas of university government for far too many years.

Fortunately, a sound guidepost for any discussion of aca-

---

[2] Gladys M. Kammerer, "The State University as a Political System," *Journal of Politics*, May 1969, pp. 295–297, 301; Logan Wilson, "Changing University Governance," *Educational Record*, Fall 1969, pp. 388–404.

[3] W. L. Deegan, T. R. McConnell, K. P. Mortimer, and H. Stull, *Joint Participation in Decision Making: A Study of Faculty Government and Faculty- Administrative Consultation at Fresno State College* (1970); Deegan and Mortimer, *Faculty in Governance at the University of Minnesota* (1970); Mortimer, *Academic Government at Berkeley: The Academic Senate* (1970); McConnell and Mortimer, *The Faculty in University Governance* (1971). (These four monographs were published at the Berkeley Center).

The case studies were based on secondary sources, constitutions, committee minutes and other institutional documents, and more than 200 in-depth, semi-structured interviews with faculty members and administrators.

demic government is provided by the remarkable document which in 1966 was sponsored jointly by the AAUP, the American Council on Education (ACE), and the Association of Governing Boards of Universities and Colleges (AGB). The *Statement on Government of Colleges and Universities* is successful because it provides a succinct model reflecting the existing state of our norms and knowledge. As Louis Joughin, one of the Statement's principal creators, recalls, the AAUP in 1957 began preparation of a document on the role of the faculty in academic government. After six years of work, a draft was approved by the AAUP Council. At about the same time, President John Millett's book, *The Academic Community*, appeared and was read "with enthusiasm" in the Washington office of the AAUP, particularly because of its "conspicuous harmony" with the thoughts expressed in previous years in AAUP circles. As a result, in the spring of 1963, the AAUP's Committee T on College and University Government met in joint session with the Commission on Administrative Affairs of the ACE (which was chaired by John Millett) – the first sitting down together of two bodies with highly similar concerns each of which had been in existence for more than fifty years. Shortly thereafter, the AGB came in too, and in March 1965, a Committee of Nine, representing the national associations of faculty, administration, and trustees, met to consider the preparation of a joint statement on university government. This committee produced a mutually agreed final draft in August 1966, the *Statement on Government of Colleges and Universities*. The Statement was adopted as policy by the AAUP's Council in October 1966, and by the AAUP's Fifty-Third Annual Meeting in April 1967. It was endorsed officially by the Board of Directors of the ACE and the Executive Committee of the AGB in late 1966.[4]

The Statement's basic concept is the principle of shared authority ("Joint Effort") by three components – trustees, administration, and faculty – for the government of the institution, with emphasis falling on the powers of the administration and the faculty. It notes further that students have a stake, and that their role requires further study. Shared au-

---

[4] The ACE Board and the AGB Executive Committee recognized the Statement "as a significant step forward in the clarification of the respective roles of governing boards, faculties, and administrations," and commended it to their members.

thority is essential because "the variety and complexity of the tasks performed by institutions of higher education produce an inescapable interdependence [among the components]." The actual mix of authority "will take a variety of forms appropriate to the kinds of [decision-making] situations encountered." In some situations, the administration will take the initiative with consideration by the faculty at a later stage; in other situations, a first recommendation will be made by the faculty, subject to the endorsement of the president and the trustees. The Statement grants the faculty predominance in certain areas because of its special professional competence and to guarantee academic freedom – for example, in curriculum, methods of instruction and research, degree requirements, appointments, promotions, tenure, and dismissals. In areas in which the administration has a preponderant responsibility, it is given predominance – for example, in over-all leadership and coordination, in planning, in certain aspects of "quality control," in business management, and in the care of physical facilities. Yet, in a true "checks and balances" fashion, the Statement urges joint efforts even where clear predominance is given to one component.

As Sanford Kadish has observed, the model put forward by the Statement exists nowhere perfectly, "but it has tended to be the mode of *rapprochement* between bureaucracy and professionalism in institutions of higher education to which faculties have traditionally aspired." [5] As will be seen below, in the first chapter, the Statement's basic doctrine of joint effort or shared authority is accepted by virtually all writers on university government. Moreover, the survey in the second chapter confirms the influence of this doctrine in actual constitutional provisions; in fact, a number of constitutions contain clauses copied verbatim from the Statement. All in all, the Statement represents a remarkable consensus on principle and practice of college and university government (with some 180,000 printed copies distributed throughout academic institutions during the first thirty months of its existence). To the extent that this handbook is a successful elaboration on the themes of the Statement, it should fulfill its purpose.[6]

---

[5] Sanford H. Kadish, "The Strike and the Professoriate," *AAUP Bulletin*, Summer 1968, p. 163.

[6] The complete text of the Statement is cited in Appendix A of this study.

PRINCIPLES OF COLLEGE AND UNIVERSITY GOVERNMENT: A GUIDE THROUGH SOME RECENT LITERATURE

A. THE UNIVERSITY AS A DECISION-MAKING MILIEU

1. Non-Hierarchical Organization

The university differs radically from most other types of organizations, such as governments, business enterprises, or armies, because of the particular purposes of the academic institution. That purpose comprises two basic aims: to teach students and to advance human learning. Both tasks involve intimate personal relationships – between the professor-teacher and his student, and between the professor-researcher and his subject matter. The heart of the university's "business" is based on individual efforts of teaching, learning, or research. As Burton Clark expressed it, "what the individual professor does on his own, or in the company of a few other workers, is what the organization [the university] sets out to do." [1]

The implications for university government are clear. The people "on top" in an academic institution are not necessarily the trustees, the president, or the deans, but in many situations the professor-teachers in their lecture halls and seminars or the professor-researchers in their studies and laboratories. Decision-making in the university must involve the teacher-researcher "on the assembly line" because he chiefly knows intimately what the "production" of the university is all about; it is his immediate proximity to the personal tensions of learning and scholarly creation which gives legitimacy to much of the decision-making for the academic community.

Burton Clark posited one basic difference between academic organizations and most other organizations: "The need for coordination and integration ... is much lower, almost different in kind." Rational organization in the university requires leaving the professor alone rather than coordinating his efforts.[2] In a similar vein, John Corson emphasized the solitary

---

[1] Burton R. Clark, "Faculty Authority," *AAUP Bulletin*, Winter 1961, pp. 300, 301.

[2] *Ibid.*

and self-directed efforts of the faculty member as compared to the group efforts in business or in government; thus "the lack of programming of academic decisions" is understandable.[3]

Trustees and administrative officers have traditionally delegated to the faculty various degrees of responsibility for decision-making in the university – frequently by custom, sometimes by formal regulation. Often delegation is justified by the peculiar requirements of freedom of speech and thought on the part of the individual faculty member, which call for an autonomous position of the university and its faculty with respect to the power centers of the society in which it operates.[4] The main reason for faculty participation in academic government, however, is embodied in the "production point" arguments presented above. Since the individual faculty member executes much of the real "business" of the university, "the authority structure does not need to be as closely knit, or as hierarchical, as in most other settings"; there is rationality rather than madness in the "loose, meandering, overlapping structure of authority" which is common in most colleges and universities.[5]

In the literature on university government there is general consensus about the necessity of a non-hierarchical structure for university decision-making. There is further agreement concerning the many misunderstandings which are a consequence either of a lack of empathy for a role within this type of structure or of the misjudging of *quasi-hierarchical* features which, confusingly enough, are present on the academic scene. Corson notes how firmly the hierarchical principle is "embedded in the minds of those acquainted with business, governmental and military organizations." Although this principle has no place in the university, the presumed roles of the trustee, the president, the deans, the department heads, and the various ranks of faculty members "have a surface similarity" to hierarchical organization and thus cause confusion.[6] Again, John Millett observes how few persons – particularly among trustees, administrative officers, and even faculty members –

---

[3] John J. Corson, *Governance of Colleges and Universities* (New York, 1960), pp. 129, 130.

[4] John D. Millett, *The Academic Community: An Essay on Organization* (New York, 1962), pp. 55, 56; Corson, *Governance*, p. 97.

[5] Clark, "Faculty Authority," p. 301.

[6] Corson, *Governance*, p. 15.

"realize the extent to which their own ideas have been influenced by the [hierarchical] organizational concepts around which we have built so much of our knowledge about public and business administration." And, superficially, there seems to be a hierarchy of offices on campus, from the junior instructor to the member of the board. Thus, it is "customary to describe a board of trustees as having ultimate or final authority for all activities of a college or university." Since this description is invariably found not to correspond to the facts of decision-making in a university, "great generosity" or "great self-denial" on the part of the trustees is offered as an explanation for the reality of faculty decision-making. The real explanation, of course, relates to the basic purposes of the university – teaching and research – which invariably imply a non-hierarchical academic structure.[7]

Nicholas J. Demerath and his fellow authors, in their case study of academic power at the University of North Carolina, describe how "laymen" believed that "administrators give orders to full professors, who give orders to associate professors, and so on 'down' through the assistant professors and instructors." These same "laymen" found it "exceedingly strange" that a dean or chairman would forsake "the power and glory" of his office to be a "pure" professor again. There is a formal status hierarchy in the collegiate structure which superficially resembles a government agency or industry, "but these hierarchies do not work in the same way" – except, perhaps, in the service departments such as accounting, buildings and grounds, etc., where superiors do give orders to subordinates.[8] Harold Enarson once advised a dean that "a literal reading of the straight lines on the chart" would head him straight for trouble, since on the campus orthodox administrative theory is clearly misleading and lines of command do not exist.[9] Logan Wilson found the differences between the teacher-researcher and the administrator "more analogous to those between the infantry officer and the artillery officer than to those between the captain and the general" – a "functional" rather than a "scalar" difference.[10]

[7] Millett, *Academic Community*, pp. 24–29, 34.

[8] Nicholas J. Demerath, Richard W. Stephens, R. Robb Taylor, *Power, Presidents, and Professors* (New York, 1967), pp. 22, 23.

[9] Harold Enarson, in Gerald P. Burns, ed., *Administrators in Higher Education* (New York, 1962), p. 120.

[10] Logan Wilson, *The Academic Man* (New York, 1964), p. 73.

To conclude, the hierarchical model is generally considered inappropriate for university government. In any college or university, the faculty will ordinarily resent suggestions that its relations to a dean or the president involve supervisory authority or that administrative officers can give orders to a faculty member. Many a conflict on the campus involves an "imagined hierarchical relationship," as Millett calls it, which is reflected – or which faculty members think is reflected – in the attitude of a dean or other administrator. In a true hierarchical structure, the "higher-up" commands legitimately because he "knows more"; this, as Corson remarked, is nowhere less applicable than in the university.

2. "Collegialization" of Decision-Making

John Millett, after describing the inadequacies of the hierarchical concept of university government, presents his main position, which is that universities should be organized upon the principle of a "community of authority" in which power is shared by faculty, administration, and also students and alumni. Each of these groups must possess "substantial power," with coordination to be achieved "through a dynamic of consensus." Millett is aware that even in a successfully established community of this type all kinds of conflicts may persist, between and among the four groups. He is particularly worried about professors who oppose administrative power as such; faculty members, often unconsciously, reflect notions of hierarchy by assuming automatic conflict between faculty and administration.[11]

Burton Clark describes three concepts of authority which "contend with one another in and around colleges and universities" in the United States. His appreciation of the reality reflects a mixed situation, with each concept having some influence. First, the principle of "public trust" is widely accepted for the administration of educational institutions. A board of laymen, part-time and amateur, supposedly representing the outside society rather than the "narrow" educational community, is empowered legally to give direction to the institution with respect to educational policy as well as financial needs. Then, to overcome the handicaps of the

[11] Millett, *Academic Community*, particularly pp. 61–62, 101–102, 226, 232–235, 243.

board's part-time and lay status, a second principle, the principle of "bureaucratic authority," is applied. Operating authority is either delegated to administration officers by the board, "or is assumed by the officers in the course of affairs." The board members remove themselves from actual operations, while administration officials "– full-time, expert, informed – are on the scene, making the daily decisions." The resulting hierarchical structure of university decision-making is relieved, however, by the prevalence of a third principle, the principle of "colleague authority." The idea of the self-governing community of teachers who control policy as well as practice in their institution is centuries-old and has made headway in the United States too, after initially being totally suppressed by the principles of "public trust" and "bureaucratic authority." [12] Clark's perception of the balancing-off of these three principles is crucial. A victorious principle of "colleague authority" would have eliminated the administration role in the university; by the same token, an unchecked practice of the principles of "public trust" and "bureaucratic authority" would have prohibited faculty participation in university government. The three principles "contend with one another" in American universities, and the result is not greatly different from Millett's "community of authority" shared by the different components even though conflicts persist.

Demerath et al. have developed a concept of "collegialization" of decision-making which combines a non-hierarchical view of university government with a realization of the need for improved formal structures and other devices not implied in the principle of "colleague authority." On the one hand, universities cannot meet the challenges of the present period merely through greater bureaucratization – more formal organization or more line administrators with greater authority. On the other hand, the complexity of the structures and functions of universities today does require more effective administration, particularly administration more responsive to the ever-increasing needs of academicians. This can be accomplished

by means of clear and known procedures for consultation, communication, and decision which serve to make easier and greater the faculty's participation on policy-making. To create and utilize such procedures in a university is to collegialize its management. Inasmuch as

[12] Clark, "Faculty Authority," pp. 294, 295.

these things occur over time and in degree, there is a process, and this process we call collegialization.[13]

"Complementary social ordering" is needed in the university; it is to be accomplished by means of improved administrative and management procedures which facilitate and regularize faculty participation in the spheres of consultation, communication, and decision-making. "Collegialization," thus, becomes a device for adapting the academic institution to urgent societal and academic demands by means of a more intensive collaboration between administration and faculty.

However, "collegialization" is not intended necessarily to pervade all spheres of university decision making. Professors, either individually or in committees, should ordinarily not perform "executive" tasks. "Faculty participation in university management should be confined to matters of policy, with rare exceptions. While the executive actions of administrative officers need to be reviewed regularly by the faculty and by top managers, very rarely should a professor act as an executive unless he has taken an executive appointment." Moreover, certain management functions pertaining to the "business affairs" of a university "are best conducted by qualified business officers who are accountable to the president; business policies need not be made with faculty advisors so long as the policies are consistent with the overriding educational goals and policies of the university." At the same time, even the various kinds of business managers should attempt "to collegialize" their relationships with the faculty, while faculties "should overcome their bureaucraphobic tendencies and help them." [14]

Millett, Clark, and Demerath et al. have different ways of describing the acceptable ways of structuring the academic institution, after they agree fully on the necessity of a non-hierarchical organizational pattern. Yet, all their basic concepts amount to, in effect, "collegialization" – which is another way of expressing the need for a new quality in the co-governing of academic institutions by administration and faculty.

---

[13] Demerath et al., *Power*, pp. 216, 217.
[14] *Ibid.*

3. An Untenable Dichotomy: Academic vs. Financial Affairs

This new quality of cooperation between faculty and administration cannot be facilitated by dividing the governmental task into an academic sphere, where faculty influence might be considerable, and a financial sphere, where the administration would be dominant. Archie R. Dykes, in his survey of campus attitudes at a large Midwestern state university, noted tendencies toward such a dichotomy – which would be considerably more far reaching than the distinction between policy-making and execution noted in the previous section, or the separation of strictly business-type function, also mentioned there.

The connection between "educational" decisions and "financial" decisions was, at best, quite evanescent in the minds of many respondents, who repeatedly showed a strong tendency to view educational and financial affairs as two different worlds. As a result, prerogatives were assigned respectively to the faculty and the administration on the rather simplistic assumption that everything "educational" belongs to the former and everything "financial" to the latter.[15]

As Dykes points out, such a dichotomy is arbitrary and simplistic – "this kind of thinking overlooks the interrelatedness of decision areas." Unfortunately, all financial decisions in a university directly and immediately affect academic policy, and vice versa. The very heart of governing a university may well lie in the judgments pertaining to the balancing of academic needs with the realities of an institution's financial situation. This is precisely the sphere where the faculty's "production point" insights must be incorporated into the board's and the administration's decision-making. Moreover, this type of decision, more than any other, requires the new qualities of cooperation which are contained in the concept of "collegialization."

A pioneering study at Brock University, in Canada, similarly insisted that "the present division of powers between the Board and Senate – between the financial which belongs to the Board and the academic which belongs to the Senate – is becoming increasingly an anachronism . . . ." The so-called "one-tier" system, suggested by the Brock study, was to provide a way to overcome this obsolescent pattern.[16] In general, di-

[15] Archie R. Dykes, *Faculty Participation in Academic Decision Making* (American Council on Education: Washington, D.C., 1968), pp. 4, 40.

[16] "The Structure of Government at Brock University," (mimeo., August

chotomizing of decision-making areas is falling into disrepute
in academic government. For example, in a later section the
"segregated" jurisdiction of student government and the separate domain of the dean of students will be critically reviewed.
Other functions which obviously concern all the components
of the university include alumni relations, intercollegiate ath-
letic policy, and the institution's public relations in general.
Needless to say, mere acceptance of the concept of "collegialization" does not make academic government any easier or
more acceptable to the community of the university and the
world outside. Neither does the acceptance of dichotomizing
shortcuts which ignore the realities of the academic institution
– its governing tasks as related to its specific "culture."

4. The Culture of the University and University Government

The report of the Foote Commission at Berkeley offered
profound insights into university government as the Commission grappled with the causes of the Berkeley troubles of 1966.
The Commission pinpoints two crucial failures of the university
in the years before the riots: one, the failure to develop a student body "which respects the value of the intellect itself,"
and, two, the failure "to order its [the university's] activities
according to a conscious conception of its unique purpose of
nurturing that intellect." The first failure relates to the educational process as such; the second, in fact, to processes of
government which were insufficiently related to the educational purpose. The Foote Commission emphasized that reform of
the university's governing structures could not in itself re-
vitalize the educational processes. Yet, the governing process
should provide the most appropriate means for recognizing
"genuine conflicts of values and functions" and for establishing
"a framework of priorities and relationships for discriminating
among the growing tasks and demands placed upon the university." Better government of the university, then, facilitates
better solutions for educational and intellectual problems.
    The concept of "campus culture" is introduced by the Berke-
ley Commission to show practices and institutions of university
government in their widest perspective:

We are convinced that modes of governance and of education are

1967), p. 13. (Hereafter referred to as Brock University Report.) The "one-tier"
system is discussed below, p. 32.

shaped by a broader campus culture and that in turn, the campus culture is affected by what occurs in committee room as well as in the classroom. By "campus culture" we mean to draw attention not only to the concrete arrangements and institutions which order the educational and governmental processes of the university, but to the intangible values, such as a sense of common fellowship, a commitment to free inquiry and rational discussion, and pride in belonging to an institution which refuses to judge itself and the behavior of its members by any but the most demanding standards. More briefly, by a campus culture we mean that complex of tacit assumptions about what is important that leads the members to ask not what is the letter of the law or the prerogative of status and authority, but what is appropriate to an institution concerned with the cultivation of the mind and spirit.

Or, as stated by the Commission in similar terms:

It is more enlightening to think of governance as a complex set of relations, powers, and influences embedded in a broader, more general campus "culture." The context in which governance operates helps to shape the actions and style of the participants; at the same time, the manner in which governance operates, the procedures it follows, and the spirit in which it treats problems and people will, in turn, help to shape that broader context. Campus governance, then is not simply a method for arriving at decisions about educational policies; it is itself a method of educating those who participate in it or who are affected by it. How well such a system operates is not to be determined solely or even primarily by criteria of efficiency, but must be evaluated by reference to the quality of life appropriate to an educational community.[17]

The governmental structure of a university, as well as the quality of its educational processes, are dependent on the "culture" of the particular campus – which, however, is in turn dependent on governmental as well as educational factors in a complex series of interrelationships.

An aspect of campus "culture" particularly affecting faculty members presents a curious dilemma: on the one hand, the professor, as Clark Kerr notes, is "of necessity elitist – the elite of merit"; on the other hand, Kerr observes that he operates in a campus environment usually dedicated to a social-demo-

---

[17] *The Culture of the University: Governance and Education* (University of California, Berkeley, 1968), pp. 10, 15, 16. This is the report of the Study Commission on University Governance, co-chaired by Caleb Foote and Henry Mayer. This joint student-faculty commission had been established in January 1967 by the Berkeley Division of the Academic Senate and the Senate of the Associated Students of the University of California. The report, which was published on January 15, 1968, will hereafter be referred to as Berkeley Report. (A somewhat expanded version of this report was published in 1968 by Jossey-Bass, San Francisco. The references in the present study are to the original Berkeley version.)

cratic philosophy. An "aristocracy of intellect" must survive in the liberal-radical milieu of the campus.

There is a kind of "guild mentality" in the academic profession, as in many others. The guild was isolationist toward society, devoted to producer as against consumer sovereignty and committed more to guild rules than to quick adaptation to popular demand. The guild was egalitarian, full of senatorial courtesy, selective of its own members.

The individual faculty member, and particularly the political liberal on the faculty is often torn between the "guild" and the "socialist" views of the university. The guild view stands for self-determination, and for resistance against the administration and the trustees; the socialist view, for service to society which the administration and the trustees often represent. The guild view is elitist toward the external environment, conservative toward internal change, conformist in relation to the opinion of colleagues. The socialist view is democratic toward society, radical toward change, and nonconformist. And the political liberal is drawn toward both views. Here is a paradox. Few institutions are so conservative as the universities about their own affairs while their members are so liberal about the affairs of others; and sometimes the most liberal faculty member in one context is the most conservative in another. The natural radical, within the context of the guild, is radically conservative. The faculty member who gets arrested as a "freedom rider" in the South is a flaming supporter of unanimous prior faculty consent to any change whatsoever on his campus in the North.[18]

This paradoxical mixture of conservatism and liberalism within the faculty influences the "culture" of many academic institutions. It may well provide a conveniently solid base for campus government and politics, with the faculty in a comfortable middle position between the conservatism of most boards and administrations and the radicalizing of the more activist students. If a faculty can maintain an open mind about the ferments in the air, its natural attachment to traditional structures and procedures may well provide the vehicle for effective peaceful change. Of course, a blind and lethargic, or highly polarized, faculty may miss all the opportunities to prevent escalation of violence or authoritarianism on the campus. Although experience with well organized and powerful faculty "parties" is hard to document, some evidence points to the potential ability on the part of such "parties" to manipulate, bargain, and reconcile among the other components of the university. Demerath et al. provide one example of a successful faculty "party," based on the local AAUP chapter, which apparently played an important role at the

[18] Clark Kerr, *The Uses of the University* (Cambridge, Mass., 1964), pp. 97–99, 121.

University of North Carolina during the change of regime described in their book.[19]

Another "cultural" trait of the university affecting government is depicted by the Berkeley Commission in its attack on the "interest group conception" of university politics.

We are asked to assume that the campus consists of three components, the "students," "faculty members," and "administrative officers," each having an area of primary concern. Clearly the campus "society" is here viewed as a collection of status-bound interest groups; each having a special preserve and each possessing claims to participation in varying degrees – subject to negotiation – in the activities assigned to the other components. The political problem set by this approach is one of devising institutions and procedures which will enable each group to pursue its particular concerns as efficiently and harmoniously as possible in areas which overlap with the other groups. Politics, in this view, consists of finding techniques for promoting particular interests and conciliating conflicting ones. Although this view may be an accurate description of our present situation, we do not regard it as an adequate, much less ideal, process for creating an educational setting fit for the cultivation of the mind and the strengthening of the human spirit. Most issues of university policy are questions requiring qualitative judgments rooted in values and principles. Such questions cannot readily be broken down into component units over which highly politicized interest groups can bargain and for which some mutually agreeable form of distributive justice can be decided on the basis of which group has the most bargaining power. To pursue university policy as a task of trading off the interests of competing groups is especially damaging because the interests themselves often remain unexamined and no process exists by which the community as a whole can openly assess the cumulative effect of many isolated exchanges on the value and direction of the institution. Hence, a major weakness of the interest group conception of university policy-making has been that it has imposed narrow and artificial limits upon the process of discussion and decision in the university. Moreover, it has obscured the special character of a university, by regarding it much as one does any other pluralistic society populated by diverse interest groups and lacking a common commitment to anything more than the bargaining process itself.[20]

As Millett, of course, has also maintained, the university differs from the typical Western political system where the bargaining process and its rules are said to be the only norm and purpose. Very emphatically, the "culture" of the university does *not* permit us to consider the three main components – students, faculty, and administration – merely as competing interest groups which play political games for a slice of the

[19] Demerath et al., *Power*, pp. 138–139. But, note fn. 64, below, for evidence of dysfunctional faculty "parties."
[20] Berkeley Report, p. 10.

university's cake. If the human agents among the components ignore the "culture" of the university and proceed to fight the ideological and political battles of the outside world among themselves, they have in effect destroyed the university.

Clark Kerr seems to challenge Millett and his former colleagues at Berkeley when he goes out of his way to identify conflicts among groups in his "multiversity."

The multiversity is an inconsistent institution. It is not one community but several – the community of the undergraduate and the community of the graduate; the community of the humanist, the community of the social scientist, and the community of the scientist; the communities of the professional schools; the community of all the nonacademic personnel; the community of the administrators.

A community, like the medieval communities of masters and students, should have common interests; in the multiversity, they are quite varied, even conflicting. A community should have a soul, a single animating principle; the multiversity has several – some of them quite good, although there is much debate on which souls really deserve salvation.[21]

It could be maintained that the several sub-communities of Kerr's multiversity are, nevertheless, significantly part of the larger campus "culture."

Three aspects, then, of the "culture" of the university affect its government. First of all, the quality of government is related to the quality of the particular "culture" of a university and its educational processes; in the second place, faculty members reflect a paradoxical "cultural" pattern featuring mixtures of conservatism and liberalism; in the third place, the different groups on a campus do not play their political games in the usual ways of Western political systems. These three factors help to explain why universities have developed altogether unusual structures and rules for governing themselves.

5. *Structural Patterns for Government Among Interdependent Components*

As was noted above, the AAUP's 1966 *Statement on Government of Colleges and Universities* recognized an "inescapable interdependence" among three components of the university – the board, administration, and faculty. Two basic principles of this interdependence are stipulated in the Statement:

(1) important areas of action involve at one time or another the initiating capacity and decision-making participation of all the institutional

21 Kerr, *Uses*, pp. 18–19.

components, and (2) differences in the weight of each voice, from one point to the next, should be determined by reference to the responsibility of each component for the particular matter at hand as developed hereinafter.[22]

In other words, while each component may have something to say about all the decisions affecting the university, different kinds of decisions require different weights of decision-making power for each component, depending upon the relationship of the particular component to the decision at hand. Thus, university governance can be seen as numerous layers of pancakes, with each pancake representing a decision-making situation. While each pancake is made up of several slices, representing the components of the university, the size of each of the slices differs with each pancake – representing different weights of decision-making power for each component as required by each particular situation.

Interdependence of the components will in most decision-making situations necessitate, as a minimum, meaningful consultation processes among them. Consultation, to be effective, requires delicate management and political skill on the part of all participants; the consulted party must feel that its opinions count even where they cannot be fully respected by the party initiating the consultation. Real statesmanship produces success in a consultation situation if it can also convincingly reflect concern for the welfare of the entire university rather than for the power of one component. Moreover, as Clark Kerr emphasized, to make governance of the university – and the "multiversity" – effective,

the moderates need to be in control of each power center and there needs to be an attitude of tolerance between and among the power centers, with few territorial ambitions. When the extremists get in control of the students, the faculty, or the trustees with class warfare concepts, then the "delicate balance of interests" becomes an actual war.[23]

"Moderate control" and minimal "territorial ambitions" are preconditions for the successfully governed university; the inevitable interdependence among the components leads to chaos or tyranny where these preconditions are lacking, even in just one of the components.

As to governmental structures, universities do reveal a cer-

[22] *Statement on Government of Colleges and Universities* (1966), p. 6.
[23] Kerr, *Uses*, p. 39.

tain amount of uniformity in the United States. As Corson points out, there usually exist "two structural arrangements operating to a large degree on a parallel basis." [24] One resembles "line" relationships, emanating from the President and involving vice-presidents, provosts, deans, and – perhaps – departmental chairmen. The other structural arrangement consists of several layers of quasi-legislative bodies dominated, presumably, by faculty members, from the level of the professoriate of individual departments to college faculty assemblies, a university-wide faculty assembly, and a university-wide representative senate. The connections between the two structures are at several levels: the departmental chairman presides at the departmental meeting, the dean presides over the college faculty, and the president usually presides over institution-wide bodies. Besides, senates usually contain the more important administrative officers from the "line" structure. Finally, specialized committees at the various levels usually contain faculty members as well as administrators.

Successful government of the university requires the uniting of these two parallel structures into an "operating whole." [25] The administration's "line" structure must not be used as a monopolistic power device in relation to which the various levels of quasi-legislative faculty bodies play symbolic but basically insignificant roles. Yet, even where good statesmanship accomplishes a meaningful welding of administration and faculty power, the other components are often not effectively tied into the administration's and faculty's decision-making structures. The board of trustees in most universities has to channel its influence through the president; only in relatively few cases do members of the board have direct communications with other administrators, the faculty, and students – usually through the device of special committees containing representatives of all four components. Student involvement with the dominant structures of governance is certainly increasing; nevertheless – for all kinds of reasons – student representation at present tends to be "tokenish" at best. In later sections more attention will be paid to the special problems of board and student relations to the structures of administration-faculty government.

Two factors of some significance for the comparative study

[24] Corson, *Governance*, pp. 34–35.
[25] *Ibid.*

of structures of governance are the size of an institution and the nature of its support or special purpose. The former can be expressed in terms of numbers of students or numbers of faculty members; the latter, in terms of public, private, or denominational affiliation and such special categories as teachers colleges or community colleges. Lazarsfeld and Thielens, for example, suggested the following dual-level typology: (a) institutions with fewer than 700 students, with 700–2500 students, with 2500–9000 students, and with more than 9000 students; (b) tax-supported, private, private Catholic, and private Protestant institutions, and teachers colleges.[26] Obviously, the categories can be expressed differently; yet both of these kinds of factors are bound to have effects on structures of university government In fact, Ralph Brown has asked for the construction of "inductive outlines of government by types of colleges and universities" along the lines suggested by Lazarsfeld and Thielens.[27]

A final structural consideration has evolved particularly from the Berkeley crisis of 1966 – although assuredly not from the Columbia crisis of 1968. Clark Kerr found his multiversity vital and dynamic only at the departmental level, and consequently became a strong advocate of decentralization "below the campus level." [28] The Berkeley Commission, too, called for greater responsibility and autonomy to be lodged in smaller units, such as colleges and departments. "The principle which ought to govern these changes is that autonomy should be lodged in groups that are intimately and vitally involved in the substantive processes of teaching." [29] Decentralization, of the right kind, was also the main cure for current campus troubles advocated by Burton Clark in an article published in 1968. According to Clark, "traditional collegial forms of campus governance have lost their efficacy" and many universities today can no longer be described as communities. The crucial reform in American higher education must now be "to devise substructures on the large campus that promote informal influence and a sense of personal contact" to replace the existing

[26] Paul F. Lazarsfeld and Wagner Thielens, Jr., *The Academic Mind* (Glencoe, Ill., 1958), p. 18.
[27] Ralph S. Brown, Jr., "Rights and Responsibilities of Faculty," *AAUP Bulletin*, Summer 1966, p. 139.
[28] Kerr, *Uses*, p. 120.
[29] Berkeley Report, p. 26.

substructures "that build walls of impersonality and formal (and seemingly arbitrary) authority." [30]

Martin Trow, on the other hand, delivered a severe attack on the "communitarians" of the Berkeley Commission who offer "a Utopian vision of small . . . educational units built on participation and consensus against the anti-Utopia of the mass impersonal, conflictful, and interest-ridden multiversity. . . ." The Berkeley Report, says Trow, is an expression of faith and ideology rather than a description of reality. Many faculty members and students at Berkeley, he asserts, actually prefer the multiversity to small, participatory communities. Besides, we just can't go back to "pre-industrial" forms of academic organization. Also McConnell and Mortimer expressed strong doubts about decentralization. A faculty member cannot just do "his own thing," and the sum of individual departmental decisions does not necessarily add up "to a coherent institutional whole." Decentralization encourages the development of conflict and results in an unmanageable "multiversity." In fact, the authors believe that centralization is needed at present, for two main reasons. In the first place, an academic institution must today define its particular "controlling goals" and "educational priorities." In the second place, the institution's increasingly scarce resources require central allocation and central control of academic standards of performance. These tasks can only be performed by campus-wide organs in which the various components of the university are represented appropriately.[31]

While many aspects of decentralization may be beyond realization today, it appears probable that for real progress toward student participation, in any case, the departmental level is crucial. Yet, other aspects of university government may have to be reformed or cultivated at a very centralized level, requiring more effective representative institutions at a university-wide level.

[30] Burton R. Clark, "The New University," *American Behavioral Scientist*, May-June 1968, pp. 2, 4. (Clark's article is part of a special issue devoted to "The State of the University: Authority and Change." Among other contributors to this issue are Martin Trow, Terry F. Lunsford, and Troy Duster, who will be cited below.)

[31] Martin Trow, "Conceptions of the University: the Case of Berkeley," *American Behavioral Scientist*, May–June 1968, pp. 20–21. McConnell and Mortimer, *The Faculty in University Governance*, pp. 129–132, 136–138, 153.

6. Ambiguities of University Government

Burton Clark maintained that "anyone who seriously and intensively probes the authority structure of his own college ... and presents his observations for public consumption, is likely to make enemies and may have occasion to travel." Questions of university government, he insists, "are considered nasty by many...." In any case, "academic authority is a peculiarly subtle and complex matter, a murky business that has caused highly intelligent men to veer away and throw up their hand." [32]

The "murky" point of the above opinion, at least, is also brought forward by Corson:

No student of the administration of higher education has effectively revealed how and why the power is distributed among trustees, president, deans, department heads, and faculty as it typically is in this country's institutions of higher learning. Nor has there been an effective assessment of the strengths and weaknesses that accrue from the distribution of authority that is customary. [33]

The main difficulty, of course, results from the degree to which final responsibility for making various decisions is diffused in the university among trustees, president, deans, department chairmen, the entire faculty, and individual faculty members. This diffusion of final decision-making powers makes university government hard to understand even for persons who have spent all their lives in academic institutions. It is doubtful whether most members of a university component are really aware of what their component's share of power or jurisdiction in a particular decision-making situation is, or should be. The board's "legal" and "final" responsibility; the administration's "executive" and "delegated" authority; the collective faculty's powers flowing from "consultation" and more or less binding "advice"; the totally undefined rights of students to participate – all of these descriptions or allotments of decision-making powers beg the question of the real share of power of the respective component.

[32] Clark, "Faculty Authority," p. 293. As Morris Keeton put it, "campus governing structures and processes will need a flexibility and complexity uncommon in our presently complex society." (M. Keeton, *Shared Authority on Campus* [American Association for Higher Education: Washington, D.C., 1971], p. 21.) Or, "a modern American university is by far the most complicated type of organization yet devised by man." (Paul L. Dressel, F. Craig Johnson, and Philip M. Marcus, *The Confidence Crisis* [San Francisco, 1970], p. 236.)

[33] Corson, *Governance*, p. 14.

The Berkeley commission pointed to another source of ambiguity – the way in which the symbols and reality of academic government have been confused by the injection of the governmental symbols and reality of the outside world's political arena. The commission is much disturbed by this "fundamental error," which ignores all the consequences flowing from the uniqueness of the university's purposes and "culture."

Traditional concepts of democratic government have been used as verbal arsenals, pushing debate in directions which needlessly build up mutual distrust, concealing the real issues, and rendering sensible institutional solutions politically unobtainable. Debate becomes a tiresome competition in which each protagonist seeks to find "authority" in alleged controlling principles drawn from governmental or administrative models quite inappropriate to the unique environment of a university. On the one hand is the repeated demand by students for governmental autonomy, which is understandable if the model of self-government is taken at face value, but which as a goal is both unobtainable within the constitutional structure of the university and undesirable in a collaborative educational enterprise. On the other hand, University policy mixes constitutional analogies with administrative rules, and this produces, as in the controversy over the enfranchisement of graduate students, a debate more appropriate to Gilbert & Sullivan than to a university community.[34]

Of course, political analogies from traditional Western political dogma are far easier to grasp than the "murky" reality of academic governmental relationships.

Two well-known and rather dour observers of the academic scene, Theodore Caplow and R. J. McGee, insist that whenever there is a crisis in university government the resulting stresses are resolved by "a kind of lawlessness, consisting of vague and incomplete rules and ambiguous and unmodified procedures." Academic authority is "essentially illegitimate," according to Caplow and McGee, even in non-crisis periods: it "is exercised largely by means of the personal control which the administrator has over the salary, rank, and prerogatives of the working professor." This kind of extra-legal control, which can easily become capricious, "serves in default of a workable system of academic government." Needless to say, the two authors regard this system of loose-lying powers as partly responsible for "the extraordinarily high incidence of conflict reported in the universities ...." [35] The "academic market-

---

[34] Berkeley Report, p. 33.
[35] Theodore Caplow and Reece J. McGee, *The Academic Marketplace* (New York, 1961), pp. 206–208, 228.

place" may not be quite as anarchical or capricious – nor, for that matter, quite as venal – as Caplow and McGee allege. Yet, they do depict vividly the ambiguity of the typical atmosphere of academic government.

This ambiguity is further illustrated, perhaps in its most extreme form, by the on-going debate about the unionization of faculty members, which will be described in the following section.

7. The Faculty's Status: Professionals or Employees?

Faculty participation in university government is *not* an expression of some kind of democratic principle adapted from the outside world; it is, rather, the consequence of the unique professional expertise of the professor which makes his contributions to decision-making essential to the success of the university. It is characteristic of the "murkiness" and ambiguity surrounding the principles of university government that the current preoccupation with the unionization of college and university faculties has often overlooked the possible contradiction between unionization and professional status.

A professor's position in the university is comparable to the physician's position in the hospital – neither the professor nor the physician can be considered employees in the union's sense of that term. The crucial difference between the employee-management relationship and the faculty-administration relationship lies in the fact that the faculty – rather than the administration – is the primary authority on much of the "business" of the university. After all, in what industrial enterprise are the employees or workers the key experts on manufacturing policy, product lines development, purchasing policies, and quality standards? The faculty member has the undisputed right to decide what and how to teach, just as the physician is not challenged in his diagnoses and treatments of diseases. But, what employee can determine the nature of the product and the method by which he will produce it? There is little analogy between employees and professors in their relationships to employers and university administrators.[36]

[36] For these and similar points, note Ralph N. Campbell's address at the Exploratory Conference on Faculty-Administration Relations, American Council on Education (Hotel Biltmore, New York, May 7–9, 1957), p. 38 (mimeo.). Christopher Jencks and David Riesman, in their recent volume on *The Academic Revolution* (New York, 1968), have a revealing section on "Professionalism and Its Consequences" (pp 199–207).

This kind of reasoning was critically analyzed in a study on faculty participation in university government completed in 1967 by the American Association for Higher Education (AAHE). The unique status of the faculty member was found to relate to the nature of the "production" of universities:

Although various elements of support can be provided by the adminis-tration, the basic productive activities are carried out by the faculty, alone or in concert with the students. The product cannot be specified in advance by superiors. Rather, it results from the intellectual and pedagogical capacities of faculty members and the quality of their relationships with students and colleagues.

. . . .

Ultimately, faculty members must bear the main responsibility for determining their own standards of performance. Doctors and lawyers largely determine their own standards of performance because laymen would be hard-pressed to identify the factors that distinguish good from bad practice. Similarly laymen or nonprofessionals have a limited ability to evaluate professors.

However, the study did also note certain elements of employee-status in the professor, particularly in the financial sphere. Thus, the faculty's "dual role" complicates its relationship with the administration – even if the professional role of the faculty necessitates "co-governance" with the administration.

The problems of developing a system of governance based on the concept of shared authority are rendered more difficult because of the faculty's dual role. Because they are professionals, faculty members seek to attain the rights of self-regulation exercised by other profession-als; however, because they are also employees, the delegation of authority to the faculty complicates, if not undermines, the formal employee-employer relationship. This duality does not present an in-superable obstacle to the attainment of a condition of shared authority but it does mean that in most institutions testaments of good faith will not be sufficient to dissipate the tensions between collegial and em-ployee-employer relationships and that conscious efforts will be neces-sary to reconcile these two roles.

The authors of the AAHE study suggest that the faculty, on the one hand, can share in government with the administration (for example, in an academic senate) with respect to education-al policy, *and*, on the other hand, can be represented by a union in a bargaining relationship with the administration with respect to employee-status matters. Yet, in the end this combination of roles is found to be "unstable":

While we support a division of issues between a bargaining agency and an academic senate when both are well established on a campus, we recognize that any such demarcation is likely to be unstable over time.

The record of collective bargaining in industrial settings reveals a steady expansion of union concern and influence to topics previously identified as management prerogatives. A parallel series of developments may take place in higher education. For example, the determination of admissions standards may be assigned initially to a senate as an issue of educational policy. This issue, however, may soon appear on the formal bargaining agenda because of the consequences of admissions policies on faculty work loads.[37]

Matthew Finkin provided a first survey of the actual impact of collective bargaining on traditional university government. He did not cover the two-year colleges and community colleges where collective bargaining has become relatively frequent but where traditional forms of university government have remained quite infrequent. Instead, he focused on the four-year colleges and universities where collective bargaining contracts were in effect at the time of his writing in 1971. Finkin found only five such institutions: Central Michigan University, Southeastern Massachusetts University, the six New Jersey State Colleges (negotiating as a unit), the City University of New York (CUNY) system, and St. John's University (New York).[38] The transitional college, typically the teachers college in transition to a multi-purpose liberal arts college, is considered a likely type of campus for collective bargaining. At such institutions, Finkin posits, "the influential older faculty may see its status threatened by the influx of a number of liberal arts oriented junior faculty and a new like-minded administration." Consequently, the older faculty may turn to collective bargaining to prevent the establishment of a senate in which the junior faculty and administration might dominate. Or, perhaps, the younger faculty may decide to turn to the union to eliminate the oligarchs in control of a senate. In any case, it is quite evident that other than transitional colleges are also likely to turn to collective bargaining.

[37] *Faculty Participation in Academic Governance* (American Association for Higher Education: Washington, D.C., 1967), pp. 20–22, 24, 65.

[38] Also the United States Merchant Marine Academy and the Bryant College of Business Administration (R.I.) have had collective bargaining relationships with their faculties, but Finkin found these institutions "too specialized" for the purposes of his analysis. Collective bargaining agencies have been established at at least ten other four-year colleges and universities, but at the time of Finkin's writing negotiations had not been completed there. These institutions are Rutgers University, Boston State College, the Polytechnic Institute of Brooklyn, New York Institute of Technology, the State University of New York (SUNY) system, Monmouth College (N.J.), the Newark College of Engineering, Pratt Institute, Long Island University Brooklyn Center, and Oakland University (Michigan).

One general problem indicated by Finkin is the composition of the bargaining unit, which tends to include not only the regular faculty but also part-time faculty, "ancillary support professionals," and "quasi-administrative faculty." Particularly the latter two groups – including, for example, counselors, placement advisors, public relations officers, and financial aid officers – could exercise considerable influence as a "swing vote" in a closely contested bargaining agent election, affecting the regular faculty's traditional position of predominance. A related problem is the position of the departmental chairman, who in traditional university government should be considered a faculty colleague but in collective bargaining situations tends to be "elevated" to a "supervisor," again a blow at the general posture of the faculty. This issue has caused a major crisis at the City University of New York, as yet unresolved.

Finkin cites Walter Oberer to suggest one likely impact of collective bargaining. "The collective bargaining agent, by its very nature, is subject to the pressures of egalitarianism and will perforce substitute the interests of the majority of the bargaining unit for the interests of the elite." To maintain their position as leaders, the collective bargaining agents "must appeal to where the votes are ... by a program of immediate across-the-board benefits for the existing majority." This constitutes "a surrender of the environment of excellence" which had always been the ideal of the university. Equally serious, of course, is the extension of the scope of negotiations to traditional areas of faculty decision making, as was already suggested in the previously quoted AAHE study. Ralph Brown, also cited by Finkin, suggested the likelihood "that negotiations on clearly bargainable matters will lead to negotiations on matters of educational policy"; thus, what used to be faculty jurisdiction will be "absorbed" into the collective bargaining process. Finkin's documentation on this kind of "absorption" is particularly impressive, as he lists intrusions into faculty or senate jurisdiction in the presently operative bargaining agreements. It is not surprising, then, that in his conclusions Finkin is unable to predict whether traditional university government, as posited by the 1966 Statement, can survive "apart from the bargaining power exerted by particular groups within the University ...." If it is to survive, all parties (including the collective bargaining agent) must have a deep commitment to the traditional ideals – which may be the case, Finkin hopes, as collective bargaining further develops in "mature" colleges and universities. Significantly, perhaps, the 1966 Statement was incorporated into the agreement in effect at St. John's University, where the local AAUP chapter and a local faculty association were the joint bargaining agents.[39]

The AAUP's attitude toward collective bargaining is basically clear. On October 31, 1969, the Council of the AAUP approved a statement on *Policy on Representation of Economic and Professional Interests*. This statement presents a working model for collective bargaining in academic institutions, and at the same time attempts to preserve the basic spirit of the 1966 Statement. On the one hand, the *Policy Statement* stipulates that the nature of the academic enterprise is such that the faculty properly *shares* in responsibilities which in nonacademic institutions might be entirely those of ownership or management, as is indeed the case in "the outstanding colleges and universities" which do afford their faculties a potent voice in educational and academic policy as well as provide adequately for their economic interests. On the other hand, the *Policy Statement* notes that numerous institutions fail to grant the faculty either an effective co-governing voice or proper compensation. These failures "demand correction" which, according to the *Policy Statement*, can be accomplished through "professional self-representation by an internal faculty agency." This kind of faculty agency, perhaps a senate or a special body elected by the faculty, can effectively represent the faculty for collective bargaining purposes "without taking on the adversary and sometimes arbitrary attitudes of an outside representative" – such as exclusive bargaining agents patterned after union procedures in industry. Thus, the Association recognizes the significant role which collective bargaining

---

[39] Matthew W. Finkin, "Collective Bargaining and University Government," *AAUP Bulletin*, Summer 1971, pp. 149–162. (This is a revised version of an article which appeared originally in the *Wisconsin Law Review*, 1971, pp. 125–149.) Finkin is the Director of the AAUP's Northeastern Regional Office. Note also, Ralph S. Brown, "Collective Bargaining in Higher Education," *Michigan Law Review*, March 1969, pp. 1067–1082; Walter Oberer, "Faculty Participation in Academic Decision Making," in S. Elam and M. H. Moskow, eds., *Employment Relations in Higher Education* (Bloomington, 1969), p. 143.

Dexter L. Hanley, S.J., President of the University of Scranton and formerly a professor of labor law , suggested a "professional negotiating team" consisting of faculty members *and* administrators as an alternative to, what he considered, the disastrous effects of faculty unions. The contract negotiated by such a team would not be binding upon an individual faculty member. (Hanley, "Issues and Models for Collective Bargaining in Higher Education," *Liberal Education*, March 1971.)

may play in bringing agreement between faculty and administration on academic, governmental, and economic issues –
while not supporting policies or legislation which leave faculty
members "no alternative to exclusive representation derived
from some models of industrial collective bargaining." A local
chapter of the Association may offer itself as the faculty's
representative where conditions of governance or compensation require a collective bargaining agent. Such a chapter may
not require any person to become a member of or make a
financial contribution to the Association as a condition of his
enjoying the benefits of representation; also, a chapter may
not call or support a faculty strike or work stoppage except
under extraordinary circumstances of gross abuse of faculty
status and rights – but specifically not for the purpose of
economic benefits.[40]

[40] The *Policy on Representation of Economic and Professional Interests* appeared
in the *AAUP Bulletin*, Winter 1969, pp. 489–491. Earlier Association statements
on collective bargaining can be found in the AAUP Handbook, *Academic Freedom
and Tenure*, 1969 edition, pp. 348–353; also, in the *AAUP Bulletin*, Summer 1968,
pp. 152–159, and Summer 1969, p. 179.
   The Council of Rutgers AAUP Chapters was certified on February 2, 1970, as
exclusive bargaining agent for all faculty members at the three campuses of
Rutgers University. In order to meet the requirements of Public Law 303 of New
Jersey, which provides for a system of collective bargaining in public employment,
a 50 per cent vote of the Rutgers faculty was necessary to designate the official
bargaining agent. Actually, two thirds of the faculty voted for the AAUP Council,
which had been formed by the AAUP chapters of the three Rutgers campuses.
(*Academe*, April 1970.) As was mentioned above, the AAUP chapter at St. John's
University, serving together with the local faculty association as the collective
bargaining agent for the faculty, negotiated an agreement which was ratified in
January 1971. The Oakland University (Mich.) chapter was certified as the
faculty's collective bargaining representative. Petitions for certification as bargaining agents have been filed, for example, by the chapters at Wayne State
University, Eastern Michigan University, Fordham University, Adelphi University, and the University of New Haven. At quite a few other institutions, AAUP
chapters are reportedly considering active roles for collective bargaining purposes.
(*Academe*, February 1971.)
   Two other national organizations contend in the area of academic collective
bargaining, the AFT (American Federation of Teachers, AFL-CIO) and the National Education Association – in addition to state organizations of civil service
employees and local or state-wide associations of faculty members. Recently, the
AFT suffered two major (if narrow) defeats in the state of New York. In January
1971, the State University of New York (SUNY) system's 16,000 faculty members
and non-teaching professionals voted in favor of a system-wide faculty group as
their bargaining agent. Earlier, in December 1968, the City University of New
York (CUNY) system's 5000 full-time faculty members had also voted for their
own faculty group, although the 6000 temporary and part-time teachers at CUNY
had opted for the AFT.
   For two examples of academic senates acting as collective bargaining agents,
see chapter 2, p. 134.
   On June 18, 1971, the AAUP filed a petition to the National Labor Relations
Board for "proceedings for rule-making in representation cases involving faculty

It remains to be seen whether the 1969 *Policy on Representation of Economic and Professional Interests* can provide an
effective model for collective bargaining within the bounds of
the 1966 Statement. In any case, the Association's Council in
1969 affirmed its belief that collective bargaining could be
used by a faculty as a means of effecting those goals which
some other faculty might be able to attain directly under the
terms of the 1966 Statement.

The university as a decision-making milieu has been depicted in the previous sections; analogies from business or
government were found to be inappropriate in academe. More
detailed discussion on the various components and levels of
government will follow. It was the Ford Foundation's president who recently claimed that governance, not money, was
the key to the present-day crises of the universities: the economic problems of higher education are immense but soluble;
it is the "reshaping of the political process" which he found at
the heart of the academic matter today.[41]

B. THE BOARD OF TRUSTEES – THE REALITY OF
LIMITED POWER VS. THE MYTH OF
UNLIMITED SOVEREIGNTY

As Corson pointed out, what is needed most with respect to
boards of trustees is a clearer definition of their actual power
and responsibility. "It is idle to say that all authority flows
from the board," for, obviously, there are many areas of academic decision-making where the board's authority is not at
all involved.[42]

In Millett's characterization, the board "is a peculiar kind of

members in colleges and universities." (The Board, in a 1970 decision, had asserted
jurisdiction over private colleges and universities.) The petition's text included a
detailed discussion of the uniqueness of the relationship between faculty members
and their academic institution, a relationship which "has no counterpart in any
industrial setting. . . ." The Board, on July 16, 1971, denied the AAUP's petition
on the ground that "to adopt inflexible rules for units of teaching employees at
this time might well introduce too great an element of rigidity and prevent the
Board from adapting its approach to a highly pluralistic and fluid set of conditions." However, the Board promised to take into account "certain practices
and organizational structures [in colleges and universities] which do not parallel
the traditional practices and organizational structures in private industry."
Moreover, the Board welcomed "the fruits of any research" in this area, for the
use of its members and professional staffs.

[41] McGeorgy Bundy, "Faculty Power," *The Atlantic*, September 1968, p. 41.

[42] Corson, *Governance*, pp. 57–58.

representative device ...; the keeper of the social conscience, the protector of the public interest ....'' [43] A Canadian study, the Duff-Berdahl Report, elaborated on the same theme as it stressed the need for the board. The university is depicted as a "closed society" that tends to ignore the outside world; its capacity for self-reform is limited. For example, at Oxford and Cambridge, "it took an absurdly long time" before the sciences were allowed equal status with the humanities, and until the present the whole range of social sciences "is underprivileged and neglected." The Oxford-Cambridge model, in the Duff-Berdahl view, is an extreme example of academic government without influence by a board – that is, without an agent of the outside public. "We received many briefs from Faculty Associations arguing that professors were just as capable administrators as business men and knew more about the particular business of running a university." This may be perfectly true, maintain Duff and Berdahl, but the real point at issue is not the board's ability to administer but its primary function as representative of the world outside the university.[44] Corson, too, took this view of the board's main function. It should interpret to the faculty "the evolving needs" of the outside world so that the faculty can improve its efforts of equipping students to enter that world. While Corson grants that board members are not necessarily more accurately sensitive or even aware of the needs of society than historians or social scientists, he nevertheless thinks that "board members should be able to light up angles of the problem not apparent to the professors and to provide an additional, more comprehensive and pragmatic interpretation of society's course." [45]

The board is the representative of the outside world in the academic community, the protector of the public interest. It has considerable powers at its disposal to carry out this most crucial of its functions. Yet, no argument or principle comes to mind which would entitle a board of trustees to act as the final or supreme authority in all the important affairs of the university – legal provisions in the board's charter notwithstanding. All the principles, traditions, and longstanding customs of

[43] Millett, *Academic Community*, p. 183.

[44] James Duff and Robert O. Berdahl, *University Government in Canada* (Toronto, 1966), pp. 13–14. (This report was sponsored by the Canadian Association of University Teachers and the Association of Universities and Colleges of Canada. It will be referred to hereafter as Duff-Berdahl Report.)

[45] Corson, *Governance*, p. 58.

university government point to the delegation of formal board powers to administration and faculty, and to the cooperation of all the institution's components in deciding on matters of importance to the institution.

Besides, as Glenn Morrow has pointed out, "the sheer necessities of administering such a complex organization as the University" require diffusion and delegation of the legal powers of the board. The effective execution of any decision or policy that concerns the University as a whole is so dependent upon the cooperation of the members of the faculty that they inevitably enjoy "a kind of latent veto power." [46] Moreover, even if a board uses its formal powers to override faculty opinion, this could turn out to be somewhat of a Pyrrhic victory, according to Morrow.

Despite the long record of Senate successes [at the University of Pennsylvania] there have been cases in which faculty opinion, whether rightly or wrongly, has been overridden. It requires more than the normal amount of political wisdom to realize that an opinion clearly stated and strongly supported, though it may seem to have produced no impression on the administration, has not necessarily been a fruitless expenditure of time and effort. Faculty dissent has become a matter of record, so that the image of a monolithic university is dispelled; and the dissent itself may have a delayed effect in modifying future decisions, if not the currently relevant one. [47]

McGeorge Bundy has argued that in times of crisis it is the faculty rather than the board which is likely to hold the real power; therefore, he advocates an adjustment "of legal forms to the political reality." [48] The Duff-Berdahl Report, on the other hand, does not object to a continuation of the formal status-quo as concerns the board's position – to exercise "ultimate de jure sovereignty." The Canadian commission further emphasizes the board's other primary function, next to the representation of the outside public, its "ultimate fiscal responsibility." The board "must have the last word on fiscal matters." [49] The AAUP's 1966 Statement merely urges boards to "undertake appropriate self-limitation"; boards should maintain "a general overview," but for the rest should leave

---

[46] Glenn R. Morrow, "The University of Pennsylvania – Faculty Participation in the Government of the University," *AAUP Bulletin*, Winter 1962, p. 115.

[47] *Ibid.*, p. 121.

[48] Bundy, "Faculty Power," p. 45.

[49] Duff-Berdahl Report, pp. 26–27.

the conduct of administration to the president and the deans and the conduct of teaching and research to the faculty.[50]

The extent of the board's fiscal powers is not sufficiently delineated in the literature. Obviously, in the case of private institutions, the board does make the basic investment and certain overall budgetary decisions; in the case of a public university, it involves itself with the general appropriation before the legislature. Yet, these financial duties of a board should by no means be compared with the budget powers of, for example, a parliament or, even less, an exchequer. The specific educational-research output of a university is to a considerable extent determined by financial decisions, but by financial decisions which are made, *in fact*, by the other decision-making centers of the university, not by the board. The board provides ultimate financial limits concerning the size of the cake – or rather, the outside world's willingness to support the university's budget is estimated and packaged by judgment of the board; the more crucial and flexible decisions on the size of the various slices of the cake are made by full-time academics. In this sense, the board's fiscal function is not as important as it may seem, and is certainly less penetrating than its other primary function, the representation of the outside public.

Corson raises a delicate point as he refers to the average board member's inevitable concern with educational policy as such. Trustees often join these boards because they are interested in education and they resent "being told to keep hands off the most interesting part of the activity . . . ." Corson offers no precise solution, but recognizes that the board should be informed about the central educational problems and programs of the institution, while at the same time it should "not substitute its untutored judgment for the judgments of educators on educational questions." [51]

[50] *Statement on Government* (1966), p. 10.

[51] Corson, *Governance*, p. 57. A study undertaken at Duke University distinguished between three conceptions or models of board behavior: "controlling," "supportive," and "passive." The *controlling* board, found at small denominational colleges and community colleges, is undesirable because in practice such a board cannot maintain continuing involvement and thus its actions often tend to become uninformed, precipitate, and arbitrary. A *passive* board, largely honorific ("except when the sensationalism of political issues . . . goad the trustees to intervene"), is seen as "at best harmless but scarcely useful." The ideal model, the *supportive* board, remains informed but does not dominate; it does not involve itself in day-to-day affairs but neither does it abdicate its responsibilities for institutional development, the determination of ultimate priorities, fiscal support,

In summary of the discussion on powers of boards of trustees, the board is "supreme" and "sovereign" in a legal sense only. In reality, on the probable evidence of the experience of most universities, the board interferes only sporadically and superficially with a university's decision-making. The key function of the board relates to the representation of the outside public. The board reminds the university that it is part of "ordinary" human society, and that society may impose definite limits either on academic aloofness from or on academic involvement with the outside "culture." In the most favorable sense, the board shields the university from dysfunctional public pressures; or, far less acceptably, the board tells the university what "extremes" of academic freedom cannot be tolerated. In the language of the 1966 Statement, "when ignorance or ill will threatens the institution or any part of it, the governing board must be available for support." In grave crises the board is expected to serve "as a champion" of the university; this protection rendered by the board constitutes, in fact, "a fundamental defense of the vested interests of society in the educational institution." The second key function of the board relates to financial management, to assure the basic fiscal integrity of the institution. Boards do, or should, realize that they are not the "owners" or the "managers" of the university. Their two primary functions must be exercised with care and consummate statesmanship, particularly since concepts such as the public interest or fiscal integrity are not clearly definable. Many boards have managed to establish useful and "non-meddling" relationships with their administrations and faculties; yet, some boards have not seen fit to forget about provisions in their charter which, for example, authorize a board to hire faculty and approve educational programs. The reality of board powers, as opposed to legal provisions, is meaningful enough and permits fascinating preoccupations and influences with respect to the life of the academic institution.

Another kind of problem is presented by the composition of boards. Frequent criticism is heard about the kinds of persons who are, or are not, appointed to the body which is supposed to represent the world outside the university. The Duff-Ber-

and administrative review. In order to perform its tasks, the supportive board must establish procedures for regular contact with faculty, students, and employees as well as the administration. (Duke University Commission on University Governance, *The Board of Trustees* [Interim Report, Jan. 16, 1970], pp. 10–11.)

dahl Report's observations appear as applicable in the United States as in Canada.

There should be more variety than is commonly found at present among Board members. Business men and lawyers tend to predominate. Both are admirably suited for the fiscal and constitutional aspects of the Board's duties, but what we may describe as the "window on the world" ought to be wider open.

... It was almost tragic to hear senior members of faculty say that they had never met a member of their Board socially, and pathetic to hear Board members regret that they knew hardly any of the professors by sight. Of course, these contacts exist in some universities, perhaps in most, but not in all. And that is quite wrong. We hope it is not offensive to say that business men and professors, as types, have exceptionally different standards of value, each tending slightly to disapprove of the other. Both need help to cross the gulf. Such help could be given by adding to the Board members of other professions, scientists, writers, men of mark in any of the arts, or those who have retired from any branch of public service, not excluding former academics.

... Boards should not be self-perpetuating, nor should members hold office for life. This will not happen in those provincial universities for which the Government appoints a majority of the Board. It can happen in a "private" university. Members serve too long, and the Board becomes too elderly. And when a vacancy does occur, the test of suitability looked for in selecting a new member is likely to be: "Will he fit in with our ways and our ideas?" Yet new ways and new ideas may be urgently necessary.[52]

A survey of more than 5,000 board members, made public in 1969 by Morton A. Rauh, confirmed the lack of "variety" among them – with respect to occupational background as well as with respect to attitudes on academic issues.[53]

Still controversial is the inclusion of faculty members of an institution on the board of that institution. Professor Robert MacIver, in 1955, argued that the president is not a sufficient link between the board and the faculty, and that, therefore, faculty members should participate at the board level. This is particularly necessary, MacIver said, because members of the board are not "experts in education" in the sense in which the directors of a business corporation are experts in their field of

[52] Duff-Berdahl Report, pp. 19–20.
[53] Morton A. Rauh, "The Trustees of Higher Education," *AGB Reports* (Association of Governing Boards of Universities and Colleges, Washington, D.C.), January 1969. According to the survey, 86% of all trustees are male, 75% are over fifty years of age, 98.7% are white, 75% are Protestant, 58% are Republican, and 33% are Democrat. The median income of trustees is in the thirty to fifty thousand bracket; the average *annual* time devoted to university business, including travel time, is 85 hours per trustee. Also, Rauh, *The Trusteeship of Colleges and Universities* (New York, 1969).

business enterprise. Board members must exercise their function in ways "integrally related to the work of educators," and this requires educators on the board – persons from the faculty "with maturity of comprehension truly reflecting the faculty." [54] The Duff-Berdahl Report also recommended that faculty members should be included on boards, particularly professors who are members of the senate of the institution. Specifically,

> Beyond the minimum of three [faculty] members to permit proper rotation in office, the number of faculty members on the Board should vary with the size of the board, not exceeding 25%. The faculty should definitely be in a minority, because otherwise there would be a danger that the professors, being more vocal by nature and training than most lay members of the Board, would tend to monopolize the discussions.[55]

The main arguments in favor of a faculty presence on the board are two. In the first place, as has been suggested above, it is simply not feasible to distinguish between "fiscal" questions to be decided by the board and "educational" questions to be left to the faculty; the intertwining of the two areas is too complete to expect effective decision-making by a two-tier, segregated system of governance. In the second place, and this is only partly a consequence of the point just mentioned, deliberations by the board on educationally related questions require a closer touch with teaching and research than can be provided by the president; a faculty presence on the board is urgently needed to make possible the effective execution of the board's tasks. However, the Commission on University Governance at Duke University, whose report was cited above (fn. 51), took a decided stand against faculty and student membership on boards – mainly because such membership "smacked of 'tokenism,'" and would involve some danger of conflict of interest. In elaboration of this position of the Duke commission, it can be argued that a faculty and student presence might invite the board to scrutinize more closely certain details of the academic operation with respect to which other components of the university should have primary jurisdiction and responsibility. Because of the representation of the other components the board may come to view itself as the one genuinely repre-

[54] Robert M. MacIver, *Academic Freedom in Our Time* (New York, 1955), pp. 100, 191.

[55] Duff-Berdahl Report, pp. 24–25. McConnell and Mortimer believed that boards should include a substantial proportion of voting faculty members, perhaps 20 percent or one-third. (*The Faculty in University Governance*, p. 186.)

sentative group on the campus, in spite of the inevitable "tokenism" of the faculty and student presence.

If the presence of faculty members from an institution on that institution's board is not feasible or desirable, other measures are available to lessen the board's isolation. In the first place, faculty members from *other* institutions can be invited to serve on the board – a practice quite frequent today, especially on the part of smaller colleges who invite faculty members from neighboring, prestigious universities to serve on their boards. In the second place, the faculty can be authorized to elect some of the board members from among persons from the outside, as was provided in the constitution of Columbia University. In the third place, the faculty can participate in the nominating process. The Duke commission went as far as to propose that all trustees be nominated by a committee consisting of four trustees, two elected members of the faculty, and two elected students; moreover, it also proposed that the term of office of all trustees be limited to two six-years terms. Finally, joint committees of board members and faculty members be set up, as has been done, of course, in numerous colleges and universities.

An entirely different approach was suggested by a study at Brock University in Canada. The Brock committee suggested a so-called "one-tier" structure which would, in effect, draw together the policy functions of the board, the president and deans, and the faculty senate into one body, to be called the University Council.

Our thinking at the moment is based on the premise that there is an *artificial* division between the *academic* interests of the Senate and the *fiscal* interests of the Board of Governors. No real, precise or valid line of demarcation exists in practice. This split has brought about not only an unreal bifurcation of university affairs but at the same time has placed an almost inhuman burden on the office which is the formal link between the two disparate bodies, i.e., the President of the University.

This University Council is to be superior to the senate *and* the board of trustees. It would be composed of elected representatives from the senate, the board, the administration, and the students.[56]

The feasibility of Brock's "one-tier" proposal is not at issue at this point. The proposal is significant because it points up the anomaly of the typical board's position with respect to the

[56] Brock University Report, pp. 28–29.

other components of the university. Considering the dubious prospects of major structural reforms in the usually arch-conservative milieu of the university – arch-conservative as far as its internal practices are concerned – "one-tier" tinkering attempts might as a matter of fact lead to clearer definitions of the position of boards, their *real* powers and their *real* functions.[57]

C. THE ADMINISTRATION – RELATIONSHIPS TO THE ACADEMIC PROCESS

1. The Need for the Administrative Component

As Millett emphasized, administration (as this component of the university is called somewhat misleadingly because it too much recalls governmental or business hierarchies) is obviously essential to the academic community: it provides the specialized and full-time effort to free the energies of faculty and students for the pursuit of learning. Yet, warns Millett, administration can easily defeat its crucial function if its powers

[57] Another unusual proposal for university government reform was made on November 22, 1968, by a political scientist, J. David Singer, of the University of Michigan. As printed in the *Michigan Daily*:

"In order to reduce faculty and student involvement in the time-consuming details of university administration and at the same time to assure administrative responsibility, why not adopt one possible version of what we call parliamentary government? Thus, the administration (president, vice-president, deans and certain upper-level officials) might be thought of as 'the government' in the British sense.

"The Government would hold office at the pleasure of the faculty, and could be removed by the Regents following a vote of no confidence at any time, requiring the negative votes of perhaps two-thirds of the entire professional staff (assistant professors and above). And just as the faculty would be equivalent to a House of Commons, the student body of the various colleges, plus the alumni, might be thought of as the constituencies, and the Regents as a modified House of Lords.

"The students would, as I see it, have no direct vote but would have unlimited rights of petition, coupled with much greater access to both the faculty (Commons) and the administration (Government). In practice our constituents would probably exercise their influence either directly upon the faculty, or indirectly upon the administration, via the faculty. If the faculty, either in response to student petition or independently, were dissatisfied by the performance of the administration, it could call for specific policy changes, the resignation of certain officers, or in extremis, the resignation of the president and his 'government,' with the Regents perhaps holding some sort of veto power.

"Such an agreement should, hopefully, do the following: increase student influence over university faculty control, minimize faculty (and student) involvement in matters which should be the responsibility of the administration, and yet assure greater responsiveness of the administration to both students and faculty.

"This general proposal, many of whose details remain to be examined, is offered as a tentative basis for discussion, and as an alternative to the increasing 'politicization' of the University's decision making process."

are so pervasive that the faculty is denied its power to participate or if the administration begins to see itself "as a supreme
echelon in a hierarchy of authority." [58]

More specifically, five tasks can be identified for which administrators may have a natural or functional advantage
among the components of the academic community – in addition, of course, to the administration's major responsibility
for carrying out the functions of "business" management.

A first and fundamental role is that of *overall leadership*, combining the
interest and efforts of a diverse constituency and achieving a commitment by all of the various groups to the general objectives of the institution, without stifling individual fulfillment.

A second role of administration is that of *coordination*. Because top-
level administrators are responsible for the operation of the entire
institution, they presumably can help to keep the pieces fitted more or
less together.

A third role that is performed by an administration is a role of
planning and innovation. This is not, of course, an exclusive role. It is
also not a role exercised through fiat, but rather through helping to
provide leadership and by suggesting new programs or changes in
working with the faculty and students of the university.

A fourth function which administration provides within this general
rationale of shared authority is to help to assure that particular departments or divisions meet the *general quality standards* of the institution.

A fifth function is to serve as a *mediator or buffer* between the board
of trustees, general public, and the faculty. Presumably the administration, living in both worlds, can help mediate and translate between
one and the other.[59]

In all of these functions, the administrative component should
have the crucial advantage not necessarily of superior wisdom
but of detachment. Policies, and particularly innovations,
"that seem to conflict with established interests require that
the power to initiate be located outside the area of established
interest," i.e., outside the departments, schools, or colleges.[60]

An Australian author, P. H. Patridge, presents a sharp
critique of typical faculty attitudes concerning the administration's role, a critique which is the more interesting because
it is directed at European and Commonwealth universities
where most aspects of university government have traditionally been in the hands of committees of senior faculty members,

[58] Millett, *Academic Community*, pp. 180–181.
[59] C. Addison Hickman, "Faculty Participation in Academic Governance,"
Proceedings, 2nd Minnesota Intercollegiate Faculty Conference, March 1968, pp.
61–62. (Emphasis added.) The same categories are mentioned in *Faculty Participation in Academic Governance* (AAHE), pp. 18–19.
[60] Clark, "Faculty Authority," p. 299.

with very little interference from weak and subservient administrative elements. According to Patridge, faculties display hypocrisy when they pretend that administration is "something extra" that a professor can easily take care of while continuing to be a teacher and scholar. In fact, administration has become a full-time function. Patridge grants that faculties should be suspicious as full-time, professional administrators are introduced into the university and should probably insist that such administrators be former academics. But, we will be getting the worst of all worlds if we continue to produce "a race of part-time teachers, part-time scholars, part-time administrators" who cannot properly fulfill any of their tasks. And, "whatever gives under the strain, it is usually not the administrative duties." [61]

There are important functions in the university which must be fulfilled by full-time administrators, for reasons of efficiency detachment, and preservation of faculty (and student) energies. As Clark described it, the administration occupies a fascinating middle position between the authority of the board on the one side, and the jurisdiction of the faculty on the other side. "Through budget allocation, through influence on *key* appointments, through persuasion generally," the administration must play the crucial in-between role of maintaining "a rolling equilibrium" among the components.

This picture seems to downgrade administration, to offer it the least important role. But more than we realize, administrative leadership . . . requires a willingness and a capability to muddle through – to pick one's way step by step through a tangled web of conflicting values and standards – rather than the heroic ability to define goals first, then pick the appropriate means, then implement, review, and so on, in the logical sequence offered in textbooks on administration.

Rationality in college administration calls for so much muddling through precisely because neat, compelling order is less important than leaving the professor alone, and because responsibility for decision-making is diffused among groups with inherently different interests. The authority structure puts a premium on administrative action through consultation, persuasion, patient gaining of a working consensus. Persuade or perish may become as much of a dictum for administrators as "publish or perish" is for the faculty.[62]

"Persuade or perish" is a perfectly clear characterization of the heart of the administration's task. And, no more chal-

[61] P. H. Patridge is cited in Francis E. Rourke and Glenn E. Brooks, *The Managerial Revolution in Higher Education* (Baltimore, 1966), pp. 158, 169.

[62] Clark, "Faculty Authority," pp. 301–302.

lenging task can be imagined in the university than the "patient gaining of a working consensus" among faculty, board and, not to be forgotten, students. The myth of administrative leadership suggests neat and even "heroic" acts of policy determination; the reality imposes upon the administration the more pedestrian and immensely more difficult chores of behind-the-scene diplomacy and statesmanship which alone can make faculty participation a meaningful and effective instrument of university government. Even such a "neutral" commentator as Corson suggests *engagement* of the faculty as the core responsibility of the administrator:

The function of the university makes it essential that the faculty – its effectiveness, and the zeal and continuing growth of its members – shall be the central concern of a university's administrators. The characteristics of the faculty – of the roles its members play as individuals, of the training they bring to their tasks, or the views they hold, and of the kind of people they are – constitute an essential part of the context to which administrative process must be adapted.[63]

More specifically, Deegan et al. urged administrators to play an active role in reducing faculty polarization. Attempts must be made to bring about "an accommodation between the major 'parties'" and to mobilize faculty moderates as a constructive third force on the campus.[64]

2. What Role for the President?

Corson provides a schematic analysis of the presidential role in university government as divided into six sectors of juris-

---

[63] Corson, *Governance*, p. 25.

[64] Deegan et al., *Joint Participation in Decision Making*, pp. 61, 90. The authors undoubtedly emphasized this function of administration because of their disturbing findings at Fresno State College, where the faculty was split into two opposing factions, the "conservatives" and the "liberals." The highly polarized and politicized faculty clashed mainly in two arenas, the senate and open meetings of senate or college committees. Political methods used included caucusing, getting out the vote, organizing pressure groups to attend open committee sessions, and active recruiting of new faculty members (who "are asked early to choose sides or are co-opted into a tightly knit faction . . . .") During 1968–69, the majority faction succeeded in denying the minority any representation on the Executive Committee. This "monopoly" was defended by the majority "as more efficient and less time-consuming than a divided committee" – although the authors discovered that meetings were as long and as frequent as at the time that the committee still contained both factions. The "liberals" caucused every Wednesday noon to discuss senate and campus affairs; the majority "conservatives" did not caucus weekly but controlled enough votes "so that a few telephone calls could muster the votes necessary to pass or block legislation." (*Ibid.*, pp. 9, 86–7; McConnell and Mortimer, *The Faculty in University Governance*, p. 34.)

diction – educational programs, faculty selection, student affairs, finance, physical facilities, and public and alumni relations. The president has a role in each of these principal areas of academic decision-making, "but in each area he is opposed by countervailing forces – the faculty, the trustees, the students, the alumni or other constituencies." Accordingly, the extent of the president's influence "varies markedly in each area in accordance with his ability to cope with these forces." In Figure I, "the profile of the governance role of a typical president is suggested by the darkened center portion ...."

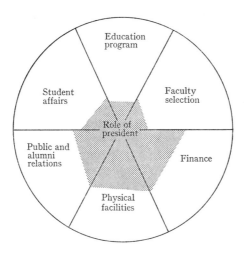

Figure I. Role of the President

As is evident from Figure I, Corson sees the presidential role as least significant in educational programs and in faculty selection, and only slightly more important in student affairs. He finds that in practice the president is seldom "the author of big, new ideas about educational programs" nor "the stimulus that evokes such ideas from others." In fact, the president is not often "permitted to participate in the give and take of faculty discussion of educational program proposals." There are, says Corson, presidents who are in fact "the educational leaders" in their college or university, but "their number is small." [65]

More substantial presidential powers exist in the financial

[65] Corson, *Governance*, pp. 63, 70–71.

sphere. Through control of the budget presidents exercise much influence over the character of their institution; at times, even educational policy may be affected through "indirect financial levers" used by the president. Corson sees the institution's physical plant program as perhaps the key domain of the president. Accordingly,

The hallmark of the president's office in American universities is a large plan to scale of the campus, showing the new buildings planned or for which funds are sought. And it is not the unusual president who may appear at a faculty committee meeting or a cocktail party with mud stains on the cuffs of his trousers, having just tramped through the rising foundations of a new building.

Finally, the president plays an important role in the general area of public relations, more so, according to Corson, than is often imagined.

A greater proportion of his [the president's] time is devoted to the making of speeches before selected groups. Through the statements he makes before public, educational and alumni groups, he determines, in significant part, the posture that the institution shall have in the minds of important constituencies. These statements constitute, in terms of the influence they exercise over important supporters, as well as in terms of their indirect influence on the thinking of faculty and staff, a far more significant element in the governance of the institution than is recognized by most observers of the presidential role.[66]

The study by Demerath et al., *Power, Presidents, and Professors*, provides unusually frank analyses of presidential attitudes and particularly frustrations. The most common complaint of presidents seems to relate to what they conceive as their general lack of power, particularly with respect to educational matters, in spite of their qualifications for the exercise of such power as a result of their presumed detachment from the parochialisms of the departments and other "vested interests."

Most presidents ... feel that where they and their administrations are held responsible, they should in fact be responsible. The university complex, and the intricacies of compromising numerous faculty viewpoints demand centralized authority. This authority, moreover, should not be vested in groups whose interests are involved. The president commonly sees himself as above the vested interests of departments, alumni, students, etc. He thinks he sees the university as a whole and is responsible for its over-all growth and success. Such responsibility demands commensurate power.[67]

[66] *Ibid.*, p. 67.
[67] Demerath et al., *Power*, p. 84.

To the outside public, at least, the claims for greater presidential power seem quite legitimate, not only because of imagined analogies from the industrial or governmental scene, but also because of the generally favorable public image of the president.

In contrast with the mumbling professors who seem to pursue the esoteric and forget their overshoes, there is the president as seen by the trustees and the public. He stands trim in his executive suit, young in spite of his fifty-odd years, a figure with both feet on the ground and a big proposition to put over.

Unlike the controversial professor, the unconventional intellectual, or the seemingly unsuccessful schoolteacher, the president rarely offends with his educational pronouncements.[68]

Presidents may desire more influence; yet, they may not be able to obtain it, particularly not in educational matters. The current and apparently rapidly increasing institutionalization of contacts between boards on the one hand and faculty and students on the other hand, is eliminating one traditional position of strength of presidents – the monopoly of communications between the board and the other components of the campus. Other duties impose burdens upon presidents, such as incredibly heavy demands upon their time for fund-raising or public relations functions. At times, in the pessimistic view of Demerath et al., "in attempting to cope with their difficulties, presidents may adopt mechanisms of personal behavior which have the effect of removing them from the social realities of their jobs and their universities." Three such "escape mechanisms" are mentioned: isolation, platitudinousness, and inertia or excessive busyness. Isolation seems the style of life imposed upon American university presidents, whose contacts with faculty members and students are by necessity indirect and impersonal. "There are too many meetings to attend, too many trips to make, and too many conferences to be held for the president to maintain intimate campus relationships." [69] Similar causes are cited for the platitudes which are said to characterize many a president's approach to educational issues:

Relatively few presidents, either academically or non-academically trained, have the opportunity to visit quietly and consult with one another or with other learned men about broad educational ideas and policies. Certainly their traveling is extensive, and they frequently talk about education, but to the alumni, the legislators, the businessmen,

68 *Ibid.*, pp. 97, 111.
69 *Ibid.*, pp. 220–221.

and at celebrations, and centennials. Such pronouncements are often accumulations of secondhand knowledge or mazes of superficialities, or both.[70]

The Brock University Report urges presidents to make every possible effort to remain real members of the academic community. They should have tenure in a department, be active in teaching and research, and be eligible for sabbatical leave. However, as the report points out with obvious justification, any chance for the successful carrying-out of this academic re-entry of presidents would depend on relieving them to the greatest possible extent particularly "from routine representational and public relations duties." [71] A similar proposal was made by a president, Robert F. Goheen of Princeton University. Goheen suggested that Princeton be headed by two officials, a president and a chancellor. The president would be "the chief executive officer, directing all internal operations, overseeing the curriculum, the student body and the faculty." The chancellor "would head fund-raising operations and represent the university in external functions, including alumni affairs." Goheen favored the dual-head concept because under the present system the office of president had become "more and more like that of a business manager and less and less academic." Goheen further specified that the chancellor too, under his proposal, should have "some academic background." [72]

[70] *Ibid.*, p. 113.

[71] Brock University Report, p. 14. Mark Ingraham, in his survey of the working conditions of administrators, was most emphatic in concluding that entertainment was "overdone and its importance overrated" among administrators in general and presidents in particular. (Mark H. Ingraham, *The Mirror of Brass* [The University of Wisconsin Press, 1968], p. 106.)

[72] Joseph G. Herzberg, "Goheen Suggests Dual Leadership," *New York Times*, December 26, 1968. A Commission on University Governance at Duke University agreed with Goheen on the necessity of dividing the functions of the academic chief executive between two officers. The commission discussed three models of dividing the labor between a president and a chancellor. The first model was that proposed by Goheen, a division of responsibility between internal and external operations, which the commission found undesirable because it could lead "to separate power bases for the two officers," resulting in divided responsibility and dysfunctional competition for policy control. A second model of the president-chancellor relationship would place the president as the "chief executive or policy-determining officer" and the chancellor as the "chief administrative or policy-implementing officer." This model, said the commission, would isolate the president from much of the university community. The commission's third model, its preferred one, would "deliberately blur the line between the President and the Chancellor who is to be seen as the President's alter ego." Responsibility for decisions would rest solely with the president, while the chancellor would serve in effect as an executive vice-president. (Duke University Commission on University (Governance, *Central Administration* [Interim Report, March 30, 1970], pp. 4–5.

The AAUP Statement on Government of 1966 assigned to the president the role of chief planning officer, innovator, and initiator on the campus. This task will have to remain beyond fulfillment unless presidents can establish a close, personal relationship to the heart of the academic process, teaching and research. Unfortunately, even if presidents were relieved of most of their ceremonial and representative duties, it is doubtful whether the ever-increasing burden of real pressures and real dilemmas from inside and outside the university would permit a president to devote himself to true academic work. The presidency, in most cases, is likely to remain a position remarkably far removed from the spheres of action academicians like – with as one compensation the prestige attributed to the presidency by the outside world.[73]

3. Administrative Organization

Administrative organization in the university places "distinctive demands" upon administrative practice and procedure because of the relative difficulty – again, in contrast with business or government – of evaluating quality and efficiency. In Corson's words,

The crucial activity for which these institutions exist takes place in the minds and characters of individuals – faculty members and students. It cannot readily be measured as a basis for exercising administrative control or for evaluating individual performance.[74]

Two groupings of administration exist in all academic institutions: the president and his academic staff (the provost, the academic vice-president, the academic deans – and to some extent the director of admissions, the dean of students, the registrar); and the president and his auxiliary staff (the business manager, the dormitory and food service managers, the physical plant supervisor, the security police chief, etc.). "Two cultures," administratively speaking, co-exist on the campus: a sphere of operations pertaining to auxiliary and housekeeping

[73] McConnell and Mortimer point to Clark Kerr, who was Chancellor at Berkeley from 1952 to 1958, as an example of effective presidential leadership under difficult conditions. His style and effort with committees; his view of the senate as "the basic instrumentality of the university"; his success in working with the faculty through informal associations; his reliance on functional or collegial rather than positional authority – all these elements enabled Kerr to play the role of the academic leader who can significantly influence the life of the university. (McConnell and Mortimer, *The Faculty in University Governance*, pp. 142–144.)

[74] Corson, *Governance*, p. 22.

matters which can be more or less tightly rationalized, and the
sphere relating to teaching and research which must be non-
hierarchically loose and unstructured. Yet, even in the "ordinary" administrative sphere – for example, dormitory management or security police operations – the academic sector will
infiltrate with "non-rational" demands of its own. Therefore,
administrative officers from the academic side, with faculty
assistance, have to play a role in the auxiliary and housekeeping administration of the university. This is also important, for example, in the news and public relations operations
of the institution, where journalistic expertise, as such, may be
totally insufficient to handle affairs without appropriate inputs
of academic expertise. Nevertheless, Rourke and Brooks are
quite right in insisting that modern methods of management,
such as computers, can be applied in certain areas of campus
administration.[75]

The academic dean is at the very opposite pole of administration from the computerized sphere of the auxiliary services.
His effectiveness depends on his influence on the strictly academic side of the university, particularly the individual faculty
member in the shelter of his department. In the opinion of
Deegan et al., the academic deanship is in many ways "the
most difficult administrative position in a large college or university." The relationship between a dean and the president
is quite different from the relationship between the president
and a vice-president. The dean is truly the man in the middle,
"the chief medium of communication" and "creative link"
between faculty and administration. The dean must work
with both the president and the faculty and may not move
out of the middle position; he cannot agree with the president
and disagree with the faculty over an important issue, or vice
versa. This "peculiar" status of the academic dean "calls for a
special style, characterized by openness and integrity." [76]
Chancellor Kimpton of the University of Chicago thought that
"a good dean is a very pleasant thing to have around, but he
shares the weakness of the head of the institution – he rarely
knows what is going on." This weakness is attributed to tendencies on the part of deans to devote their time to the wrong

[75] Rourke and Brooks, *Managerial Revolution*, pp. 10, 127. The Duke University Commission on University Governance suggested the appropriateness of selecting an institution's top public relations officer through mechanisms of faculty
consultation. (*Central Administration*, p. 12.)

[76] Deegan et al., *Joint Participation in Decision Making*, pp. 62–63.

things – administrative "chores" rather than direct contact or confrontation with the faculty on subjects close to the heart of academic life.[77] The Brock University Report took a strong stand on the question of the dean's close relationship to the faculty.

The Dean should remain an active member of the academic community. This implies that he should retain his academic appointment, have tenure in a departmental position, at his discretion be active in teaching and research, be eligible for sabbatical leave, and enjoy the other rights and privileges of his academic colleagues. Upon retirement from the office of Dean, there should be no reduction in salary or benefits, and additional sabbatical leave may be appropriate and annual increments should be considered in the same light as for all other academic staff.[78]

One way of keeping academic deans close to the faculty was suggested by the Duke University Commission on University Governance. It insisted that academic administrators should be appointed for a five-year term, "once renewable upon mutual review." A third term should be considered "only in highly unusual circumstances." Similarly, Deegan et al. recommended "stated terms" for deans (and vice-presidents), perhaps five years – "as a further check on unacceptable administrative performance and as another measure of administrative accountability ...." [79]

This kind of suggestion places the dean in a position very similar to that of the department chairman, whose effectiveness as a link between faculty and administration has been due, indeed, to his usually undisputed status as a full member of the faculty component – as will be demonstrated in some detail in a later section. The question arises, as in the case of the president, whether the burden of deanly work will ever permit his rejoining of the faculty ranks while still taking care of his non-faculty duties or even after completing his term. If deans have to remain full-time deans, as is likely, special attention will have to be paid, of course, to the relationship between the administration and the faculty.

[77] Corson, *Governance*, p. 78. (Chancellor Kimpton is cited by Corson.)
[78] Brock University Report, p. 18.
[79] Deegan et al., *Joint Participation in Decision Making*, p. 85. The Duke commission also emphasized the function of the provost as the "chief academic officer" of the institution who has the special responsibility "to insure the ascendancy of the academic component in the highest councils of the university ...." The commission thought that the typical undergraduate dean's functions should be divided between two officers – a Dean of Faculty for central academic and faculty matters and a Dean of Undergraduate Education for specific undergraduate programs and students. (*Central Administration*, pp. 6–7, 12.)

D. THE ADMINISTRATION – FACULTY RELATIONSHIP

I. Shared Authority

The basic concept in the governmental model of the 1966 *Statement on Government of Colleges and Universities* is that of shared authority among the components of the institution. The faculty and the administration particularly participate jointly in influence and decision-making. As was indicated above, the model makes the faculty predominant in issues where its special knowledge or status so require; in other issues, the administration has natural advantages and therefore a predominant voice. However, the concept of shared authority prescribes carefully adjusted patterns of joint action even in matters where either the faculty or the administration is clearly predominant. While this model exists nowhere perfectly, it has become, as Sanford Kadish remarked, "the mode of *rapprochement* between bureaucracy and professionalism in institutions of higher education" which faculties have come to prefer. "Certainly at our more distinguished and pace-setting institutions it is invariably the operational model ...." It is therefore appropriate that when Kadish marshalls his arguments against professorial use of the strike weapon, he refers chiefly to the strike's disastrous consequences for the shared-authority principle, which he calls the system of university government holding "the greatest promise for the effective progress of the main business of research and education." [80]

Rourke and Brooks reach the same model through an altogether different approach. They come to the conclusion – writing in 1965 (and not in 1971!) – that both faculty and administration have profited greatly in a "growth industry," higher education. While both faculty and administration may be after "power," they are playing a "non-zero-sum game"; *both* components are increasing their influence, prestige, and decision-making potential in the university. "With booming enrollments and the growing demand for technical skills generated by automation, new opportunities have been opened up for colleges and universities to play an expanding role ...." As a result, both administration and faculty have been able "to increase ... [their] winnings without decreasing the total

[80] Sanford H. Kadish, "The Strike and the Professoriate," *AAUP Bulletin*, Summer 1968, p. 163–164.

available to the other." Administrative offices and functions have multiplied, while faculty horizons have been expanding and competition has sent academic salaries upward. Administration and faculty power have grown in a complementary rather than a competitive way; a dichotomy between faculty and administration "simply does not exist at most institutions of higher education today" – campus politics, observe Rourke and Brooks, "are far more complicated than that." [81] In somewhat similar terms, Martin Trow talks about a governmental "arrangement" between administration and faculty: on the one hand, there exists an elaborate system of administration rules largely for handling the masses of undergraduate students with respect to admission, organizing their programs, housing, etc.; on the other hand, there is an intricate system of departmental rules for the content of teaching, faculty recruitment and promotion, recruitment and training of graduate students, and research. These two forms of government – the administrative one and the departmental one – "exist side by side" in most universities, and it is this "arrangement" which makes for relatively non-competitive and coordinated relationships between faculty and administration.[82] Whether faculty and administration share in decision-making because it is the best way to run a university, or merely because they are both "fat cats" with respect to the other components and want to keep it that way – the model of the 1966 Statement holds in any case.

Dykes' study does not contradict the model either: "faculty power and administrative power are, in a sense, fused, and each depends in considerable measure on the other"; "it is possible for administrative and faculty power to increase simultaneously." However, Dykes is deeply concerned about the misconceptions which he found among faculty and ad-

[81] Rourke and Brooks, *Managerial Revolution*, pp. 14–15, 117. This point is confirmed in Edward Gross' empirical study: "By and large ... the faculty and administrators tend to see eye-to-eye." ("Universities as Organizations: A Research Approach," *American Sociological Review*, August 1968, p. 538.) Note also a main conclusion of a large-scale empirical study by Gross and Paul Grambsch: "... the dichotomy is not between administrators and faculty members: It is between the 'outsiders' (legislators, the state government, regents ...) and the academicians.... In short, our analyses give no support to the contention that administrators differ so much in outlook from faculty members that the goals they emphasize, when they have power, run counter to faculty interests." (Edward Gross and Paul V. Grambsch, *University Goals and Academic Power* [American Council on Education, 1968], pp. 114–115.)
[82] Trow, "Conceptions of the University," p. 19.

ministration about each other, since he is convinced that shared power between the two components is essential for effective leadership in the university. Many members of the administration and faculty suspect that any increase in the other's power must necessarily result in a decrease of their own power; they assume erroneously that the university is "a closed system with a finite power potential." New perspectives, Dykes urges, must be developed on the administration-faculty relationship in order to upset the conventional wisdom about the dichotomy between administration power and faculty power – "as attractive as that idea may be in its simplicity." [83] Paul Lazarsfeld made a similar point during his presidential address to the American Sociological Association in 1962. A "crippling malaise" in our universities keeps them at a "dangerously low level of institutional development": the tendency on the part of the faculty to keep administration out of academic affairs, while at the same time considering administration "beneath its dignity." The faculty and administration must realize that academic leadership involves "intellectual as well as administrative tasks." [84]

The process of "collegialization" was identified by Demerath et al. as crucial for the effective sharing of administration and faculty power, as was mentioned earlier.[85] Two additional – rather awkward – terms are introduced to clarify this process: "professional-administrator" and "professor administrant." The professional-administrator (the ideal dean!) provides the type of authority "which is an accommodation between the organization's need for the pattern of superordinate control and the professional's need for the colleague control pattern of authority." The professional-administrator must be a professional himself who can work with other professionals but who can also "exercise superordinate control when necessary"; he must be able to grant autonomy as well as provide over-all direction and coordination.[86] The ideal professor, in turn, must act as professor administrant; he serves on committees or senates and, besides his main functions of teaching and research, generally participates in his university's government. Thus, the effectively governed academic institution features a faculty-administration continuum. At one end is the "pure"

---

[83] Dykes, *Faculty Participation*, pp. 40–41.
[84] Paul Lazarsfeld, as quoted by Demerath et al., *Power*, p. 7.
[85] See above, p. 5.
[86] B. Barber, as quoted by Demerath et al., *Power*, p. 36.

professor who acknowledges no obligations except teaching
and research, who refuses membership even on departmental
committees; at the other end is the "pure" dean who devotes
his efforts exclusively to administration and makes no attempt
to find out faculty opinion nor in other ways to remain close to
interests of the faculty. Between these extreme poles are what
Demerath et al. call "the participants in the collegial structure
of the university" – the professors administrant on committees
and senates whose efforts count in policy matters, and the
professional-administrators who remain active teacher-scholars
or associate intimately with the faculty. These persons in the
middle of the continuum make possible successful government
and preservation of the "historic mission" of the university.[87]

Professional-administrators and professors administrant
make for collegialization, i.e., effective processes of shared
authority between administration and faculty. As to the exact
details of the sharing, some more precise coverage will be provided below. In any case, with respect to both structural and
jurisdictional arrangements, James Darlington's general advice seems useful:

> ... there is no single or unique answer to the problems of appropriate
> faculty-administration relationships. There can be no prototype be-
> cause the human elements cannot be equated from campus to campus.
> The size of the institution, the research emphasis, traditions, charter
> restrictions, are further variables which oppose conformity.[88]

2. Irritants Between Administration and Faculty

In spite of the need for administration and faculty to co-
operate, irritants between the two components abound. For
example, there is a definite tendency to grant higher prestige
and salary to administration than to faculty, regardless of
merit or seniority. In some institutions, the "officers" of administration deport themselves in the style of an aristocracy,
while to the mere "members" of the faculty is delegated the
role of overseer or non-commissioned officer. On all kinds of
official or social occasions, the more elevated status of administration is implied. For example, when visiting dignitaries
come to the campus, it is not at all unusual to invite to the
reception the entire "corps" of administration officials, but

[87] Demerath et al., *Power*, pp. 24–25, 178.
[88] James M. Darlington, "Faculty-Administration Relationships," *AAUP
Bulletin*, Autumn 1960, p. 265.

only a handful of faculty members or none at all. Such practices reflect an entirely arbitrary preference for administration
status, based frequently on the administration's own policy
directions.[89] Fortunately, at least the salary of the senior
faculty is presently catching up with the deans', if the so-
called nine-month salary base of the professors is granted as
compared to the deans' eleven-month year.

In a comparative study on the status of university teachers
throughout the world, Richard Shryock cited professorial complaints in the United States about salary and status outside
and inside the university. American academics are particularly
jealous of the prestige of European professors "as co-equal
participants in the government of universities – a dignity
denied in varying degrees in the United States because of the
status and authority of administration and trustees." Even
within academic circles the low prestige of the professor is
acknowledged; otherwise, not so many professors would want
to become deans and presidents![90] Lazarsfeld and Thielens
point to the large number of professors in the United States,
as compared to Europe, and their distribution over a great
variety of institutions – from very good to very poor in academic standards. The outside public, at least, is unable to
distinguish between the many lower quality faculty members
and the elite; all are put into the low-prestige category.[91]

From the administration's point of view, some faculty members may be irritatingly difficult:

they object to coming early for registration, to compulsory roll calls in
classes, and to smoking regulations; they will not report grades on
time, or give examinations when they are scheduled, or serve on committees, or take their student-advisory roles seriously, or place their
textbook orders; they fail to attend university ceremonies and exercises, and they avoid most faculty and student social gatherings.[92]

Frequently, and particularly in the better-known institutions, the administration official has no choice but to tolerate
careless or even callous behavior on the part of faculty members; a professor's career depends largely on his nation-wide
reputation within his discipline and relatively little on the
"authority structure" of his particular campus – the greater

[89] Campbell, address, p. 42.
[90] Richard H. Shryock, in R. H. Shryock, ed., *The Status of University Teachers*
(Ghent, 1961), pp. 193–194.
[91] Lazarsfeld and Thielens, *Academic Mind*, pp. 148–149.
[92] Demerath et al., *Power*, p. 226.

his merit (or even, potential merit) as a scholar, the more he might enjoy a kind of veto power over his "local" administration.[93] Administration officials have the most frustrating obligation to adapt, on the one hand, to the faculty member's "lack of an institutional perspective," and, on the other hand, to his insistence to be involved in all decisions.[94]

Burton Clark described the "banners" under which faculty and administration tend to go into battle:

The faculties march under the banner of self-government and academic freedom, emphasizing equality of relations among colleagues and de-emphasizing administrative hierarchy. The administrations move forward under a cluster of banners: let's bring order out of chaos, or at least reduce chaos to mere confusion; let's increase efficiency, utilize our scarce resources of men and money effectively; let's give the organization as a whole a sense of direction, with knowledgeable hands on the helm. . . . [95]

Fortunately, Clark also discovered a set of six "conflict-reducing mechanisms" which operate in many universities to reduce the tensions between faculty and administration. The first such mechanism is *separation of powers*. Formally, or tacitly, spheres of influence are designated in which either the faculty or the administration predominates. Clark's examples show the limits of this mechanism – the curriculum is to be set aside for faculty hegemony, and student affairs for administration control. Obviously, strong counter-influences of the administration on curriculum, and the faculty on student affairs, are hardly avoidable. The second conflict-reducing mechanism is *joint appointment*, as is universally practiced, says Clark, in the case of the departmental chairman who is "clearly both in the faculty and in the administration" – the "man-in-the-middle" who understands the views of both camps and manages to reconcile conflicting pressures. Again, some conflict-reducing undoubtedly comes out of the chairman's "hide." But, as will be argued later, the chairman is clearly not of the faculty *and* the administration; at least in the current view of the chairmanship, he is a faculty member primarily, if not exclusively. A third mechanism is called *bureaucratization of the faculty* by Clark, consisting of the development of committees and representative bodies and the elaboration of jurisdictions and proper channels. Thus, the volatile and unpredictable output of mass

[93] *Ibid.*, p. 29.
[94] Corson, *Governance*, p. 29.
[95] Clark, "Faculty Authority," p. 296.

meetings of the faculty is moderated and regularized through the habit of committee study and reporting. Of course, another name for this mechanism, in a sense, is shared authority – which does serve to reduce tension, among other things. The fourth mechanism, *institutionalization* or *formalization of conflict*, is closely related to the previous point; it transforms "raw conflict" into socially approved conflict by the creation of legitimate rules and procedures. The fifth conflict-reducing mechanism is *oligarchy in the faculty*.

The faculty oligarchy may be seen as a quasi-administrative component of the faculty. The faculty oligarchs are in frequent contact with the central administrators, much more than the average faculty member. The faculty oligarchy is more conservative than the faculty as a whole .... On the large campuses, academic matters are handled increasingly by a combination of the faculty oligarchs and the middle and lower echelons of the administration .... The majority of faculty members gravitate toward research, toward scholarly reading that grows increasingly burdensome, into consulting and the pursuit of other interests aside from the governing of the college – and they, unconsciously or deliberately, "delegate" authority to the oligarchs. The *partial* centralizing of faculty authority, in the hands of professors who are oriented strongly to the local institution and who have chosen governance as their first concern, is a mechanism of prime importance in the amelioration of conflict between faculty and administration.

The last conflict-reducing mechanism, *disengagement or withdrawal*, is complementary to the one just mentioned. It is equally pertinent. While the faculty oligarch specializes in government, the faculty "cosmopolitan" is "proudly impatient" with such "local" chores. The "cosmopolitan" is oriented to external, disciplinary matters; he combines mobility and professionalism, is "on the move or ready to move," and has little interest in "campus politics." His withdrawal or disengagement from the campus leaves the administrators and the faculty oligarchs even less challenged in their control over the university's affairs.[96]

[96] *Ibid.*, pp. 296–298. Note the discussion of faculty oligarchs, below, p. 61. Trow saw institutional and "geographical" insulation as another conflict-reducing device; however much historians and chemical engineers may disagree about the goals of the university, they hardly ever confront one another. Keeping the basic decision-making in the departments provides such insulation. (Trow, "Conceptions of the University," p. 17.)

With respect to Clark's fourth mechanism, institutionalization or formalization of conflict, McConnell and Mortimer saw this as "the great problem of governance in the next decade." Universities must recognize "the normality of conflict and adapt their structures and functions in ways that will make controversy serve organizational purposes"; internal conflict must be translated into constructive

Entirely new types of irritants between faculty and administration are discussed in Rourke's and Brooks' previously cited book, *The Managerial Revolution in Higher Education*. Computers and related techniques have dramatically focused certain basic beliefs that have long been prevalent among faculties:

(1) that educational outputs cannot be measured, and that any attempt to do so is ludicrous if not actually subversive of the purposes for which academic institutions exist; (2) that there is an inherent conflict between administrative efficiency on the one hand and academic effectiveness on the other; (3) that efforts to improve management efficiency are really designed to increase the power of administrators at the expense of faculty members.[97]

Particularly the department's autonomy, the crucial organ for a faculty member's independent status, is considered threatened by the computer. The establishment of a centralized information system in a university milieu inevitably will affect the department's power, say Rourke and Brooks.

Strictly hierarchical organizations accept the idea that information processed by any constituent unit should be subject to surveillance by higher administrative echelons. In theory, at least, the subordinate is not expected to conceal anything from his superior. But in a university setting, where authority is not hierarchical and where individual departments operate with a great deal of autonomy, departmental officers may be understandably reluctant to supply information to the central authority when their position of independent power may largely depend on the fact that they alone have access to certain kinds of data.[98]

The interference with the department's traditional status is the more effective because the new information flow is a one-way process. While the central administration gains new kinds of information about departments which enhances its central powers, the departments are usually *not* given access to the new data – for example, information about differentials in salary scales or teaching loads. Knowledge of such data would strengthen a department's position in bargaining with the administration.[99]

educational policy. (McConnell and Mortimer, *The Faculty in University Governance*, p. 9.)

[97] Rourke and Brooks, *Managerial Revolution*, p. 8.
[98] *Ibid.*, pp. 37–38.
[99] *Ibid.*, p. 108. According to Dressel et al., deans prefer to impose information screens between departments, especially with respect to salary differentials, to avoid difficult confrontations. But, say the authors, in the long run open communications are wiser. "If inequities exist among departments, they should be brought to light and remedied; if differences exist for a reason, the reasons should be stated and defended." (Dressel et al., *Confidence Crisis*, p. 14.)

Rourke and Brooks conclude that the new techniques of management create "a greatly enhanced potential for administrative dominance" in the university. If the faculty wants to retain its traditional scope of power in the "rationalized" university, it must develop "more effective techniques for participating in university government than the town-meeting devices" that have often prevailed in the past.[100] The threat of the computer will be particularly severe in new or "radically changing" institutions (e.g., former teachers colleges), where faculty members felt underprivileged even before the new techniques arrived. Greatly intensified antagonisms between faculty and administration, and a deepened sense of faculty alienation, are predicted for these institutions.[101]

The previous section, on shared authority, ended with the observation that the precise structural and jurisdictional arrangements for joint government by faculty and administration cannot be specified in any generalized form. This basic truth, in itself, may produce what could be a major irritant between administration and faculty. In the diffuse and non-hierarchical milieu of the university, neatly delineated spheres of jurisdiction and sovereignty cannot be provided. Terry Lunsford emphasized the conflicts which were the result of "the very absence of a clear technical separation between faculty and administration in the processes of governance"; particularly the academic senate and the administrative hierarchy have to co-exist on the campus without a "simple and understandable division of specific responsibilities." [102] In fact, most exercise of shared authority involves the supremely vague concept of consultation. The heart of shared academic decision-making probably lies in the quality and intensity of the consultation processes between faculty and administration. If these two parties do *not* act in the interest of the university as a whole rather than of their own component; if they are *not* convinced of the supreme importance of the teaching-research process and its essential feedback on decision-making; if they are *not* sufficiently empathic to each other's basic positions –

[100] Rourke and Brooks, *Managerial Revolution*, p. 118.
[101] *Ibid.*, p. 102.
[102] Terry F. Lunsford, "Authority and Ideology in the Administered University," *American Behavioral Scientist*, May–June 1968, p. 6. McConnell's and Mortimer's data indicated "that there is little, if any, clear-cut distinction between faculty and administrative activities . . .," and there are "no discrete categories of pure faculty as opposed to administrators." (*The Faculty in University Governance*, pp. 24, 26.)

then, the concept of shared authority may lead to ever increasing doses of irritants which are bound to leave the institution in chaos.

Lunsford expressed considerable pessimism concerning the future relationships between administration and faculty. In an article entitled "Authority and Ideology in the Administered University," he emphasized the insecure status of the "new university 'executives'" of today's "administered university." His paper is concerned with the administrators' often vain attempts to establish a legitimate basis for their authority; "bureaucratic, rule-based authority" is becoming more and more insecure in the academic setting as it has to compete "with a complex interplay of professional and consensual principles." The *special* competence of the academic administrator is "highly precarious and contingent" since administrators, *as a group*, cannot convincingly claim "any distinctive expertise which might clothe their bare formal positions with 'professional' legitimacy." In the highly professionalized contemporary university, administrators cannot expect implicit acceptance of their authority just because of their organizational position; they must forever try to justify their decisions to their various publics in a milieu where there seldom is "a simple and clearly applicable rule covering the case" and where their very "jurisdiction" in the particular decision may be in doubt. It is this growing sense of insecurity flowing from the administrator's precarious standing as a legitimate academic decision-maker which Lunsford explores.

Moreover, Lunsford notes increasing symptoms of isolation of administrators from the rest of the campus. More and more, administrators find themselves excluded from the university's "substantive" activities – teaching, research, and professional consultation; and more and more, they have to devote their energies "*exclusively* to the problems of institutional support and coordination." As administrators "spend most of their time coordinating the work of other administrators," they have less and less "official reason for direct contact with either faculty members or students." Thus, administrators lose their feeling for the "subcultures" of the students and faculty; their expertise depends increasingly on their past personal experiences as students and faculty members, and these are rapidly becoming outdated. Besides, the administrator's interpretations of these subcultures are "highly colored by his own immersion in an 'administrative' subculture." Also in their social relations university administrators and faculty members are becoming strangers as "each is encouraged toward contacts mainly with his own 'kind.'" Administrators are so busy that many social contacts with the faculty are simply out of the question; further, the necessary associations with trustees, legislators, alumni, federal bureaucrats, "community leaders," and other administrators make "some accommodation to these groups' way of thought ... almost inevitable"; finally, "for some administrators the respect and even awe accorded them when they meet the outside world ... contrasts pleasurably with their lower prestige as administrators inside academe."

Isolation and alienation from the rest of the campus is frequently rationalized through myths. For example, administrators tend to ascribe to themselves a greater and less parochial awareness of responsibility to "the institution" – not realizing that administration may also create "a narrow perspective of its own" and may involve the irresponsible abuse of power. Also, administrators often claim that only their decision-making is truly non-political, rational or technical – ignoring the fact that much administrative decision-making, too, has to be inherently political, based by necessity on "brute opinion, doctrinal preferences, ... existing relations of power," and pressures from the outside community.

Lunsford predicts a further accentuation of the isolation of administration as "a distinct and even alien segment of the university." Yet, effective government of the university requires easy, informal relationships between administrators and faculty, based on mutual trust and appreciation. What can be done? Lunsford advises administrators to cultivate close personal friendships with representatives of influential faculty groups ("hoping that these will not be seen as 'palace cliques' by those who are not included"). Also, respected faculty members should be appointed as part-time, special assistants to administrative officers, so that the "pure" academic view of things can be better appreciated.[103] Of course, a proper realization by the faculty of the administration's internal problems, such as indicated by Lunsford, is urgently required for any kind of improved relationship between the two components who are so dependent on one another for the operation of the academic institution. In the previous section, the need for

[103] Lunsford, "Authority and Ideology," pp. 5–12.

the administrative component was stressed. Perhaps, if this component could be made somewhat more attractive for the academician, the right kind of academician would be more willing to join its ranks – for the right reasons. At present, becoming an administrator almost inevitably means giving up the academic life; too many campus administrative milieus seem too tightly bureaucratic and hierarchical. There may be, as Troy Duster remarked, "little room for the eccentric and little reward for innovation," and the most certain path to promotions, as in "ordinary" bureaucracy, may be to play with the "team" and to follow faithfully the orders of one's "line superior." [104] Above all, perhaps, the administrator must regain some sense of creative leisure, so as to have the time, at least, *to think* about the decisions he has to make. The gap between administration and faculty will close rather than widen to the extent that the administration task can be related more directly to the academic. The proper exercise of the principles of shared authority in academic government should encourage this process.

E. FACULTY PARTICIPATION IN UNIVERSITY GOVERNMENT

1. Faculty Participation as a Right and Duty

Ralph Brown called faculty participation in academic government "a complement to the right and responsibility to teach conscientiously and to investigate freely." Not only do faculties have "a right to participate in practically every aspect of university affairs"; they also have "a responsibility to do so, limited by considerations of efficiency and division of labor ...." [105] Richard Adams saw faculty participation not merely as a reflection of principles of democracy but above all as the prime insurance of the supremacy of the academic purposes of the university – "it [faculty participation] is to insure, as much as insurance can, that administrative authority is always used in the service of academic authority, and never allowed to get in the way of learning." [106] Harold W. Dodds

---

[104] Troy Duster, "Student Interests, Student Power, and the Swedish Experience," *American Behavioral Scientist*, May–June 1968, p. 22.

[105] Brown, "Rights and Responsibilities," p. 131.

[106] Richard P. Adams, "Tulane University: Faculty Participation in the Government of the University," *AAUP Bulletin*, Autumn 1963, p. 221.

makes a similar point. The fundamental reason why the faculty should participate at the highest policy levels "is the cardinal truth that if an institution is to prosper, it must utilize the intellectual application and imaginative thinking of more than the president, vice-presidents, and deans." [107] Sanford Kadish, finally, relates faculty participation to the autonomy which must be guaranteed professionals in their professional activities.

Autonomy in exercising that competence is an important ideal of professionalism. The professional himself must have final responsibility, though with advice and consultation among colleagues, to determine how his work is to be done – what problems should be dealt with and how, what values should be striven for, what the criteria of distinction are. And this autonomy extends to the admission of others into the professional ranks as well as to the work done.

. . . .
Like other professionals, the highly specialized character of his calling disqualifies others from making the principal judgments about how he should carry on his scholarship and his instructions. Standards and performance must reside in the judgment of the scholarly community if the judgment is to be reliably made.[108]

2. Conditions for Faculty Participation

The reasons for faculty participation in academic government are easily stated: participation is complementary, as a right and duty, to teaching and research, and must be undertaken to uphold academic purposes and professional autonomy. Less easily stated, of course, are the precise conditions, jurisdictions, and structures for effective faculty participation. As the AAUP's Committee T stated some years ago, what seems important is an understanding concerning the philosophical basis for educational administration rather than insistence upon any particular set of institutional arrangements.[109] Faculty participation requires effective demonstration of faculty influence, which does not necessarily depend on formal institutions:

Faculty participation in university government can perhaps be effective to about the degree that faculty members are able to influence the thinking of others both among their colleagues on the faculty and among the officials in the administration. The media through which

[107] Harold W. Dodds, *The Academic President – Educator or Caretaker?* (New York, 1962), p. 97.
[108] Kadish, "Strikes," pp. 161–162.
[109] Darlington, "Faculty-Administration," p. 268.

this kind of influence flows, *whether formally constitutional or not*, are very often, if not always, the real means of governing the levers by which power is actually manipulated.[110]

Neither does the nature of a university's affiliation or its size determine the extent of faculty participation; faculties can play significant or insignificant roles in large, medium-sized, or small public, private, or church-related institutions.[111]

Three bases for a faculty's effective participation in university government have been specified: delegation of real powers to the faculty, formally or informally; establishment of deliberative organs for purposes of decision-making and consultation; willingness of the faculty to assume governing responsibilities. The delegation of powers is useless unless the administration and the board restrain themselves from interfering in areas which have been declared to be under faculty jurisdiction. The deliberative organs can function only if they are involved by the administration and board when decisions have to be made and if the deliberations in these organs are then appropriately respected. Last but not least, faculty members must take time out for formulating their positions on university government and must be willing to support its organs and institutions.[112] All components must be convinced that effective faculty participation is essential to the institution; and, a set of clearly formulated and well-understood procedures must be instituted. Undoubtedly, faculty participation makes an administration's tasks more complicated and time-consuming in the short run; however, in the long run decisions made with the faculty are bound to be more effective. Capacity for organizing faculty participation has been posited as the major test for judging the ability of an administration.[113]

3. Faculty Reluctance

Faculty participation in government is by no means the most desirable investment of time for a considerable number of faculty members. One important reason for this view, undoubtedly, is the ignorance, misunderstanding, and suspicion which prevail in many faculty circles with respect to faculty

[110] Adams, "Tulane University," p. 221. (Emphasis added.)
[111] Shryock, *Status*, p. 27.
[112] Morrow, "University of Pennsylvania," p. 115.
[113] "Faculty-Administration Relationships: The School of Medicine at The University of Miami (Florida)," *AAUP Bulletin*, Spring 1961, pp. 31–32.

roles in academic government. As has been mentioned before, the rules of academic government are often unclear and the jurisdictions diffuse; the "ultimate" fact of administration hegemony through such devices as budget manipulation seems simplistically clear; the dependence on the "supreme" legal authority of the board seems equally inevitable. As the Berkeley commission stated, "the power of the faculty is considerable, but it is exercised within a milieu of confusion and uncertainty" as to precise jurisdictions and the extent of finality of faculty recommendations and other advice.[114] It is not surprising, then, that numerous faculty members are reluctant to spend time and energy on an activity which seems dubious, confused, and useless.

Several other reasons can be cited for faculty members' reluctance to participate in government: faculty time is an increasingly scarce item in the modern university; the more reputable activity for faculty members is said to be research, and perhaps teaching – but not service on committees; many faculty members feel more attachment to their discipline at the national level than to the "local" affairs of their university; the main campus attachment – if there is any – of numerous faculty members is to the department rather than to the college or the entire university.

Philip Denenfeld described the problem of government involvement as many faculty members see it:

> ... a Senate requires a great expenditure of time by many faculty members, imagination, serious study of problems, regular attendance at meetings, all of the requisites of persuading and accomplishing, rather than just complaining. It requires, in short, assuming responsibility in a joint enterprise and sacrificing the comfort of a convenient scapegoat whom one can blame for all the deficiencies, real and alleged, of the University. It is in some ways a strange role for many faculty members, certainly not one that they entered the profession to play, and full acceptance of it cannot reasonably be expected.[115]

The Berkeley commission, too, expressed concern about the burden of time which senate and committee work imposed upon the faculty, even before the Berkeley riots. "For many faculty members the demands of administration consume as much time and energy as either teaching or research, and have

---

[114] Berkeley Report, p. 15.
[115] Philip Denenfeld, "Western Michigan University – Faculty Participation in the Government of the University: The Faculty Senate," *AAUP Bulletin*, Winter 1966, p. 396.

no compensating good effect upon teaching." The commission realized that its recommendations pertaining to student participation would further aggravate the faculty's time problem. Yet, the solution must never be found in reducing the faculty role in decision-making. Relief might be provided, however, by more adequate staff assistance and avoidance of involvement in routine administrative chores.[116]

As to the problem of the lack of prestige of government activities among faculty members, Caplow and McGee remark quite rightly that the "publish or perish" syndrome has not only affected teaching but has equally depreciated the value of service on committees and similar work. Formerly, a professor could make a career either in his discipline or in his university; currently, as the generation of campus-oriented elder statesmen retires, most of the younger faculty will not want to take their place because the institutional orientation, say Caplow and McGee, has ceased to be attractive to the up-and-coming academician.[117] Dodds makes the same point: "Perhaps the most serious handicap under which faculty self-government labors is the questionable standing attached to participation . . . ." Dodds was told more than once "that no man who views committee work as an important duty can be a true scholar." Dykes' investigations discovered the same conditions: little inclination among many faculty members for participation in governance, partly because it was not important in promotions and salary increases. Moreover, there was a definite tendency "to denigrate" the efforts of those who did become involved in governance – "at least 50 percent of the faculty look down on those who participate." Particularly younger faculty members tend to avoid committee work in their efforts to get ahead: "the younger members of the faculty who desire advancement and tenure have learned to concentrate on their personal teaching, research, and writing and eschew involvement in the corporate life of the campus." [118]

Among the crucial differences between the university on the one hand and business, industry, or government on the other hand, Corson notes that in the latter, the activities of the staff and officers are judged in terms of their participation in the organization's operations. The academician, in contrast, carries

[116] Berkeley Report, p. 42.
[117] Caplow and McGee, *Academic Marketplace*, p. 85.
[118] Dykes, *Faculty Participation*, pp. 18–19.

out his scholarship "more in concert with colleagues at other institutions specializing in his field than with colleagues in other departments and schools of the university." [119] And, as was suggested above, whatever institutional loyalty the younger "careerist" may have is usually consummated in his department, or perhaps only among the younger colleagues in his department. In fact, isolation from the rest of the university within the safe shelter of the departmental peer group is a typical academic attitude.

What can be done about faculty members' reluctance to participate in university governance? Logan Wilson suggests that "proper credit" be given for performance of such functions, and that department heads specifically point out to their colleagues the importance of participation.[120] Obviously, it would help to make committee and senate membership a more rewarded chore for salary, promotion, and tenure purposes; moreover, active participants in such duties should be considered eligible for reduced teaching loads or special administrative assistance. In any case, a major effort must be undertaken to improve the faculty's general attitude toward participation in government. As Dodds reflected, it is certainly illogical for the faculty to demand discretionary powers on policy and general autonomy, but then to "fail to honor" those who occupy themselves with these newly won rights.[121]

The notion that good scholars must find "sitting on committees, arguing about university affairs or haggling about the wording of regulations" distasteful is just "a romantic reflection," notes Darlington with obvious justification.

The satisfaction that a faculty member, passionately interested in teaching and scholarship, would get from the burdens of policy making would certainly not arise from the deliberations of committee meetings but would come with the knowledge that a better climate for both teaching and learning had been engendered by his efforts.[122]

In the long run, at least, only a faculty which is not reluctant to participate in policy decision-making will confidently leave day-to-day routines to the administration. Also, a faculty which does participate in government will attach itself more deeply to the institution.

In a sense, a faculty that captures control is also captured in return,

[119] Corson, *Governance*, pp. 26–27.
[120] Wilson, *Academic Man*, p. 103.
[121] Dodds, *Academic President*, p. 105.
[122] Darlington, "Faculty-Administration," pp. 266–267.

committed to the college by involvement in policy-making. After a half-dozen years, a man often has invested too much of himself to leave. In short, faculty authority attracts, involves and commits faculty personnel.[123]

As President Dodds exclaimed, "that institution is fortunate which has a substantial number of distinguished teachers and scholars who regard participation in the general affairs of the university as an obligation . . . ." [124]

McConnell and Mortimer paid particular attention to the faculty activists – or "oligarchs" – in their case studies. At all three institutions participation by individual faculty members on senate committees followed a similar pattern: approximately 65 to 80 percent of those eligible to participate on committees did not do so at all; most faculty members who did serve on committees did so only once; however, at each institution from 10 to 20 percent of those who served on committees did so three or more times. In his analysis of activists at

[123] Clark, "Faculty Authority," pp. 299–300.

[124] Dodds, *Academic President*, pp. 104–105. Archie Dykes' survey of faculty attitudes at one state university revealed reactions which could be termed neurotic. Respondents clamored for a strong faculty role in decisions but, at the same time, showed extreme reluctance to give the time and energy demanded by such a role – and even refused to accord to other faculty members the right to do so. Also, many faculty members held an exceedingly simplistic view of the distribution of power in their own institution and attributed to the administration vastly more power than it actually possessed. Moreover, "during the interviews, faculty members repeatedly lamented the lack of faculty involvement in decisions of considerable moment when, in fact, the faculty had been intimately involved; the administration was often criticized for failing to consult with the faculty, when, in fact, the faculty had been consulted; and criticisms were often voiced that decisions had not been taken through proper channels when both protocol and university statutes had been followed scrupulously. In short, serious misconceptions existed about the processes through which decisions are made and about the role of the faculty in them. The major result was a widespread sense of suspicion and distrust." Many faculty members in Dykes' sample "proudly recounted how long it had been since they had attended a meeting of the faculty at any level," and seemed to consider prolonged absence from faculty meetings as "a mark of distinction"; yet, all of these also decried "their lack of information" and criticized their administrators for "subterfuges" in handling the faculty. (Dykes, *Faculty Participation*, pp. 10, 41–42.)

Logan Wilson went so far as to complain about the large number of "deviants" on faculties whose presence makes faculty participation in government difficult. He even distinguished three common types of faculty "deviants": first, the "fundamentally disordered personalities" or "screwballs," who often appear on faculties because professors are selected on the basis of technical competence, regardless of personality traits; second, "the frustrated and disgruntled" or "troublemakers," who channel all their frustrated energies "into schemes of protest"; finally the "misfits" who fail to teach and fail to research but act exclusively as partisans of causes and as missionaries. According to Logan Wilson, "deviants" seldom occupy administration positions, because administrators – he asserted – are more carefully screened in terms of their personality. (Logan Wilson, address at conference noted in fn. 36, above.)

Berkeley, Mortimer found that full professors tended to dominate, especially those who had been at Berkeley for a rather long period. Also, and "contrary to what was expected," the activists "had *higher* mean publication scores and, in some areas, the differences were significant." Apparently, to be chosen to committees "involves having been at Berkeley long enough to exhibit a degree of commitment to the institution," and a more than average degree of scholarly productivity.

McConnell and Mortimer believe, with Michels, that faculty oligarchies are inevitable. In any case, the oligarchs constitute a much needed bridge between the faculty and the administration. The danger of oligarchical rule is that the oligarchs may become insulated or remote from the feelings and perceptions of their constituents, particularly when moods change in the body politic of the faculty. For example, during Berkeley's loyalty oath controversy the oligarchs advised President Sproul that there would be no insurmountable faculty opposition to the oath; they proved to be quite ignorant of the feelings of the faculty majority, especially its younger component. At all three institutions the oligarchs, with few exceptions, were persons who – in the words of McConnell and Mortimer – subscribed to the views of the "academic establishment." [125]

4. Levels of Faculty Participation

Levels of faculty participation can be discussed in two ways, structurally and functionally. According to the 1966 Statement on Government, "agencies for faculty participation in the government of the college or university should be established at each level where faculty responsibility is present" – the department, the division, the college or school, the entire university, and (if applicable) the system of coordinated universities. Structures and procedures should permit joint action by the components of the university, with faculty representatives selected by the faculty where a structure does not include all the faculty members.

As to functions, the faculty should participate in the de-

[125] Mortimer, *Academic Government at Berkeley*, pp. 14, 61–65, 164–171; McConnell and Mortimer, *The Faculty in University Governance*, pp. 24, 171–172. Dressel et al. have an interesting sketch of the discipline-oriented assistant professor developing into the department-oriented associate professor and finally into the university-oriented full professor. (*Confidence Crisis*, pp. 78–79.)

cision-making for each kind of function, but with varying degrees of influence with respect to the other components. The AAHE study, for example, depicts a faculty-administration continuum of influence for decisions on the totality of functions in the university under five headings: administrative dominance, administrative primacy, shared authority, faculty primacy, and faculty dominance. Thus, both components can influence a particular area of decision-making. Furthermore, "effective influence may or may not be synonymous with legal authority, because there may be a de facto shift of decision-making power away from the party with the de jure authority." [126]

The 1966 Statement on Government assigns "primary responsibility" to the faculty for such functions as "curriculum, subject matter and methods of instruction, research, faculty status, and those aspects of student life which relate to the educational process." With respect to these kinds of functions, the power of review or final decision lodged in the board or delegated by it to the president "should be exercised adversely only in exceptional circumstances and for reasons communicated to the faculty." Following such communication, the faculty should have opportunity for further consideration and transmittal of its views to the president or the board. The Statement envisages "budgets, manpower limitations, the time element and the policies of other groups, bodies and agencies having jurisdiction over the institution . . ." as possibly setting some limits to faculty primacy in these functions.[127]

Planning is a chief example of an important university function which the faculty may not be able to influence to any large degree, although some kind of faculty participation is highly desirable. The Duff-Berdahl Report goes into detail:

An academic plan involves careful and detailed stocktaking of where an institution is, where it wishes to go over the next five to ten years and with what priorities. In addition to the obvious fact that it takes an enormous amount of time and work, the task of developing such a plan is often a delicate one for the faculty because it involves making difficult and sometimes invidious judgments about the comparative values of different offerings and research programmes, both existing and proposed. Disagreements will inevitably occur. But the point is that, given the scarcity of resources that besets all universities, judgments will have to be made by someone at some time.

[126] *Faculty Participation in Academic Governance* (AAHE), pp. 14–15.
[127] *Statement on Government* (1966), pp. 12–13.

Duff-Berdahl insist that even in this sphere of administration primacy "purely administrative ad hoc decisions" must be avoided. However tempting it may be for the administration to bypass the delays and arguments inherent in committee deliberation, in the long run predominantly administrative decisions are made effective if a faculty consensus is permitted to evolve. According to Duff-Berdahl, the heart of the presidential function is leadership in precisely such situations; a good president should be able to persuade a reluctant faculty that his plans are sound.[128]

By the same token, Corson urges that even at the very center of the faculty's primary jurisdiction, educational policy, the administration should participate in decision-making in view of its possibly greater awareness of societal needs and its relative immunity from departmental parochialism.[129] The evidently universal principle of shared authority makes clear-cut functional levels of faculty or administration jurisdiction undesirable, since the administration must be heard in typical faculty functions, and faculty participation is necessary in spheres of administration primacy.

The Duff-Berdahl Report attempts to minimize uncertainty and confusion by urging that a "careful" distinction should be made between policy functions, in which administration and faculty must collaborate, and functions pertaining to day-to-day execution, which the administration would carry out by itself.[130] It is doubtful whether such a functional distinction can in fact be made, carefully or not so carefully. Nevertheless, some kind of division of labor, perhaps roughly or at least allegedly along these lines, will sooner or later develop in the institutions which take their faculty participation seriously at all the different structural and functional levels.

A "quantitative" overview of the actual distribution of decision-making power between administration and faculty in various functional spheres was provided in 1971 by the Survey Subcommittee of the AAUP's Committee T on College and University Government. The subcommittee designed a ques-

---

[128] Duff-Berdahl Report, pp. 33–34. Yale's president, Kingman Brewster, Jr., said: "The harassed administrator's instinct is to believe that all consultation is a drag on decisive action. In fact, failure to take account of the ideas and feelings of those affected by a policy decision courts a far greater disaster." (Yale University, *The Report of the President*, 1967–1968, p. 11.)

[129] Corson, *Governance*, pp. 105–106.

[130] Duff-Berdahl Report, p. 55.

tionnaire which it sent out in September, 1970, to the chief administrative officer and the chapter president at institutions where the Association has a chapter. Usable replies were received from approximately one thousand institutions. The questionnaire covered thirty-one types of decision-making situations in the university, for each of which the respondents were asked to describe faculty participation in their institution according to a five-level scale: 1) determination (by the faculty exclusively); 2) joint action (with the administration); 3) consultation (of the faculty by the administration); 4) discussion (by the administration with the faculty); 5) no faculty participation. A revealing summary table of replies to the questionnaire was among the materials released by the subcommittee and is reproduced as Appendix B to this study. On the average, the subcommittee concluded, the responses show that "faculty participation in college and university government in the United States is viewed by faculties and administrations as being at the level of *consultation,* a far cry from the ideals envisaged by the 1966 *Statement on Government of Colleges and Universities.*" [131]

5. Improved Structures for Faculty Participation

Harold Dodds put his finger on a major problem of the structures of faculty participation when he noted the "love of democracy, town-meeting style" which "haunts" the campus despite enormous increases in the size of faculties; "faculties have been slow to accept the principles of representative government ...." [132] Dykes reflected the same lack of confidence in the devices of direct democracy, which have become "cumbersome and impractical." New representative techniques must be developed by faculties if they are to be effective

[131] Note the subcommittee's report, *AAUP Bulletin,* Spring 1971, pp. 68–124. (The summary table appears on p. 69.) The report includes a graphic presentation of the responses for each of the thirty-one decision-making situations at each of the approximately one thousand institutions (pp. 73–121). The subcommittee emphasized that these data were obtained from a self-survey at the participating institutions; "neither the Survey Subcommittee nor any other agency has audited or otherwise checked (by, say, visits to the campus) the uniform application and interpretation of the definitions, instructions, and specifications of the questionnaire."

[132] Dodds, *Academic President,* p. 99. Mortimer describes the intense disputes at Berkeley over the proposal to change the Senate's structure from that of a town meeting to a representative body of the Berkeley Division. (Mortimer, *Academic Government at Berkeley,* pp. 68–70.)

decision-makers; "the quixotic perception of university government as pure democracy" must be abandoned.[133]

Rourke and Brooks provide elaboration and quite novel
suggestions on this theme in the light of their investigations
on the managerial revolution in higher education. The large
faculty gathering (the general faculty assembly) has become as
cumbersome as a vehicle of government as the town meeting in
rapidly growing New England towns. Therefore, representative
institutions are needed, and also "academic administrators"
who will represent faculty interests "in the day-to-day management of university affairs." [134] In fact, Rourke and Brooks
call for a kind of faculty-executive structure, which would
function parallel to, and in cooperation with, the administration's structures.

> Throughout modern society there has been a trend toward the growth
> of executive power resulting from the increasing need for speed of
> decision and continuity of attention to the critical problems on the
> agenda of all organizations. Colleges and university faculties must
> come to terms with this trend by creating and delegating authority to
> committees and individuals empowered to represent the faculty point
> of view in the on-going business of a university. ... The faculty role in
> university government is often less than it should be in many areas of
> policy. This power can be effectively asserted on a day-to-day basis
> only by a continuously functioning instrumentality, either a faculty
> committee or a cadre of academic administrators. Indeed, the most
> effective response by the faculty to the bureaucratization of the uni-
> versity today will be the development of *its own academic civil service*,
> which will reflect faculty rather than administrative points of view in
> the management of the university.[135]

The faculty's civil service is needed, evidently, for the same
reasons that faculty participation in general is needed – to
present crucial "production point" views where the decisions
are made. A faculty civil service is appropriate at the present
time because of the growth of executive power in all phases of
modern society, including the university.

Least dispute about the necessity for a faculty civil service
should be forthcoming with respect to the increasing number
of academic decisions which are being reached at the state-
wide "system" level. The AAHE study gave proper attention
to the problems of faculty representation at this level. State-
wide "superboards," state budgetary agencies, and legislative

133 Dykes, *Faculty Participation*, p. 39.
134 Rourke and Brooks, *Managerial Revolution*, p. 128.
135 *Ibid.*, p. 129. (Emphasis added.)

mechanisms have been imposed on the traditional academic "hierarchies." While such developments are understandable in terms of a more rational allocation of resources at the state-wide level, these novel bureaucratic superstructures pose all kinds of problems for faculty representation. The AAHE study concluded that the faculty was likely to have inadequate access to the system-wide levels of administration where crucial economic and academic issues are decided, and called for "new and imaginative" solutions.[136]

6. Roles for the AAUP Chapter

The Duff-Berdahl Report came out strongly against suggestions that the Faculty Association at each campus should assume *formal* functions in governmental structures of the university. (The Faculty Associations in Canada are, very roughly only, comparable to chapters of the AAUP – they usually

[136] *Faculty Participation in Academic Governance* (AAHE), pp. 25, 31–32. Note also, Hickman, "Faculty Participation," pp. 67, 69. Rourke and Brooks described the bureaucratic problems of the "system" level without even considering the further problems of faculty participation. "In California as in other multi-campus systems the central administrative structure is duplicated by administrations on each campus. For example, the president and vice-presidents at the state-wide office are paralleled by chancellors and vice-chancellors on the individual campuses. A central budget office is matched by local budget offices. Now, partly in response to the existence of a central office of institutional research, local campuses in the University of California system are beginning to develop their own institutional research offices. This multiple layering of administrative officials may be an unavoidable consequence of growth in size (although the point is hotly debated), but it is also a common source of conflict. The number of layers in the hierarchy makes vertical communication extremely difficult. Messages tend to become blurred on their way up or down the administrative hierarchy, and even when communication is reasonably clear, local administrators may still evade the intentions of the central office. In a multi-campus setting, an inordinate amount of time must also be spent in working out agreements between counterpart officials. To some observers, the multi-campus university inevitably becomes a parody of bureaucracy in which the appearance of an administrative office at one level begets a new office at another level and these new offices then devote their primary energies to talking to each other." In the California system, even geography creates major problems: "The physical distance between campuses in California forces administrators to spend an inordinate amount of time traveling around the state in order to maintain personal contact within the system. A variety of devices has been employed to keep the campuses in closer touch with each other and with the central office. Open-line telephones between many of the offices permit administrators to talk with each other as if they were on the same campus. Eventually, integrated computer systems may tie together computer units on local campuses with a central computer facility so that information processed locally can be monitored or analyzed almost simultaneously by the central offices." (Rourke and Brooks, *Managerial Revolution*, pp. 119, 120.)

For examples of interference in academic affairs by state legislatures, note H. Eulau and H. Quinley, *State Officials and Higher Education* (New York, 1970).

contain 90% or more of the faculty at an institution, and engage in such activities as salary negotiations.) Duff-Berdahl
believe that the Faculty Associations would prosper more
without a "compromising" connection with university government; they could pursue their goals more vigorously "if they
stayed completely outside the formal structure of university
government." [137]

What is inappropriate for Faculty Associations in Canada
appears even more inappropriate for AAUP chapters in the
United States. The real importance of AAUP chapters lies in
their activities outside the formal structures of the university –
as a pressure group or a "party" if necessary. For example, as
was mentioned before, the AAUP chapter at Chapel Hill was
an informal but crucial agent for change in post-World War II
developments at the University of North Carolina. (Reportedly, six of the twenty-five most active members of the chapter
became members of the central administration after a new
president came into office in 1956.) [138]

A description of the merits of AAUP chapters as *informal*
instruments of academic government was provided by Richard
Adams. First of all, an AAUP chapter has some of the virtues
of an academic department in that it belongs to the local
campus and also to a national professional group; at the same
time, it is concerned for professors from all disciplines and is
not tied down by departmental parochialism. In the second
place, the chapter "can be a keen cutter of red tape." Normal
procedures for faculty participation and academic decision-
making "are at best slow, and perhaps best because they are
slow." But, at times important decisions have to be made in
too short a time for adequate use of the regular channels. In
such situations, the AAUP chapter can serve as a "legitimate
short circuit." In the third place, the chapter provides a most
useful "extra medium" of communication.

It has free access and right of direct communication to anyone or any
group it wishes to address, including the general public, and it gets
attention more readily than most other faculty groups because it is
part of a powerful national organization. It is especially handy for
helping to build redundancy. If a department or a college faculty
makes a statement, it has a certain force. If an AAUP chapter makes

[137] Duff-Berdahl Report, pp. 61–62. Note a sharply disagreeing Canadian
voice: W. B. Cunningham, "Within or Without? – The Location of the Faculty
Association," *C.A.U.T. Bulletin*, December 1968, pp. 34–45.
[138] Demerath et al., *Power*, pp. 138–139, 153, 159.

substantially the same statement at approximately the same time, its range and force may be considerably increased.

In the fourth place, chapters frequently serve as consulting bodies on national norms for academic freedom and tenure, on faculty salaries and fringe benefits, and on faculty participation in university government. In this capacity, "where relations are good, that is, where communication channels are open, the chapter is likely to be consulted by administrators as often as by faculty members, if not more often." Thus, by combining their various functions, chapters "can help to build the whole system of institutional relations and communications so strongly" that difficulties can be forestalled or solved more easily.[139]

AAUP chapters should be beneficial in a faculty milieu which tends to be highly unstructured. Faculty members sit on faculty assemblies and senates which have no political parties to regulate and lubricate the conduct of business or to crystallize issues. The frequently present quasi-parties, the "liberals" and the "non-liberals," are usually quite unrelated, as such, to the academic problems at hand. Moreover, departmental interests within the faculty assembly or senate may produce patterns of log-rolling and senatorial courtesy. AAUP chapters can serve as organizational cores for university-wide preparation of policy positions which could greatly facilitate the conduct of business in the various structures of faculty participation. In general, the AAUP chapter may present the most effective format for discussion and compromising on campus issues for purposes of the faculty.

The Duff-Berdahl Report suggests a change in membership practices of local Faculty Associations to the effect that deans and other administrators, even those on the "business" side, could be admitted. "The gulf between faculty and administration needs to be bridged ...." [140] Since the government of the university depends so much on cooperation and empathy between faculty and administration, it may be entirely appropriate for the unofficial structures of the campus to reflect this by granting membership to both components. The importance and special convenience of the local chapter to both components should, after all, be beyond question. Of course, if

[139] Richard P. Adams, "Faculty Participation in College and University Administration." (Address, Florida Association of Colleges and Universities, April 1968.)

[140] Duff-Berdahl Report, p. 64.

a chapter acts as the formal bargaining agent for a faculty – as is possible under current AAUP policies – it does become part of the formal governing structure of the institution, and can hardly be expected to bridge the gulf between administration and faculty.

F.   UNIVERSITY SENATES

In any institution where the general meeting of all the faculty members has become too large to permit effective transaction of business – and this is probably the case in that overwhelming majority of colleges and universities with more than one hundred faculty members – a senate consisting of elected representatives should be the decisive institution-wide agent of faculty participation. To be effective, say Duff-Berdahl, a senate must be considered "the central educational forum" of the institution. This requires the delegation of substantial authority from "above" and from "below." "On the one hand the President should use the Senate and its committees as a principal source of advice on academic policies; on the other, departments and Faculties must transmit to the Senate for review many of their decisions on internal affairs." However, care must be taken "not to drown it in trivialities" if the senate is to meet its great responsibilities.[141] Senate membership requires a considerable investment of the faculty member's – and administrator's – scarce time. Nothing could be more damaging to the concept of shared authority between administration and faculty than a senate that is no more than a "toy" – a senate whose advice is taken or ignored depending merely on the policy preferences of the board or the president. As is the case in almost all critical situations of university government, the crucial indicator is the administration's and the faculty's attitude toward the complex concept of consultation. The senate must be consulted on all major policy issues, which does not mean that the senate can necessarily impose its actions on the administration or the board – but which also does not mean that the board or administration can simply ignore the outcome of the consultation as put forward by the senate. As Lunsford puts it, "a vital premise of this conception of decision-making is the notion that the consultation signifi-

[141] *Ibid.*, p. 32.

cantly affects the decision that the ... [administration] would otherwise have made." [142] The proper handling of the consultation process is *the* test of the administration's leadership and statesmanship in a university; it presents the kind of challenge which should once and for all stifle the rumors about the faculty's desire to reduce administrative officers to clerk's status. To handle a senate in the non-hierarchical milieu of the university is a far more challenging task for an administrator than to sit on top of a hierarchical structure and merely tend to the chains of command.

In the literature on university government there is little coverage of the problems of university senates, as will be evident in the following discussion of the size and composition of senates, the importance of administration membership, and some factors pertaining to the general weakness of senates. However, the next chapter will contain much additional material on senates.

1. Size and Composition

As Duff-Berdahl pointed out, the size of a senate often determines its effectiveness. Since it should be a deliberative body, "not a mass meeting," an upper limit of about fifty is suggested. If the senate is larger than that, "there is every likelihood that its Executive Committee will play a disproportionate role and will tend to make most of the real decisions." A senate often cannot be much smaller than fifty members, say Duff-Berdahl, because in the larger universities the administration group, which "must not form the majority," may total up to twenty.[143] Their first point is certainly well taken; a predominant executive committee would make that committee, in fact, the senate, but a far less representative and

142 Lunsford, "Authority and Ideology," p. 9. Deegan et al. emphasize that information is not equivalent to consultation. Simply informing the other component of an action or a disagreement does not satisfy the requirement of consultation. Consultation must involve the process of seriously attempting to resolve differences and to arrive at constructive proposals which both sides can support. Moreover, consultation may require the use of informal communications and the cultivation of informal relationships – yet, say the authors, for the final decision the formal lines of communication should be "scrupulously" followed. (Deegan et al., *Joint Participation in Decision Making*, pp. 83–84.)

143 Duff-Berdahl Report, p. 28. Deegan et al. are also critical of overly powerful executive committees. In general, executive committees should serve only "as an agenda and coordinating agency...." (*Joint Participation in Decision Making*, p. 48.)

legitimate one. Senates were created because general faculty assemblies were too large, which usually had meant domination by an executive committee. If senates are to avoid the preponderant influence of such committees, they must be kept within manageable size – about fifty, as suggested by Duff-Berdahl. Their second point, about the administration group not forming the majority, would be found far too weak a prerequisite in many United States faculty circles. While most American universities include administration members in their senates, they are usually outnumbered by the faculty in a proportion anywhere from 8:1 to 2:1.

Duff-Berdahl made other suggestions about senates which correspond to the practice in United States institutions of higher learning. First, the faculty should elect the majority (at least!) of the members of the senate from its own ranks, for staggered three-year terms and "with rotation considered as normal but re-election not ruled out." Second, elections for senate seats should be conducted by each college or school, "with a quota of seats approximately conforming to the size of each ... [college or school], but in no case exceeding a ratio of 3:1." In other words, colleges of the university should not be equally represented in the senate; yet, the largest college should not have more than three times as many senators as the smallest – a rule surprisingly universal throughout the United States, although probably not always quite as restrictive on the larger colleges as the ratio of 3:1. In the third place, senates should have monthly meetings (which should be followed by board meetings "at appropriate, regular intervals"). In the fourth place, provision should be made for having a number of senate seats reserved to junior faculty members.[144]

---

[144] Duff-Berdahl Report, pp. 28–31. Actually, Duff-Berdahl's suggestions on this last point are more intricate, reflecting their belief that junior faculty members form too high a percentage of the total faculty and that a "youth lobby" or "government by juniors" would be worse than gerontocracy. Accordingly, they suggest that only professors and associate professors, or perhaps only persons with tenure, should be eligible for election to the senate, except that three seats should be reserved for junior faculty without tenure, to be elected by that group. Senates in the United States are usually open to elected representatives of all ranks. However, some constitutions (e.g., Columbia University) do have provisions for guaranteeing some seats to the junior faculty – with fears of "youth" predominance apparently not presenting an issue in the United States.

2. The Importance of Administration Membership

There appears to be considerable agreement that senates are most effective if representatives of the administration sit in it as regular members. "Pure" senates – i.e., those consisting of faculty only – are considered inappropriate in view of the need for faculty-administration cooperation in university government.

For example, Philip Denenfeld, advocating a "mixed" senate, is particularly concerned to point out the irrelevance of fears about possible intimidation of faculty representatives by the presence of administrators in the senate. "It would seem that if sixty professors, most of whom are tenured, could be silenced by the presence of ... administrators, the Senate would be a sham in any case." The administration members of the senate are usually in the possession of facts and perspective not widely available to faculty members; therefore, their contributions to senate debates have been consistently valuable. Moreover, even if some faculty ideas have been unduly moderated by the administration's presence, this deficit may be balanced by the fact that the president is less likely to use his veto power for policy decisions in which he has participated.[145] The study of the American Association for Higher Education, *Faculty Participation in Academic Governance*, provides an extensive discussion of the rationale for senates and a set of guidelines. It also endorses the "mixed" senate, mainly because in such a senate there is less likelihood "that the administration and the faculty will develop hardened positions, insulated from the rational arguments of the other side." However, according to the study, "pure" senates may be preferable *temporarily* where faculty members "lack a tradition of active participation in the affairs of the institution," or where "there has been a history of centralized, if not arbitrary, administration ...." Under these circumstances, a "pure" senate may be necessary as a *transitional stage* to a "mixed" body "to develop an independent role for the faculty in the government of the institution." [146]

Duff-Berdahl advocate a "mixed" senate and emphasize particularly the importance of the president's chairmanship over the body.

[145] Denenfeld, "Western Michigan University," p. 394.
[146] *Faculty Participation in Academic Governance* (AAHE), p. 40.

We were surprised to come across the idea that he [the President] should not preside over the Senate, lest the members feel inhibited by his doing so. We realize that at some universities professors fear that outspokenness may jeopardize their own prospects. ... If professors are too timid to say what they think, they should not be on the Senate. *We regard it as virtually the most important task of the President* to preside over the Senate. Faculties should realize that if a President does not preside over the Senate, he will feel less obligation to be the Senate's effective spokesman to the Board. From the chair of the Senate better than anywhere else, he can focus the discussion of academic policies, can guide them in the light of his full knowledge of any external factors involved, and can exercise the right kind of leadership, which is leadership by persuasion.

Duff-Berdahl are worried about one possible consequence of administrators' presence in senates – that separate administrative caucusing will take place, resulting in a tight administration "party" and bloc-voting.

Nothing will weaken the effectiveness of the Senate more quickly or seal the image of a President's "party" more firmly than an administrative caucus which produces an automatic and unreal unanimity of ex officio opinion. The Senate needs the ideas and experience of senior administrators but it must have them straight in all their variety and not filtered into a dull monochrome.[147]

It is impossible at this point even to guess at the extent of administration bloc-voting in university senates. There are voting situations where administration members in the senate are entirely on their own; undoubtedly, there are other situations where the "whips" are on, so to speak, and "party" discipline is tight. Intra-administration relations frequently reflect an almost military sense of hierarchical organization and "loyalty" to a presidential "team." As Duff-Berdahl indicate, this kind of spirit has no place in the senate – even assuming that it has a place within the administration. Senates are not intended to be a battleground where an administrative "team" faces the faculty and the rest of the university in some kind of "class" war between the components. Nevertheless, administrators might not be able to distinguish between their hierarchical role on the administration "team" and their academic-parliamentary role in the senate. To the extent that administration members cannot distinguish between these roles, their presence in the senate will not be entirely functional. Yet, "pure" senates are likely to be even less functional. And for the rest, faculty members may just be jealous because their

[147] Duff-Berdahl Report, pp. 45, 46. (Emphasis added.)

own semblances of parties in the senate lack cohesion and discipline, and thus tend to be outvoted by the administration even where the administration is outnumbered.[148]

3. The Weakness of Senates

Duff and Berdahl visited most Canadian universities and found that few had effective senates; moreover, they reported the "firm opinion" that the ineffectiveness of senates was a major cause of tension at universities. They gave a variety of reasons for this ineffectiveness. Some senates are too large, or too heavily "diluted" with "non-academic" members, or contain too few elected faculty members. Other senates have no significant business, or largely formal business, while the real decisions are made at other levels. An opinion expressed even at some of the strongest universities was that the senate had the power but lacked the "guts" to use it. "When we asked why, the commonest answer was that the 'administrative group' on Senate ... is predominant and tends to speak with one voice." Also, senate agendas tend to be exceedingly crowded, mostly with formal business from the colleges and committees "all of which had to be passed through Senate lest one item in a hundred needed further discussion." Consequently, even if a senator has succeeded in placing a policy-question on the agenda, "it will not be reached until the meeting has gone on so long that the members' one overwhelming desire is to go home." Finally, Duff-Berdahl found many senates in moods of "despondency" or even "despair" because of their helplessness in budget-related questions.

The theory that the Board is in complete control of finance can be and sometimes is interpreted by the Board and/or the President to mean that *any academic policy involving expenditure*, or even *an order of priority between academic projects*, is ultra vires for the senate.

Duff-Berdahl suggest one general remedy: senates must be authorized to make recommendations directly to the board on

---

[148] If McConnell's and Mortimer's research has established anything, it is certainly the impracticality – if not absurdity – of the Berkeley senate's suspicion of an administrative presence on committees and elsewhere in structures of faculty government. "Exclusion [of the administration] sets the stage for confrontation"; "joint deliberation, negotiation, and shared decision-making are preferable to disjunctive and adversary relationships." As Chancellor Meyerson told the Berkeley senate in 1965, "the gap between faculty and administration saps the morale of administrators, and has a negative effect on both faculty and students." (McConnell and Mortimer, *The Faculty in University Governance*, pp. 50, 52, 76.)

any major policy matter of interest to the university – presumably without regard to the financial implications of the question.[149] The Berkeley commission also took up the problem of financial business in senates. The commission insisted that the level of senate debate had to be enhanced by the formal introduction of the budget on the senate agenda – several times per year and after due consideration by an appropriate committee.

A relatively simple device for promoting intelligent discussion would be to reserve a specific set of dates on the Academic Senate's calendar for the sole purpose of discussing the budget. On these occasions members of the Chancellor's staff would be prepared to explain and defend the policy decisions reflected in the proposed budget. The Senate's role should be to concentrate on the general policies and preferences and their implications, avoiding the temptation to divert itself by discussion of specific items and subheadings. Such discussions would enable the administration to allay such misconceptions as exist and to make clear what specific constraints are imposed by budgetary and fiscal decisions taken at the statewide level. To raise the level of this debate and to sharpen its focus, we also recommend that the proposed new Committee on Academic Planning which is charged to consider budget policy submit in advance an independent analysis of the budget, stressing in particular the educational implications of the priorities and allocations proposed.[150]

For the rest, most of the Berkeley proposals relate to decentralization. Institutions of faculty representation must be improved not only through reform of the main senate but also through the introduction of several little senates. Genuine faculty involvement in government can only be promoted through wider participation in a multiplication of forums. "We foresee senates at the level of colleges, schools, and small clusters of departments where issues are more comprehensible, more manageable, and more likely to evoke spontaneous participation." Such "local senates" would offer excellent opportunities for directly involving students; moreover, the commission suggests hopefully (but realistically?), "decentralized senates would reinforce decentralized administration." In any case, the lethargy resulting from the most superficial form of participation, voting for representatives, would be lessened by

[149] Duff-Berdahl Report, pp. 9–10, 32. (Emphasis added.)
[150] Berkeley Report, p. 39. The Budget Committee at Fresno State College was clearly in need of this kind of advice. Deegan et al. found that much of the business referred to it concerned "such matters as the distribution of travel funds rather than the broad allocation of resources in the college." (*Joint Participation in Decision Making*, p. 36.)

more direct participation in the little senates where the effects of decisions would be more visible and the range of problems more "within human grasp." [151]

Of course, decentralization is a cure only for a limited range of problems; the need remains to make central senates more effective and to overcome faculty reluctance to relate to a university's representative institution. Fortunately, this latter need is hardly a problem at the departmental level, to be discussed next.

G. THE DEPARTMENT — CORE UNIT OF THE FACULTY

The importance of the department to the faculty can hardly be exaggerated. It is the one structure of the university where loyalty to the discipline is often combined with loyalty to the institution. Moreover, it is – in many institutions – the one place where meaningful participation in important decision-making is experienced by all faculty members. The department is autonomous in many crucial respects and provides shelter and protection to its faculty.

These points are recognized by many authors. For example, Burton Clark emphasizes the department's role in protecting academic freedom:

The autonomous department is commonly viewed as a curse in college administration; it is a narrow, self-serving veto group. But the autonomous department, by and large, is a shield for its members, a strong line of defense against the academic man doing other than what he wants to do. It is a most important sustaining condition of day-to-day academic freedom in a large proportion of universities, and, in some colleges, on a par perhaps with tenure in providing protection.[152]

Duff-Berdahl consider the department the one "place on campus where the teacher can participate in a direct, meaningful way in some of the decisions which affect his professional life." While at many of an institution's levels indirect, representative devices of government must be used, the department is the one level where direct participation should be maximized – for all, not just the senior members. Although, say Duff-Berdahl, senior professors may have to play a large role in departments

---

[151] Berkeley Report, pp. 12, 41. Martin Trow, however, insisted that only the "communitarians" who wrote the report want more senates at lower levels; most members of the Berkeley faculty and the students do not wish to sit on additional bodies. (Trow, "Conceptions of the University," pp. 20–21.)

[152] Clark, "Faculty Authority," p. 301.

where there are many inexperienced persons, the department
is in any case "the natural place for junior staff to begin to
participate in university government ...." [153] Dykes' survey
confirmed how important the decision-making in the department was to the individual faculty member and also how near
the department comes to being a real community of scholars.

> The respondents' comments suggest that departmental staff meetings
> are most useful in providing opportunity for participation primarily
> for one reason; it is there that most decisions of real consequence to the
> individual professor are settled. As one observer has put it, "Just as
> water will always find its own proper level, so will a professor find the
> point or points at which his participation is important to him. ...
> The department is apt to be at the very center of attention of most
> members of the faculty."
> The department comes nearer to being a community of scholars than
> anything we have today. Here we can decide what it is we want to do
> and go ahead with it; we can and do agree on something one day and
> implement it the next. And because of a considerable degree of self-
> determination, we can do just about what we like. [154]

Demerath et al. also saw departments as real communities.
The chairman's power, in the departments at Chapel Hill, was
typically restricted to lesser items, while the more important
matters were often decided by the department as a whole.
"Though mixtures of bureaucracy and collegia, [the depart-
ments] were mainly collegial groups." [155] Finally, Corson recognized the power of departments, which he ascribed partly to
their undisputed rights of initiative "for a great deal of educational policy, for personnel appointments and evaluation,
and for the budgeting of equipment and educational facilities ...." [156]

Departments can fulfill many of these crucial and beneficial
roles only if they do not exceed certain limits of size with
respect to numbers of faculty members (and students). The
Berkeley commission sees the upper limit somewhere between
20 and 30 faculty members, 200 undergraduate majors, and
75 graduate students. [157] If a department becomes larger – as

---

[153] Duff-Berdahl Report, p. 50.
[154] Dykes, *Faculty Participation*, p. 30.
[155] Demerath et al., *Power*, p. 201.
[156] Corson, *Governance*, p. 87.
[157] Berkeley Report, pp. 26–27. The Commission advocated the deliberate use
of physical space facilities for fostering a collegial departmental milieu – such as
lounges for intellectual and social discourse set aside for limited groups of students
and faculty who share some academic interest.

many have become, with some containing more than one hundred faculty members – it can hardly be expected to fulfill some of the important and beneficial roles indicated above. Representative institutions will then be required at the departmental level too, and the individual professor may never again enjoy direct participation in government of the collegial group.

The department's role as the most successful of academic structures also depends on the qualities of the chairman. According to Caplow and McGee, the chairman resembles "the working foreman in industry"; his orientation to the discipline puts him in much closer relationships to his departmental colleagues than to the administration, yet in order to succeed he must also be close to the administration – although he may try to hide his ties to the administration before his colleagues.[158] Corson, too, concluded that the chairman remains "basically a teacher in function and in loyalty," even while he may be looked to by the dean as his channel of communication to the departmental faculty. Corson believes that the "anomalous," in-between position of the chairman may handicap administrative effectiveness. "Chairmen are only part-time administrators," and are given "little financial incentive to devote their time to the responsibilities of the chairmanship." They spend much of their time with regular professorial duties, rather than devoting themselves to administrative tasks.[159] Yet, Corson could hardly expect a more administration-oriented chairman to fit appropriately into the collegial group of the department – and such a "fit" has advantages far beyond the level of administrative efficiency.

As to the selection of chairmen, Duff-Berdahl suggest that the departmental perspective should be predominant, but not exclusive. Duff-Berdahl object to "outright election" of chairmen by the departmental faculty; instead, they propose "a mixed process of nomination and selection," with departmental as well as administrative participation. This is needed because the person chosen will not only act as departmental chairman "but also as a member of the administration and as such must be able to work well with other administrators." Moreover, there may be a time that a department badly needs upgrading, but the current departmental faculty might not

[158] Caplow and McGee, *Academic Marketplace*, p. 195.
[159] Corson, *Governance*, p. 88.

want to elect a person devoted to such a change.[160] The AAUP Statement on Government specifies that a chairman be selected either by departmental election or as a result of consultations between the departmental faculty and the administration; in the latter case, "appointments should normally be in conformity with department members' judgment." The AAUP position, it must be assumed, agrees with Duff-Berdahl on the necessity of administration participation in appointing chairmen in the case of the department which badly needs upgrading. However, Duff-Berdahl assign to the chairman an administration role, as Corson did, while the AAUP may see the chairman more exclusively as a faculty member. Consequently, in the AAUP view, the chairman does not have to suit the administration team's tastes as closely as Duff-Berdahl seem to require.

Both the Statement on Government and Duff-Berdahl agree on the principle of a limited term of office for the chairman, to assure his "faculty-ness."

Although we recognize certain instances ... when prolonged or indefinite tenure may be necessary, we feel that normally the term of office should be limited to, say three or four years, subject to reappointment after renewed consultation. Some Faculty Associations urged that tenure be limited to one term, and others proposed only one possible reappointment. But we consider it unwise to regulate this matter rigidly as long as the processes of consultation are required for reappointment. We recognize that faculty members have especially strong feelings that their Chairmen should remain "one of them" and that, for this purpose, rotation in office is desirable.[161]

---

[160] Duff-Berdahl Report, p. 48.

[161] *Ibid.*, p. 49; *Statement on Government* (1966), p. 13. If a chairman "lingers" in office for more than a few years, say Dressel et al., "he may be beyond the point of no return" with respect to his teaching and research. Those chairmen who enjoy the job could be suspected of having left the community of scholars to seek the shelter of "routine duties." (Dressel et al., *Confidence Crisis*, pp. 13, 82.)

A study by Frederick S. Lane provided some data on chairmen, particularly on their role with respect to tenure decisions. In general, the principal tasks of chairmen were viewed by Lane's respondents as relating to budget-making, salary recommendations, tenure and promotion recommendations, faculty recruitment and selection, and curriculum development. (Frederick S. Lane, *A Study in Role Conflict: The Departmental Chairman in Decisions on Academic Tenure* [University of Florida, Studies in Public Administration No. 29], 1967.) An investigation by Winston W. Hill and Wendell L. French attempted to measure "the power imputed to department chairmen by professors ... and to determine whether variations in such power were associated with variations in the satisfaction and productivity of departmental faculty." The results of this study, in which the chairmen were seen mainly as administrators, appear inconclusive. ("Perceptions of the Power of Department Chairmen by Professors," *Administrative Science Quarterly*, March 1967, pp. 548–574.)

Departments are the most collegial unit of the university, but they are not always successful. Needless to say, Caplow and McGee found stresses and factions to abound in departments. "There is always an ample supply of standing issues around which personal conflict can crystallize." Caplow and McGee even furnished a list of seven typical "party" divisions in academic settings. Departmental rebellions against chairmen are frequent, according to the same authors, but are usually suppressed by the chairman with the dean's assistance or at least benevolent neutrality – after which the rebellious members tend to leave the institution. On the other hand, departmental rebellions against deans are rare, and usually end with the rebellious department's withdrawal from the affairs of the college – leaving the department "unmolested" and perhaps even "prosperous" in its isolation.[162] Indicative of the potential stresses and tensions within departments is the importance to all departmental members of the filling of a vacancy.

Every appointment changes the department as a work group. Since the group is relatively small, every appointment will have some impact. To choose a man for the department, then, is to modify one's own future as a member.[163]

Notwithstanding Caplow's and McGee's findings, the department is likely to be the most effective and collegial unit of the university. Only the smaller professional school may develop departmental-like ties and loyalties among its faculty members, but, then, the professional school in many respects is like a department.[164]

H. STUDENT PARTICIPATION IN GOVERNMENT

1. Reasons for Student Participation

In the Berkeley commission's view, student participation in university governance is primarily desirable because of its

[162] Caplow and McGee, *Academic Marketplace*, pp. 192–193, 204–205.
[163] *Ibid.*, p. 170.
[164] Corson provides a penetrating view of the milieu of the professional school. (*Governance*, pp. 80–81.) Dressel et al. found that the "operating style" of the eighteen low-rated departments in their sample (low-rated with respect to scholarly reputation) tended to be "oligarchical," while the eighteen top-rated departments were "mostly democratic." Also, those departments had done better in the Cartter report ratings whose operation was more democratic – and whose concern for students and the rest of the university was less. (Dressel et al., *Confidence Crisis*, pp. 39, 142.)

educational value – to deepen the educational experiences of the student. "Incorporating students into academic policy-making is essential if today's large university is to create an environment which more successfully promotes the realization of its still unfilled educational ideals." [165]

Rourke and Brooks emphasize the students' "proletarian" status as casualties of the ever-increasing powers of both administration and faculty – and the computer. Therefore, participation in decision-making by students is also intended to relieve or prevent the kind of unrest, and perhaps violence, which flows from what some students regard "as the double indignity of impersonal treatment by computerized administrators and desertion of teaching responsibilities by the faculty." [166]

A major – or, probably, the major – reason for the students' participation in academic government flows from their consumer status, so to speak, in the learning processes in the university. As Addison Hickman puts this point:

> The logic of our position would also dictate that the student should have a voice, and one that should be heard, in decision-making on matters affecting his broader academic experience – the quality of his instruction, the intellectual environment of the campus, and even the physical environment. To be sure, the student is young and perhaps immature, he is not there very long, and there are all kinds of rationales for saying that he really doesn't have much perspective. He does, however, bring his own body of experience which is uniquely valued. He is the person doing most of the learning. He is the person that is the object of all this tender loving care. Discount his reactions as we may for limited perspective, he has something meaningful to tell us. There is a feedback here, that we are not getting at the moment, that might be profoundly helpful.[167]

According to McGeorge Bundy, "if a majority of students should come to believe that the disruption of the university is more important than their own education, there will be no future for the institution as we know it." [168] All the reasons for student participation relate to this basic danger. Accordingly, it is not surprising that at the locale of the first major disruption among American universities, Berkeley, a commission

---

[165] Berkeley Report, p. 33. In Martin Trow's critical view, the report's conception of the intellectual fellowship of students and teachers, learning and self-governing – and learning through self-governing, "has the attractive appeal of all arcadian Utopias." (Trow, "Conceptions of the University," p. 21.)

[166] Rourke and Brooks, *Managerial Revolution*, pp. 14–15.

[167] Hickman, "Faculty Participation," p. 65.

[168] Bundy, "Faculty Power," p. 44.

composed equally of students and faculty was set up to study
and make recommendations on various levels of student decision-making in the university – to be exercised exclusively by
students or jointly with faculty and (or) administration. The
Berkeley commission's report remains one of the most profound statements on the subject of student participation.

2. Principles and Basic Restrictions

The Joint Statement on the Rights and Freedoms of Students, published by the AAUP in 1968, laid down certain very
general principles:

As constituents of the academic community, students should be free,
individually and collectively, to express their views on issues of institutional policy and on matters of general interest to the student body.
The student body should have clearly defined means to participate in
the formulation and application of institutional policy affecting academic and student affairs. The role of the student government and
both its general and specific responsibilities should be made explicit,
and the actions of the student government within the areas of its
jurisdiction should be reviewed only through orderly and prescribed
procedures.[169]

Even more basic is the linking by the Berkeley commission of
the development of student participation with a "rebirth in
education":

Significant, long-range development of student participation must
ultimately rest upon informal individual absorption in the enterprise of
education in an atmosphere of honest searching and mutual respect.
For this university and this society, a rebirth in education and the
development of the student role in governance are closely dependent
upon one another.[170]

At a more operational level, Louis Joughin distinguished
four general kinds of student involvement in university government – giving and receiving information, consultation, voting
participation in decision, unilateral decision-making. First of
all, Joughin saw "an obvious need for a vastly enlarged exchange of information and opinion" involving students.

Very, very few institutions in this country systematically make available to their student bodies information which the students have a
right to have, and, more importantly, have a capacity to use compe-

---

[169] "Joint Statement of Rights and Freedoms of Students," *AAUP Bulletin*,
Summer 1968, p. 260.
[170] Berkeley Report, p. 43.

tently for the good of the institution. Virtually no institution regularly sounds out student opinion, systematically and comprehensively.

In the second place, students should be consulted. "The visceral responses of the students are as important as those of the faculty member or administrator ...." In any case for consultative purposes, there should be student membership without vote on organs and committees at all levels – departmental, college-wide, and university-wide, and even on the board. In the third place, Joughin thought that there were numerous situations where students should have the vote, at all levels of the university such as the department or the senate. Finally, "there is an area of exclusive decision where only the students decide." This area will always remain narrow, "simply because the operations of an institution of higher education are so complex that any single element of the community is seldom likely to have the only voice." In any case, a serious review must be undertaken to determine the extent of such "areas of private life which are not of academic nor even of institutional concern."[171]

The most important restriction on student participation, in more than one sense, is expressed in the following citation from the Berkeley commission:

The heart of the problem of student participation is that a university is not a natural democracy composed of members each of whom is distinguished by an equal claim to power; it is a highly artificial community deliberately arranged so that the educational relationships among the members constitute the starkest kind of contrast to relationships based on power. Properly conceived, it is a fellowship that should prize persuasion based on reason and evidence; that excludes coercion and pressure because they destroy the uncoerced agreement which is at the heart of the search for knowledge; and that relies on trust and tolerance among its members, recognizing that suspicion and dogmatism can destroy the conditions for pursuing and sharing knowledge. Although a university is organized around the principle of freedom of inquiry, it is far from being committed to the belief that any idea, opinion, or theory is as worthy as any other of a place in the university. A university is a society whose life is ordered around the necessity of constantly making qualitative distinctions, not only concerning ideas, but also concerning individual achievements, whether of faculty or students. It may perform this qualitative function well or badly, but this is only to question its performance, not the need for judgment itself.

Although "participation" or "citizenship" in a university may not

[171] Louis Joughin, "The Role of the Student in College and University Government," (address, California State College at Los Angeles, May 1968), p. 3.

take the form of majoritarian democracy, its substance is democratic in the intellectual freedom such citizenship offers all its members, the continuous opportunities it affords for making uncoerced, genuine choices, and the promise it holds for creating persons fully conscious of their intellectual and moral powers and truly free to use them.[172]

Thus, since "any mechanical analogy of a university ... to a democratic society is inapposite," a significant student contribution to shaping the life of the university must depend "upon an intense involvement by students in their own education" – and it is precisely "the infrequency of such personal engagement which constitutes our major educational problem ...." The university does need more participation by students in government, but this increased participation must be accompanied by a much more intensive relationship of the student to the academic process, which will require "slow, time-consuming, laborious collaborative efforts" on the part of all the components of the university. Without this effort, student demands for more "power" will merely be met, and can only be met, by "a tokenism which offers the premise but withholds the substance of participation ...." [173]

The path suggested above is long and laborious, and requires collaborative efforts among the university's components; it "offers neither the excitement nor the seductive appeal and militant posture of direct confrontation ...." These more appealing methods – from many student-activists' point of view – would subvert the "necessary partnership with administrators and faculty." The basic notions of student participation suggested by the Berkeley commission will hardly be popular among many "student power" advocates; they require the kind of effort from students (and the other components) "which will be hardest to elicit in the present setting." [174]

Intensive student participation in government requires intensive student engagement with academic affairs. This basic prerequisite of the Berkeley commission must be taken into consideration in addition to other frequently expressed limiting factors on student participation, such as those mentioned in the Statement on Government of 1966 – the students' "inexperience, untested capacity, a transitory status ..., and the inescapable fact that the other components of the institution

[172] Berkeley Report, pp. 32–33.
[173] *Ibid.*, pp. 31–32.
[174] *Ibid.*

are in a position of judgment over the students";[175] or, Millett's rather abrupt point that "in general ... students know so little about the component elements of academic policy that they have little if anything to contribute to its discussion." [176]

3. Levels of Student Participation

The Berkeley commission, the main source on this topic too, is quite critical of that approach to student participation which calls for separate domains of student jurisdiction, "for students only." This kind of "student government" has in fact nothing to do with university government.

> Its premise ... is that there is a separable category of functions which is both the dominant concern of students and of little or no interest to any other segments of the university community, implying that a kind of autonomous separatism is an appropriate model of governance. This conception implies that a separately constituted "government" performing specifically delegated tasks provides the principal means through which students can implement their views and interests. We believe that such an approach has serious flaws and that the time has come for a searching examination of the present model of "student self-government."

The traditional spheres of student government do not really relate to the government of the university. Rather, they were convenient ways by which students organized their own leisure-time activities such as housing, eating, social life, debating, literary, and theatrical endeavors.[177]

Real student participation in government cannot be accomplished merely by giving real powers rather than trivia to existing "student government." Instead, institutional devices must be found through which "student power" can be incorporated into regular channels of university government.

> We think it is important to distinguish between the important goal of expanding the student role in governance and the erroneous assumption that a strengthened separate, central government is the most effective means to that end. Our task, then, is to overcome such segregation by devising a variety of institutional means through which students can be incorporated into the decision-making process, rather than confined to haggling over the extent of peripheral powers delegated to a separate organization.[178]

[175] *Statement on Government* (1966), p. 14.
[176] Millett, *Academic Community*, p. 131.
[177] Berkeley Report, p. 17.
[178] *Ibid.*, pp. 18–19.

Equally inappropriate, in the opinion of the Berkeley commission, are "omnibus student-faculty relations committees." These too imply a segregated sphere of student affairs rather than participation in the ordinary channels.[179]

The primary unit for student participation should be the department. The Berkeley commission suggests students as voting members of regular departmental committees "in which problems are discussed and policies formulated," and non-voting student representatives "to attend and to participate in departmental meetings at which decisions are finally made."[180] Also, where other units than the departments have student members, such as senates and university-wide committees, the department should still serve as the main constituency-base for these student representatives. Even if a separate domain of student government continues to exist, the students serving on it should be elected from departmental constituency units, with guaranteed representatives, perhaps, for the lower division, upper division, and graduate students of a particular department. If students were elected from their academic department rather than from a fraternity house, dormitory, or a vague university-wide constituency, this might result in directing "the focus of the Student Senate from separate extra-curricular affairs to shared involvement in the major [i.e., academic] activities of the University." [181] Of course, as students participate more actively in departmental affairs, they will inevitably affect the intimacy of the collegial world of the department. Thoroughly undesirable conflicts would certainly arise if students were to enter departmental "politics" in the narrow and pejorative sense of that word, especially in those departments where the "political" situation is already tense. As Dressel et al. concluded, students can be more successfully influential in departments that have a secure and recognized faculty.[182] Perhaps, certain departments are too insecure to be able to afford student participation.

---

[179] *Ibid.*, p. 43.

[180] *Ibid.*

[181] *Ibid.*, p. 91. W. Donald Bowles supports the Berkeley Commission as he emphasizes the importance of student participation at the departmental level. He chides students for insisting that issues could be handled only at the presidential or deanly level – "in a very real sense there are no university issues, only departmental issues." (W. Donald Bowles, "Student Participation in Academic Governance," *Educational Record*, September 1968, p. 259.)

[182] Dressel et al., *Confidence Crisis*, p. 86. The authors also observed, in 1970, that "departments have not generally established any systematic way in which the student voice can be effectively heard." (*Ibid.*, p. 9.)

If "omnibus" committees of student affairs and separate student government structures are considered less effective than student participation in departments and other regular channels of government, then the traditional position of the dean of students may also be challenged. The Berkeley commission makes a distinction between "the natural authority which stems from scholarship" and the dubious authority – as far as the students are concerned – of the mere administrative status enjoyed by the dean of students.

In the professional, bureaucratized administration of "student personnel services," such officers presume to exercise authority over students in a relationship similar to the one between students and faculty. But the relationships are fundamentally different, and the unthinking transfer of authority derived from one to serve the needs of the other is the source of much misunderstanding and friction.

Thus, there is no real academic legitimacy for decisions by the dean of students in such areas as lock-out hours for a dormitory or the size of a political poster allowed to be displayed on a bulletin board.[183]

The problem of the status of the dean of students is also touched upon by Corson, who observed differences "rooted in different values" which make for conflict between the dean of students and the faculty. For example, "the dean of students' counsel to students to aid them in adjusting to campus life may be regarded by the faculty as meaningless or conflicting with the counsel the student should obtain from his instructor." Moreover, as Corson says, the dean of students is usually "the president's man" [184] – and that may make for conflict with the academic deans too. Mark Ingraham noted that "the dean of students believes that his is a central educational function, and many faculty members simply do not agree." [185]

The discussion of student participation in government is at a

[183] Berkeley Report, pp. 34–35.

[184] Corson, *Governance*, pp. 64, 111.

[185] Ingraham, *Mirror of Brass*, p. 225. Martin Trow argued that deans of students usually have good relations and communications with the communities that commit "ordinary" violations of campus laws – the fraternities, sororities, and residence halls; for these groups they have an effective control "network," such as house mothers, dormitory officers, and student leaders. However, deans of students tend to have less knowledge and understanding, and no control "networks," with respect to political activists, graduate students, and others who are currently challenging order on the campus. (Trow, "Conceptions of the University," p. 16.) As Troy Duster remarked, "once," but not at present, student body presidents were "unashamedly the handmaidens of the deans of students." (Duster, "Student Interests," p. 23.)

very early stage in the literature – and in the clauses of university constitutions. Among the many urgent questions which have defied the development of clear principles, the question of student voting is typical. Should students be voting members on committees and senates where administration and faculty have always dominated? And, if so, in what numerical strength? Or should they merely be available as non-voting consultants and "communicators"? Even Louis Joughin's reaction to this problem had to be rather general:

> Should students have a vote when they sit with departmental and college curriculum and program committees? Here, I believe, is a prime instance of a question which should be answered in terms of functional utility rather than of absolute right. If the students lack experience, cannot understand the nature of the situation, and are generally confused, it seems clear that they should not vote. Incidentally, I have enough faith in students to believe that under such circumstances they would not use their vote even if so endowed. But if the students demonstrate capacity for informed judgment, it would be folly to reject their help.[186]

Equally uncharted are questions of proportionality in relation to student representation. Morris Keeton criticized the "tokenism" of many of the "reforms" of the 1960's which placed small minorities of students on committees "with the intent of giving students a voice but preserving faculty control." In consequence, Keeton fears, the students' main instruments of participation will remain "voting with the feet" in selection and rejection of courses or programs, noncooperation or selective cooperation – and "the ability to threaten harm" to the campus. Keeton's data, based on a study of nineteen institutions, point to a lack of agreement across the country "as to the legitimate roles or voice of students in governance ...." [187]

Another puzzling matter which affects student participation differently on each campus is the great variety of student "subcultures." Burton Clark and Martin Trow use the following typology:

> the "collegiate" of the fraternities and sororities and the athletes and activities majors; the "academic" of the serious students; the "vocational" of the students seeking training for specific jobs; and the

[186] Joughin, "Role of the Student," p. 4. A pessimistic account of prospects for student participation is provided by a political scientist at San Francisco State College, John H. Bunzel. ("Some Reflections on Student Participation and Representation," *PS* [American Political Science Association], Spring 1970, pp. 117–122.)

[187] Keeton, *Shared Authority on Campus*, pp. 17, 114, 116.

"nonconformist" of the political activists, the aggressive intellectuals, and the bohemians. These subcultures are not mutually exclusive, and some of the fascinating pageantry of the multiversity is found in their interaction one on another.[188]

Obviously, important differences in the quality of student participation in government will relate to the kinds of student "subcultures" which may exist on a particular campus.

At the end of this section on student participation, it is appropriate to mention the "Draft Statement on Student Participation in College and University Government," prepared by the Association's Committee T and published in tentative form in the March, 1970, *AAUP Bulletin* with an invitation for comments from interested readers. According to this draft document, the precise mode and extent of student involvement, particularly voting rights and numbers of representatives on senates and other bodies, would typically be left to each individual campus for further decision. Students are granted the right to involve themselves with such basic problems as admissions, academic programs, academic courses and staff, academic evaluation, academic environment, and student discipline – yet, as one reads the draft document, these involvements in most cases seem to be of an advisory nature, with final decisions evidently in the hands of administration and faculty. In certain other spheres, such as budget, physical resources, and external relations, the students are specifically limited to the right "to be heard, through formal means." Only in two areas, regulations pertaining to the students' personal lives and extracurricular activities, are the students given "primary responsibility" – i.e., the power to take final action which can be overruled "only in rare instances and for compelling reasons stated in detail." In any case, student rights and responsibilities are to be exercised with "tolerance, respect, and a sense of community which arises from participation in a common enterprise." [189]

---

[188] As cited by Kerr, *Uses*, pp. 41–42.

[189] The complete text of the "Draft Statement on Student Participation in College and University Government" is cited in Appendix C of this study.

It seems impossible, at this time, to predict the role of students at institutions where a collective bargaining relationship has been established between the faculty and the administration. As Finkin remarked, "it would be ironic for students to secure representation on institutional deliberative bodies whose authority was placed in question by the bargaining agent." (Finkin, "Collective Bargaining and University Government," p. 162.)

PROVISIONS FOR COLLEGE AND UNIVERSITY GOVERNMENT: A GUIDE THROUGH SOME RECENT CONSTITUTIONAL DOCUMENTS

In the present chapter a variety of constitutional provisions are reviewed as culled from a sample of some one hundred colleges and universities. The constitutions selected here are recent [1] and represent a wide spectrum of types of academic institutions;[2] many reflect practices favored in the *Statement on Government of Colleges and Universities*. In view of the fact that constitutional texts are changing very frequently, especially in the present period, a provision cited here may be out of date at a particular institution by the time this handbook appears in print. Therefore, identifications are not ordinarily provided for the academic institutions whose constitutions – current, or perhaps not quite current – are cited; it is not the purpose of this chapter to present information about the constitutional text operative at a particular institution, but rather to give a general impression of the kinds of constitutional provisions used in various colleges and universities.[3]

I. THE FOUR COMPONENTS AND THEIR RELATIONSHIP

A. The Board

1. Composition and Overall Organization

In state universities and colleges boards of trustees are fairly uniformly composed and appointed. To cite some typical cases,

---

[1] 78% of the constitutions surveyed in this chapter were adopted in the period from 1966–1970; 17% in the period from 1960–1965; 5% in the period before 1960.

[2] 35% of the constitutions surveyed in this chapter are for state universities; 18% for private universities; 18% for state colleges; 8% for private colleges; 8% for community colleges; 6% for denominational (mostly Roman Catholic) universities or colleges; 7% for systems of colleges or universities.

[3] Columbia University is the one institution consistently identified in this chapter, mainly because the present author believes that the constitutional document describing Columbia's University Senate, as adopted in May 1969, repre-

at one university the board consists of seven members appointed by the governor, with the consent of the state's senate, for six-year terms; the board of trustees of another university is composed of the commissioner of education, ex-officio, and eight other members, six appointed by the governor and two elected by alumni associations; the board of a university system consists of sixteen members appointed by the governor for six-year terms and eight ex-officio members (the governor, the lieutenant governor, the speaker of the assembly, the superintendent of public instruction, the president of the state board of agriculture, the president of a technical institute, the president of the alumni association, and the president of the university system); at one university the board has eight members "of whom not more than two shall reside in the same county" and who "shall be a body politic." Frequently, there is a dual system of state boards. For example, in one state the Board of Regents is the coordinating agency for all the state-assisted institutions of higher education; each institution, moreover, has its own board appointed by the governor and confirmed by the legislature.

Greater variety exists among private universities and colleges. The board of one university includes the governor, the president of the alumni association, and forty other persons, divided into three classes: ten Life Trustees, twenty Term Trustees (5 year terms), and ten Alumni Trustees (elected by the alumni for 10 year terms). The trustees of another university number seventeen co-opted for life terms, virtually all from one urban area; there are three additional ex-officio members – the governor, the mayor, and the state superintendent of education – but they have not participated actively. The board of a small college consists of forty-three members, with an executive committee of twelve which includes the president. The board of trustees of a Roman Catholic university includes ten ex-officio members who are on the board of the Order of Saint Benedict and four additional members who are administrative officers of the university, a kind of composition that is no longer characteristic of the boards of most Catholic institutions.

sents the most promising adaptation of the "conventional" model favored in this handbook. Also, Columbia University is identified because of the numerous citations from a published document, the commentary to the Columbia senate's constitution. (See fn. 5, below.)

Boards have found it necessary to conduct much of their business in specialized committees composed of their own members, such as committees on finance, development, investment, educational policy, student affairs, physical plant, and, of course, executive committees. More recently, many boards have introduced joint committees, *ad hoc* or standing, which contain representatives of the other components. For example, a state university has a standing liaison committee composed of three members of the board of trustees, the president, the provost, the academic vice-president, the vice-president for financial affairs, and six elected members of the faculty; the addition of student members is under consideration. At another state university, the Regent-Faculty Conference Committee includes the board of trustees, the president, and nine elected members of the faculty. At a private university, members of the board have met with representatives of the other three components on such matters as censorship of student publications and avoidance of disruptive demonstrations. Elsewhere, faculty members are sometimes invited to meetings of the board to explain and to advise on specific programs or proposals. A Commission on University Governance at Duke University in early 1970 proposed a formal system of standing committees composed of trustees and members of the other components: a Committee on Long Range Planning (three trustees, two faculty members, two students, the President and the Chancellor); a Committee on Academic Affairs (four faculty members, two trustees, two students, the Provost); a Committee on Finance and Business Affairs (four trustees, two faculty members, one student, the Vice President for Business and Finance); a Committee on Institutional Advancement (four trustees, two alumni, one faculty member, one student, the Vice President for Institutional Advancement); a Committee on University Life (four students, two trustees, two faculty members, the Vice President for Student Affairs).

Far short of the drastic proposals to "de-isolate" boards noted in the previous chapter – particularly, the Canadian "one-tier" suggestion – a number of institutions include faculty members as regular members of the board, in one case as many as six, but more frequently two or three. Other institutions have faculty members on the board in non-voting capacity. At one private college, two faculty members from neighboring universities serve on the board, while an AAUP representative attends the board meetings of a state junior college. Student members have recently been added to the boards of a great variety of institutions, public and private, large and small.

The new constitution of the senate of a large private university, of May 1969, provides for the joint selection of six board members by the board and the faculty-dominated executive committee of the senate.

2. *General Authority*

Put briefly, as it is in numerous constitutional documents, the board has the power of final determination on all matters pertaining to the institution. At one private university, for example: "in the Board of Trustees resides the ultimate legal authority to make decisions affecting the University as a whole or any of its parts." Frequently, however, such statements suggest the presence of other components. At a state university, "the final authority" resides in the board of trustees "acting through the President of the University"; at a state college, "the powers of the President and the Faculty are delegated by the Board in accord with its policies."

A detailed description of the many aspects of the "final" authority of a board is provided in the statutes of one state university. The following powers are assigned to the board:

to hold and operate said property in trust for the state;
to acquire, hold and dispose of said property and other like property as deemed necessary for the best execution of its cooperative purposes;
to employ presidents, professors, instructors and other employees and to determine their salaries;
to create, abolish and consolidate departments or divisions;
to enact by-laws for its own government and regulations for the government of the institutions under its control;
the Board shall award with the approval of the President and a committee of the faculty of the University, academic degrees and diplomas and confer honors in the same manner as is customary in American colleges.

A more limited description of board powers is given at another state university. First of all, "for the proper use of funds appropriated by the General Assembly and for the proper administration and government of the University, the Board is responsible to the people of . . ., by whom its members are elected." But, in the second place, the board exercises primary jurisdiction in all matters *except those for which it has delegated authority* to the president, other officers, or bodies of the University. Thus, "when acting on matters having to do with educational policy and organization of the University, the Board relies upon the advice of the University Senates ..."; and, when acting "on matters concerning the administrative organization and powers and responsibilities of the officers of the University, the Board acts on the advice of the President."

The board at a small private college – in accordance with the 1966 Statement – defines and limits its functions in the following way: the Board is the "legal repository of authority" and the "final institutional authority"; yet, it must undertake "appropriate self-limitation." Thus, it entrusts the conduct of administration to the president and the deans, and the conduct of teaching and research to the faculty. In addition to its several kinds of financial responsibilities, it has "a special obligation to assure that the history of the college shall serve as a prelude and inspiration to the future"; in this, the board "should be aided by, and may insist upon, the development of long-range planning by the administration and faculty."

B. The Administration

1. Composition and Overall Organization

In a small college, the administration can remain simple; in addition to the president, there may be a dean for academic affairs and a dean of students, with full-time assistants, perhaps, working on admissions and financial aid, student records, and business affairs. One private college also has "Class Deans" as an alternative to major subdivisions along disciplinary lines. At another private college, the president is specifically designated "the head of all departments of the College."

Imposing administrative superstructures flourish in large universities, inevitably with hierarchical overtones. At one large state university all faculty members and all administrative and other officers are, "through appropriate channels," responsible to the president "and only through him to the Board of Regents." Academic deans of a college or school, directors, and even chairmen of departments are the "channels" in their respective domains. The dean of students is directly responsible to the president "for the general welfare of students in their extra-curricular life and activities."

The following is a typical list of "officers of administration" in a medium-sized private university: the President, the Executive Vice-President (for financial affairs), the Provost (for academic affairs), the Vice-President for Institutional Development, the Deans of the colleges and schools, the Dean of Students, the Director of Annual Giving, the Director of Student Records and Registration, the Director of the Junior Year Abroad Program, the Director of Public Relations, the Director of the Summer School, the Director of Alumni Activities, the Director of the University Library, the Director of Financial Aid, the Business Manager and Comptroller, the Director of Admissions, the Director of Planning, the Director of the University Health Service, the Director of Sponsored Programs, the Director of Athletics. In addition to these officers, there are directors of special academic programs and numerous associate and assistant deans or directors.

The administrative organization of a multi-institutional university system is even more complex. The president of a large state university system is described as having become the "chief coordinator and planner" rather than the "chief operating official." He presides over the President's Council of Chief Campus Officers, and his personal staff includes no less than seven vice presidents and five deans who are not attached to any individual campus. Moreover, he is provided with two "Academic Assistants," drawn on a short-term basis from the campuses to provide liaison between the president's office and the faculty of the system. This interesting attempt to circumvent the excesses of administrative layers which shield the president from the faculty is also used in one of the system's institutions where the chancellor has two similar "Academic Assistants" from the faculty.

The administrative group in a university is often formally structured. At one state university there is a Coordinating Committee, composed of the highest ranking administrators, which serves as the president's "cabinet"; a larger body, the Administrative Council, contains also lower administrators and the department heads. The university even has a formal Council of Department Heads, a device not used in most institutions, partly because the administration status of departmental heads or chairmen is – or should be – in doubt.

As to the selection of administrative officers, more and more frequently procedures are being introduced which include guarantees for faculty involvement in the selection process. At one state college, whenever a new vice-president or dean has to be named, an ad hoc five-member Selection Committee of tenured faculty is formed, elected by the faculty at large from a list of nominees who in turn have been chosen by vote of the faculty of each school and division. For each administration position to be filled, the Selection Committee recommends three names to the president for his final selection of one. When a new president of one private university had to be found, both the board of trustees and an elected ad hoc faculty committee suggested names, with each group having a veto over the suggestions of the other group. Finally, a list of five names had been approved by both the board and the faculty, and from this list the board made the final choice. According to the new constitution of a large private university, all senior administrative officials with university-wide responsibilities shall be appointed only after consultation with the senate's faculty-dominated executive committee.

2. General Authority

There are different ways of expressing administrative authority, particularly that of presidents, ranging from a strictly hierarchical model to a model allowing significant weight to the other components, particularly the faculty. The president of one large private university, for example, is "the educational and administrative head of the university" and shall be responsible to and report to the trustees. On behalf of the trustees, he shall "perform all acts ...." Similarly, the president of a state college is "responsible for the educational effectiveness and academic excellence of the college," in addition to his other responsibilities for long-range fiscal planning, business affairs, and public relations; he may delegate authority, but only to "various administrative levels." The president of a community college is, among other things, to provide leadership "in securing mutual commitment by all concerned" to an educational philosophy "appropriate to the aims of the college ...."

Different language is used at one large state university. Its president has the authority to formulate rules necessary for the "immediate government" of the university, but in carrying out this duty he is to consult with the faculty and will communicate to the board all the recommendations of the faculty which concern the welfare of the university; moreover, he may delegate in whole or in part to the faculty the responsibility for formulating the rules for the "immediate government" of the university. Almost identical terms describe the authority of the president of another state university, also with the built-in obligation to consult the faculty and delegate responsibilities to it – although all faculty members are also declared to be responsible to the president, "through appropriate channels." At one state university the board of trustees has "committed" to the president *and* a "committee of the faculty" (i.e., the senate) the authority to formulate rules necessary for governing the university. (But, again, all faculty members are, "through appropriate channels," responsible to the president and "only through him" to the board.) The president of yet another state university has "general administrative authority" over university affairs; he may suspend action taken by the senate or by any college faculty and ask for reconsideration of such action. However, significantly enough, "if the President and the Senate or college faculty do not reach agreement on the action, the question may be appealed to the Regents . . . ." Furthermore, although the president has the final authority to make budgetary recommendations to the Regents, he must first consult with and ask for recommendations from a faculty committee concerning the budgetary recommendations which "materially affect the University as a whole."

The functions of the small college president are enumerated at a private institution. He must innovate and initiate; he is to be judged largely by his capacity for institutional leadership, which – in language adapted from the 1966 Statement – will depend on "the degree to which he can envision new horizons for his institution and can persuade others to see them and to work toward them." He is to utilize the judgments of the faculty and it is incumbent upon him to insure that faculty views, "including dissenting views," are presented to the board "in those areas and on those issues where responsibilities are shared." In the interest of academic standards, the president may also seek outside advice from "scholars of acknowledged competence."

In many universities the administration works with the

faculty regardless of the provisions of constitutional texts. A president may have a constitution which contains a strictly hierarchically allocated distribution of written authority; yet, he may in fact consult most effectively with his faculty. Still, there is considerable advantage in having institutional provisions and codes reflect actual practice.

C. The Faculty

1. Composition and Overall Organization

As defined in numerous institutional documents, a faculty is composed primarily of professors, associate professors, assistant professors, and instructors; in addition, there are various kinds of lecturers and research or teaching associates, frequently not serving in a full-time capacity. In many institutions the major administrative officers are also members of the faculty, particularly the president, the vice-presidents and provost, the academic deans, and perhaps the dean of students and director of admissions. Administrative officers are often considered part of the faculty even when they do not perform any teaching duties – although many of them, of course, do. Finally, librarians, certain professional staff members such as psychiatrists, and officers of ROTC departments are frequently granted faculty or quasi-faculty status. A primary requirement for faculty status is usually the approval of each of the irregular categories of candidates by the regular faculty of a school or college, or the university as a whole. Particularly delicate problems in this regard can arise in medical and other professional schools. At times, the granting of faculty status takes place by unilateral administration action, without participation of the regular faculty.

With respect to organization, a faculty member's basic unit is the department, which ties him to the university but at the same time to his discipline and the national (and world-wide) academic scene. In view of this dual foundation of the faculty member's attachment to his department, great care is often taken to make this unit a workable, livable "home" – if possible not too large, permitting ample participation even to the junior member. Of course, numerous departments far exceed any kind of desirable limit of size, and accordingly offer less of a collegial milieu to their staff. Next in the line of organizational ties for most faculty members is the college, for example, the college of Arts and Sciences, which has regularly scheduled meetings with participatory opportunity for all ranks. Again, size is crucial; a meeting with some 300 or 400 faculty members does not permit many to participate. Parallel to the college is the graduate school, which provides a second college-size unit for many faculty members, again with possibilities for direct participation. The remaining two units may be less accessible: the general faculty assembly of a university, and the senate of a university. The former body is usually so large that it may only be used, in effect, for communications purposes, such as the delivery of presidential "state of the union" speeches. Senates, of course, are representative, and relatively few faculty members will actually serve on them in their careers.

This spectrum of organizational units for faculty members does not exist in all institutions. Small colleges frequently have no senates and in any case no larger body than the college faculty assembly. Universities often have no formal meetings for all the faculty, and a few even have no senate-like body. The faculties of some professional schools have no departmental units; on the other hand, these professional schools may resemble departments in most respects. Medical schools are *sui generis* organizationally, with their faculties at times sharply divided between full-time and part-time professors, or between M.D.'s and Ph.D.'s. Departmental chairmen tend to be extraordinarily strong if not autocratic in medical schools, and relations with other parts of the university may be minimal. However, some of the medical faculty may be active in the graduate school faculty.

One kind of ubiquitous organization must still be mentioned, the committee. Committees abound at all levels – the department, the college, the university as a whole, the senate, and the administration. Few faculty members escape committee service, which may, or may not, provide them with meaningful experiences of participation in government at one level or another of the institution's structures.

At many state colleges and community colleges, and at some smaller private colleges, a Faculty Association enjoys a kind of quasi-official status (in contrast to the entirely unofficial status of the AAUP Chapter). At one small private college, the Faculty Association "shall neither have nor seek official status, of necessity" and is specifically not a committee of the college. Yet, it is called the intermediary "between Faculty and the College," has immediate access to all administration officers, and holds its meetings directly after the regular faculty meetings. At a private junior college, it is the function of the Faculty Association, according to the constitution, to confer with the administration so as to promote "the social, economic, and intellectual welfare" of its members. Faculty Associations usually contain virtually the entire faculty of the institution. They may be badly needed in view of the backwardness of many community and junior colleges with respect to real faculty participation in decision-making, a result of historical tradition in these institutions – and of the fact that a teaching load of 15–18 classroom hours has left little time for direct involvement in governmental duties.

2. General Authority

In constitutions of academic institutions there appears to be, frequently, considerable reluctance to define with any kind of precision the extent of faculty authority. This reluctance may be an aftermath of the hierarchical myth, which most boards and administrations *de facto* have given up long ago, but which *formally* they prefer to see maintained, or at least not publicly sacrificed, in codified statements of faculty powers. Often, faculties have acquiesced in this state of affairs and have not insisted on any formal abolition of the hierarchical principle when in fact they have been successful on this point. Nevertheless, a number of constitutions include a realistic description of faculty authority.

A brief statement in the constitution of a state university system establishes the obligation for the faculty of each college "to participate significantly in the initiation, development, and implementation of the educational system," with specific reference to organs of faculty participation from the departmental level upwards to a system-wide senate. At a large state university the faculty is given "legislative authority" in all matters relating to conferring of degrees; the curriculum and the structure of the university with reference to academic matters; student conduct and discipline; faculty conduct, tenure, and discipline. Moreover, the faculty has "resolving authority," i.e., the right to express by formal resolution its opinion "on any question relating to the policy or administration of the University"; finally, the faculty exercises limited "review functions" through the specific authorization to "express its judgment on administrative action by giving an opinion and recommendation on any case presented to it which raises an issue of academic freedom, tenure, promotion, salary adjustment, or the nature or conditions of work." In the constitution of a private college – following closely the relevant text of the 1966 Statement on Government – the faculty is granted "primary responsibility" for such "fundamental areas" as curriculum, degree requirements, subject matter and methods of instruction, research, faculty status, and "those aspects of student life which relate to the educational process." This "primary responsibility" is related to the faculty's central relationship to the educational process; the board and the president should concur with faculty judgment in these areas, "except in rare instances and for compelling reasons which should be stated in detail." Agencies for faculty participation in the government of the college are to be established at each level where faculty responsibility is present. Finally, the faculty should actively participate in the determination of policies and procedures governing salary increases. At one large state university there is a specific "delegation of rule-making powers" to the faculty; the president authorizes the faculty to share with him and the academic deans responsibility for the formulation of rules for the immediate government of the university in wide areas of jurisdiction. These areas include educational policy and general welfare; policy for the regulation of student conduct and activities; scholastic policy (including requirements for admission, graduation, and honors); approval of candidates for degrees; criteria for faculty tenure, appointment and promotion; recommendations concerning the university budget; the formulation of procedures to carry out the policies and regulations thus established.

Where delegations of jurisdiction are specifically made to faculties – as in the cases just described – definitional problems may arise to cloud the issue. For example, an observer at a state college noted how difficult it is to draw the line between policy-making and policy-administering. Various administrative groups engage in the latter, while the senate is supposed to do the former in educational spheres; yet, and not just at this college, the administration invariably gets into policy-making – and the faculty at times attempts to administer. At another state college, college committees are instructed to "distinguish

clearly between policy and administration," and may engage
only in the former. Furthermore, "program and operational
planning" is specifically excluded from any policy sphere, and
committees may not become involved in the application of a
policy "to specific persons or specific problems." Also, "committees shall not be used as appeals boards from administrative
decisions."

A complex attempt to define and limit faculty jurisdiction is
made at one state college. Policy formulation is called "the
joint responsibility" of administrative officers and consultative
bodies (such as senates, faculty assemblies, and departmental
meetings) at the various levels of the institution. Yet, the
implementing decisions made under such jointly arrived-at
policies are the sole responsibility of the administrative officers. Much emphasis is put on the appropriateness of the consultative procedures which effectuate the carrying-out of the
"joint responsibility" for policy formulation. "The ultimate
purpose of consultative procedures shall be to guarantee full
participation by faculty and academic administrators in the
formulation of policies and procedures affecting the administrative and academic environment." Any member of a consultative body may request a hearing if he believes that consultative procedures have not been properly carried out. Basic to
this policy-formulation process is the so-called "determination"
stage at which the following choices must be made concerning
"a given matter":

1. is it policy or administrative?
2. shall it be dealt with at the college, school, or departmental level?
3. shall it be routed via an administrator or the faculty route?
4. does it require a "recommendation," a "decisional recommendation," a "policy decision," or an "administrative decision"?

Administrative officers or consultative bodies are specifically
designated to rule at different points of the "determination"
stage, and where no specific designation has been made, the
"matter" shall be submitted to the president or the vice-president. Each "matter" shall be determined to involve one of the
types of actions mentioned in point 4 above. A *"recommendation"* shall be presented by a consultative body to the administrator at its level; if he disagrees with the "recommendation," he shall nevertheless pass it on for final decision to

the next level(s) together with his opinion on the issue. A *"decisional recommendation"* differs from a "recommendation" in that it is "the type of action to be used when the subordinate level has major, but not final, responsibility for the decision in the matter." If such a decision is not accepted at the higher level, it cannot be amended by any administrative officer or consultative body at that level but must be sent back to the lower level; if the lower level then refuses to amend, the higher level may proceed to impose amendment if in the opinion of the president of the college "orderly administration" requires it. A *"policy decision"* must be made jointly by the consultative body and the administrative officer and shall then be policy at that level. If the administrative officer and the consultative body cannot reach agreement on a "policy decision," the matter shall be referred to the administrative officer or a faculty committee at the next higher level who may adjudicate the matter. (The question to whom the referral shall be made shall be a "policy decision" at that higher level.) An *"administrative decision"* is final, but may be taken by an administrative officer only if there is no policy to the contrary; the consultative body may call into question the correctness of the determination by the administrative officer, and then the matter shall be treated as a "policy decision." Finally, a special appeals committee of the senate has been set up to hear complaints about violations of these consultative procedures.

It is possible that elaborate rules and definitions of this type may indeed strengthen the consultative process between administration and faculty. In any case, complaints abound about the lack of effectiveness of faculty participation in decision-making. A special committee at one state university, appointed to study faculty participation in government, noted the many "grey areas" where it was not clear whether the faculty or the administration had responsibility. According to the committee, the faculty was bitter about not being consulted sufficiently on important areas of decision making; or, if it was consulted, the consultation came too late for faculty opinion to have any real impact – "liaison between Faculty and Administration is often inadequate in the early formative stages of important issues." An investigation at another state university concluded that there was little participation in government by the faculty beyond the departmental level; again it was noted how little influence the faculty had particularly during the formulation of policy. Similarly, among the most notable of a set of fifty-four critical resolutions on university government, offered by the AAUP chapter of a large private university in October of 1968, were those alleging that the prerequisite information for effective faculty participation had come "too little and too late." The chapter called for a modification of the "style of communication" in the direction of "greater openness," so that information on issues would be available *before* final decisions had to be made; moreover, regular mechanisms were to be established by which the faculty could inquire about *future* policy intentions.

A study at a large state university suggested two ways to reduce conflicts of authority between faculty and administration – the selection of administrative officers from the ranks of those faculty members who had been active in the senate or on committees, and the frequent rotation of administrative officers back to regular faculty duty. Thus, a separate class of career academic administrators would not develop and faculty-administrative relations might be maintained in a more compatible fashion. The secret of successful faculty-administration participation in government may well be found through a combination of methods: assuring empathic behavior at both the administration and the faculty level, and providing carefully drafted constitutional provisions which go somewhat beyond the old hierarchical myths of board and presidential supremacy.

Two recent constitutional drafts are illustrative of attempts at rather substantial increases in faculty authority, particularly with respect to traditional administration prerogatives. The proposed constitution of one state university provides for a president who "agrees to share his authority, in that stage where he prepares to use the power of decision residing in his office, with his constituents here on this campus speaking and acting through their duly elected representatives sitting as a university legislature." Moreover, in that "legislature," the University Senate, neither the president nor any of his administrative officials would be represented as such – even though they can run for the elective faculty seats as members of the faculty. In this proposed 100 member senate, there are to be 40 faculty members, 10 professional staff, 35 undergraduate students, and 15 graduate students. While the "academic community shall work with the President" as he carries

out his "mandated responsibilities," the senate "shall be empowered to formulate policy on behalf of the academic community with respect to budget, curricula, personnel policies,
academic standards, and the general concerns of the educational program.[4]

The new constitution for Columbia University, as adopted
in May 1969, is not quite as unconventional as the one just
noted. In its 101 member senate there are to be 9 administrative officers including the president, 63 faculty members,
"only" 21 students, 2 alumni, and 6 staff members of various
types. Many of its wide "legislative powers" can be checked by
the veto powers available to the board of trustees. However,
the senate will help nominate six trustees, and may under
certain circumstances deal with questionable conduct or efficiency of administrative officers. As the commentary to the
new constitution stated realistically:

> While powers of the University Senate cover a wide range, the nature
> of their exercise will depend on the subject matter involved. In certain
> areas, budgetary matters, for example, the Senate's role will be es-
> sentially one of review and general oversight as to concordance of the
> budget with the short-term and long-term educational aims of the
> University. In other areas – for example, the election of some Trustees
> – a Senate committee will actually participate in the nominating
> process. In some areas, the Senate may serve both a policy-making
> and an advisory function, as in the case of honors and prizes, where it
> will both set standards and work with the Board of Trustees on the
> choice of recipients. In those areas most significant for self-determi-
> nation by the University community – including matters of academic
> policy and planning, matters of tenure and academic freedom, degree
> requirement, and matters of University discipline – the Senate will
> have legislative power.[5]

D. The Students

Provisions for student participation in government have
been rare in university constitutions, even in otherwise progressive and elaborate documents. The increasingly numerous
exceptions are not necessarily impressive concessions to stu-

[4] This constitutional draft was defeated in spring of 1969, mainly due to an
unfavorable vote by the faculty – which apparently objected to the composition
of the senate.
[5] The commentary to the new Columbia constitution was prepared by the
Executive Committee of the Faculty of Columbia University, and first printed in
the *Columbia Daily Spectator* of February 17, 1969.

dent "power." At one private college, for example, it was urged – following the text of the 1966 Statement on Government – that ways should be found to permit significant student participation, even though the obstacles to such participation are considered large and not to be minimized: "inexperience, untested capacity, a transitory status which means that present action does not carry with it subsequent responsibility and the inescapable fact that the other components of the institution are in position of judgment over the students." Nevertheless, the institution needs "the strength, freshness of view and idealism of the student body." At this college three elected students are regular members of the senate. They are specifically charged to determine whether a petition coming from the student body should be considered by the senate; however, all petitions signed by 10% or more of the student body will be automatically taken up by the senate. At a Roman Catholic college, there are six students in a senate having a total of twenty-two members, while at one private university there are as many as fifteen students in a forty-five member senate.

A major breakthrough toward powerful, if not overpowering, student representation was planned at one state university. As was mentioned earlier, the senate of this institution, as proposed and rejected in early 1969, was to have 50 student members, 40 faculty members, and 10 non-teaching professional staff members. This student domination was to be somewhat tempered by the provision that the student group had to consists of 35 undergraduates and 15 graduate students.

In the new Columbia constitution, the senate contains 21 student members out of a total 101 members. The commentary to the Columbia constitution reports the rejection of suggestions "for a special student assembly or other University-wide form of student government." This rejection reflected "the dominant student point of view which regards student government as distinct from University government as both useless and unreal." The "parallel structures approach" would work only if there were "entirely separate matters for faculty and student concern which each group ought to deal with on its own"; but, in fact, in university government, such matters of exclusive concern hardly exist. The students at Columbia concluded that a separate "student government" is a sham "because it does not really have anything to govern." Another reason why Columbia rejected parallel structures was "that the

University should again become a true community"; separate governing bodies for students and faculty would "accentuate division instead of building on the common interests of the various groups that form the University."

The Columbia commentary justifies student representation in the senate as desirable in principle:

The student spends a significant portion of his life at the University, and that portion may well shape all that follows. It is neither just nor prudent to maintain that students have little or nothing to say about the decisions made by their University when it counts for so much in their lives. Student representation is also desirable as a matter of educational policy. It forces them to make difficult choices instead of simply criticizing the hard choices made by others. Such participation also offers especially fruitful contact with their elders.

If the justice of the principle of student representation is recognized, "adequate" numbers of representatives must be allowed. "The number here recommended, 21, will allow significant participation by students on University Senate committees where their participation is appropriate and will also allow students from every school and faculty to be represented." Whether "adequateness" is really determined by these necessities, and how it will be expressed in the future, is one of the great questions yet to be solved in appropriate theoretical and practical terms, against the conflicting realities of faculty professionalism and the fact of overwhelming student majorities on the campuses. After all, students *are* increasingly participating in the shaping of university policies – not necessarily through involvement in the formal machinery of academic government but through the "brute" use of mass political protest and mass organized force in a milieu where effective counter-force by or for the other campus components is notoriously difficult to apply.

The Columbia constitution has one additional feature which must be mentioned. In order that elections of student representatives "will not only reflect student interest and student participation, but will also produce representative results," a number of students equal to at least 40% of the full-time students in a constituency (school or college) must participate in an election for its results to be valid. If no representative is elected from a particular constituency because this minimum participation requirement has not been met, another election may be scheduled in an attempt to reach the 40% participation prerequisite. (While the 40% requirement is also applicable to the faculty and other components, it is obviously most burdensome for the student constituencies.)[6]

Significant governmental participation by students takes place in many universities at the committee level, where student membership can often be arranged informally without changes in the constitution or even the by-laws. At one state university, senate committees have been specifically authorized to propose the appointment of one or more student members, with each committee remaining free to determine the actual status of the student members, particularly their voting privileges. A survey of 85 institutions, undertaken in November–December 1968, indicated that, of the 59 institutions replying, 45 had voting student membership on at least one committee. (In 13 of these institutions students were serving on the senate.)[7]

II. STRUCTURES

A. System-Level Structures

Faculty participation through system-level structures – i.e., structures for two or more coordinated or, at least, related aca-

---

[6] The Council of the Princeton University Community, introduced in 1969, established a central organ, the Council, of 57 members – including 7 administration members, 18 faculty members (5 non-tenured), 22 students (14 undergraduate, 8 graduate), 4 alumni, 6 staff (library, research, office, etc.). This Council is not intended as a regular senate, and should leave largely intact the academic jurisdictions of established bodies. The Council is to concern itself with subjects "of widespread or especially intense concern" – such as the university's relationship to the Institute for Defense Analyses, counseling students about their draft status, military recruiting on campus, and particularly the making of rules of conduct which are binding on all members of the university community. The Council is to act, in effect, as "a permanent conference of the representatives of all the major groups of the University," with a deliberative rather than decision-making task. In addition to an executive committee (composed of the president, 6 faculty members, 5 students and 3 others), the Council also has a Committee on Rights and Rules, a Committee on Governance (which should give continuing attention to problems of university government, and also help select members of the board of trustees), a Committee on Priorities (to review the university budget), a Committee on Relations with the Local Community, and two other committees. Reportedly, the Council proved to be useful during the Cambodian crisis in 1970. (McConnell and Mortimer, *The Faculty in University Governance*, p. 168.)

[7] Office of Institutional Research, East Carolina University, "A Survey of Practices Related to Student Membership on Academic Committees," February 1969 (mimeo.), p. 2.

demic institutions – has become more frequent. In the following section three state systems, a city system, and a community college system will be discussed. In addition, coordinating mechanisms in two states will be mentioned.

1. A State College System

The state college system of a western state has a state-wide senate which is to serve "as the official voice of the faculties of the ... State Colleges in matters of system-wide concern"; it considers matters affecting system-wide policies and makes recommendations thereon. The areas of responsibility include, among others, general educational policy matters, state-wide curricular matters, requirements for admission and degrees, and advice to the chancellor on major system-wide administrative appointments. A significant safeguard for protecting the local jurisdiction of the various colleges of the system is provided by the possibility of referendum. Any recommendation adopted by the system-senate can be challenged in a referendum when resolutions requesting such a referendum are adopted by the senates of at least one-third of the colleges, or when 40% of the members of the system-senate support the referendum.

The senate uses a system of more or less proportional representation. Two members each are elected from colleges with fewer than 10,000 full-time students; three members each from colleges with fewer than 20,000 full-time students; four members each from colleges with more than 20,000 full-time students. Only the chancellor or his representative is an ex-officio member; all the senators are faculty members, with three year terms. The senate meets at least twice during each academic year; if the budget permits (travel expenses!), additional meetings may be held.

The system-wide senate's constitution had to be ratified by a majority of the total faculty vote cast in a system-wide referendum *and* a majority of the faculty votes cast at each of a majority of the colleges, with final approval by the trustees. The same procedures are required for amendments.

2. A State University System in the West

Prior to 1962, the university system of a western state had an unwieldy assembly containing all administrative officers and all faculty members, which was divided into two divisions: a Northern Section with three campuses; a Southern Section with four campuses. After 1962, this assembly was reorganized into decentralized divisions at each campus. Joint committees from the various divisions continued to meet, however, such as the one on Budget and Inter-Departmental Relations, on Educational Policy, and the Coordinating Committee on Graduate Affairs. The budget committee is authorized "to confer with the President on general policy concerning the University budget ...."

The reorganization of 1962 also produced the "All-University Senate Assembly," which is in effect a system-wide, representative senate with 49 faculty members and the president of the university. This system-wide representative body has the power within certain limits "to take final action" concerning "all legislation substantially affecting more than one Division [campus] or the state-wide University." Such legislative action may originate in the body, may be referred to it by a divisional (campus) senate, or may be referred to it by a special Committee on Rules and Jurisdiction if a local campus acts in a matter affecting more than one campus or the system. This system-senate meets at least three times per academic year.

3. A City University System

The senate of a city university system in a large metropolitan area is the principal decision-making body of the system with regard to those areas of activity in which the faculty has primary responsibility; in all other areas of faculty interest and concern, this senate is to be the instrument for faculty participation in the decision-making processes of the system. The areas where the faculty has *primary responsibility* include system-wide policies and procedures concerning, first, the academic status, role, rights, and freedoms of the faculty; and, second, system-level educational and instructional matters, and research and scholarly activities of system-wide import. The other areas, where the faculty merely has *interest and concern*, still require full senate participation, "directly and at all stages in the making of decisions." These other areas include:

1. the economic status of the Faculty
2. the allocation of resources for educational objectives, for research and scholarly activities
3. the establishment and location of new units of the University and the appointment of principal administrative officers thereof
4. the appointment and retention of the principal administrative officers at the University level
5. relations between the University and the local community or between the University and governmental units or agencies
6. the general public relations of the University

The senate is a "pure" faculty senate; its only ex-officio member is the chancellor of the system, or his designated representative, "with voice but without vote." The members of the senate are elected roughly in proportion to the number of faculty members in each college or school of the system. The senate meets at least four times during the academic year; it has its own budget, which includes "appropriate allotments of released time for the officers and Executive Committee of the Senate and other Senate members whose Senate duties in the judgment of the Executive Committee require release from regular teaching or related functions."

The "charter" of this system became effective after it was ratified by a majority of the constituent units of the system.

4. A State University System in the East

The university system of an eastern state comprises all publicly supported institutions of higher education in the state with the exception of the units of a metropolitan university system. Established in 1948, this system is huge, consisting at present of sixty-eight units: four universities, two medical schools, ten colleges of arts and sciences, thirty locally sponsored two-year community colleges, and several specialized colleges.

The Faculty Senate of the system is composed of from one to four elected faculty representatives from each local campus, plus the chancellor of the system and two officials appointed by him. However, the thirty community colleges are not granted representation in the senate, but have a representative organ, the so-called Faculty Council, of their own. Thus, the senate has only about forty members.

The senate's central purpose is to study matters relating to state-wide university, faculty, and educational problems and policies; it is to provide "an opportunity for the faculties of the University to act in an advisory, consultative, and planning capacity for the Chancellor ...." The senate holds three regular sessions per year.

The thirty two-year community colleges have "the most tenuous connection" with the system; they remain isolated, being dependent on local initiatives and controlled by locally sponsored trustees. The community colleges are considered "different," and the system-senate, therefore, is believed to be "not suited to their needs." To break down the sense of isolation, the Faculty Council of Community Colleges was created as an organization "which could serve the special needs and purposes of Community College faculties." The Faculty Council's key purpose is "to provide opportunity and structure for the faculties of community colleges to formulate positions on policy matters of common interest," which then can be communicated to their administrators and trustees, and also to the system-chancellor and the system-senate.

5. A Community College System

The Faculty Senate of the system of regional community colleges in an eastern state has a variety of purposes:

to provide a means of communication among faculty of the various colleges;
to provide for the welfare of the faculty;
to generate and evaluate ideas and policies for the benefit of the students, the colleges, and the communities which they serve;
to represent the faculty in dealings with the Board of Trustees for Regional Community Colleges.

Each of the colleges of the system has three faculty representatives in the senate, with an additional representative for every thirty full-time teaching faculty members. The body meets at least four times per year. The constitutional document became operative upon a two-thirds vote of the entire full-time teaching faculties; amendments require the same procedure.

6. Coordinating Mechanisms

In several states coordinating mechanisms rather than senates provide institutional arrangements at the system level. For example, a Coordinating Committee for Higher Education is to provide coordination for the activities of the state university and the state colleges and institutes of a midwestern state. The committee is to relate the various institutions to the needs of the people of the state; to recommend necessary changes in programs and facilities; and to provide for a single, consolidated, biennial budget request for all the institutions. The committee consists of fifteen members, mostly regents from the various institutions, but also "citizens." It is assisted by a special research and planning staff, and does not include faculty members.

Another committee in the same state provides coordination to a "sub-system," the two campuses of the state university. It consists of the members of the board, the president of the university, and nine elected faculty members (including one dean) from the two campuses. This committee may make recommendations concerning the university "in all its departments, colleges, schools and activities whether educational, business or otherwise." Also, "Joint Departmental Conference Committees" are to serve in an advisory capacity to the various departments of each campus on major matters of policy and standards, so as to provide for parallel development and mutual benefits.

A Senate Coordinating Council of the university system of another midwestern state is to consider all matters acted on by any of the three campus senates in the system, and to determine "whether any action affects general University policy, or is a policy of individual campus concern only." If the Council finds a matter of concern to more than one campus, it refers that matter to the other senates for consideration and recommendation. If the Council finds agreement between the senates impossible, it transmits its own recommendations to the president for submission to the board. The Council consists of twelve members who are elected from the three senates. Any member of the senate at each campus is eligible for election to the Council. This system has another coordinating device. The Senate Coordinating Council is to appoint three of its members "to act as a liaison committee advisory to the Board of Trustees (through the President), the President, and the respective Senates, in matters of special and extraordinary concern to the University."

B. *The General Faculty Assembly*

Many institutions feature a dual set of "parliamentary" devices: (1) a general faculty assembly which includes as members all, or almost all, of the faculty members and, usually, the academic deans and vice-presidents and the president of the university; and (2) a representative senate with, in most cases, 50–80 elected faculty representatives, a number of ex-officio administrative officers, and – perhaps – some students.[8] It is the former type of body which is to be discussed in the present section.

1. Functions

In the most traditional sense, the function of a general faculty assembly – as described typically at one state university – is to "receive reports and announcements from officers of the University and from the Faculty Senate" and to "formulate its opinion upon any subject of interest to the University and make recommendations thereon to the appropriate body or officer for final consideration." Or, as defined at a community college, the general faculty assembly shall provide a means for "expressing faculty aspirations for the college" and for facilitating communication within the institution. At a private university, the assembly is to hear reports on the state of the university from the president or other officers of administration and faculty members are permitted to direct questions to these personages at such occasions; moreover, the assembly may discuss "any subject of common concern" and may express its opinion thereon.

More ambitious jurisdictional grants to general faculty assemblies can be found, however. At one private college, for

---

[8] For purposes of the present chapter, a representative parliamentary body is called a "senate," while a parliamentary body containing all or most of the faculty is called a "general faculty assembly." In actual practice throughout the United States a great variety of names has been used for these two types of bodies, sometimes quite contradictory to the usage suggested here.

example, the general faculty assembly "shall determine policy relating to the academic, social and religious life of the students." At another private college, the general faculty assembly, in cooperation with the president, is charged by the board of trustees "with the fundamental responsibility for the formulation, revision and continuous review of educational policy." Moreover, the board "shall make no alterations in the basic educational policy of the College without a prior and full review" by the general faculty assembly. At a state university, the general faculty assembly "shall have charge of the immediate government of the institution under such rules as may be enacted by the Board of Trustees, together with such regulations as may be prescribed by the President." Similarly, again subject to the authority of the board and in consultation with the president, the general faculty assembly at another state university "shall have the general power and responsibility to adopt policies, regulations and procedures intended to achieve the educational objectives of ... [the] University and the general welfare of those involved in these educational processes." At a Roman Catholic university, the general faculty assembly "shall participate in determining the major educational policy in all decisions affecting the overall purposes of the University." Also, "as a deliberative body, [it] shall discuss and express its opinion on any issue considered by the members of the faculty to be within its scope of concern and interest."

General delegation of jurisdiction to the faculty and its general faculty assembly is frequently accompanied by detailed enumerations of topics assigned to the body for "legislative" purposes. To cite an elaborate example, at a state college:

It shall be the duty of the Faculty [general faculty assembly] to formulate and adopt all academic, personnel, and professional policies (including fiscal policies related thereto) for which the College itself has responsibility. Such policies, hereinafter referred to as "educational policies," include but are not limited to the following enumerated policies:

a. *academic:*
    admission and retention of students; student government, discipline, activities, athletics; courses of instruction; degree requirements; major, minor and curriculum requirements; teacher credentialling; graduate study; extension school offerings; educational television; library allocations; accepting, granting, and awarding of scholar-

ships, fellowships and research grants; college goals and plans; grading; instructional standards; counseling; released time; advising; general education; campus facility planning and fiscal matters relating to all items above

b. *personnel:*
appointment, retention, lay-off, dismissal, tenure, promotion, demotion, transfer, extension and summer school hiring, graduate and undergraduate student assistant hiring, and grievances

c. *professional:*
selection of departmental and divisional chairmen, selection of deans and president, administrative organization at all levels, research, leaves of absence, incompatible employment, professional standards and academic freedom.

Moreover, the general faculty assembly is to consult with appropriate administrative officers "to insure that policy and administrative implementation are consonant."

A briefer enumeration is used at a state university, where the faculty shares responsibility with the president and the academic deans "in such matters as":

educational policy and general welfare;
policy for regulation of student conduct and activities;
scholastic policy, including requirements for admission, graduation and honor;
approval of candidates for degrees;
criteria for faculty tenure, appointment and promotion;
recommendations concerning the University budget;
formulation of procedures to carry out the policies and regulations thus established;
research.

Since the general faculty assembly – except in a small college – tends to be much too large a body for virtually all purposes, the exercise of its powers is frequently delegated to a smaller body, usually a representative senate, with only review possibilities left to the assembly. At one large state university, "all legislative powers" of the faculty are vested in the senate, but the general faculty assembly has the power to reject certain senate actions, and also to rescind the general delegation of legislative powers to the senate. At a private university the general faculty assembly can review any action by the senate and shall also "act as a referendum body on questions referred to it for that purpose by the Senate." At a private college, the general faculty assembly has "the final right of review and referendum" over senate actions. Matters considered by the senate may be reviewed by, overruled by, or otherwise considered by the assembly in one of two ways: through submission to the general faculty assembly by a majority vote of the senate, or through a petition for a meeting of the general faculty assembly signed by at least 15% of its members. A rather complex review system is used at one state university:

Senate actions will be subject to the review and check of the general faculty through the following procedures:
1. at any convocation of the Faculty [general faculty assembly], past actions of the Senate may be brought to the floor for discussion. If a majority of those present reject a previous action of the Senate, the Senate must reconsider its action at its next meeting
2. any action taken by the Senate may be forced back to the Senate for mandatory reconsideration if within two weeks after the circulation of the Senate Minutes covering the action, a petition by at least 75 faculty members stating the objections of the petitioners is received by the President
3. in either of the above two procedures, if the Senate reaffirms its original action, the issue must be submitted to a mail ballot of the University Faculty. The majority decision of such a ballot will be final.

At a state college, a two-thirds vote in the general faculty assembly can modify or nullify decisions of the senate or any senate committee. At a private university, the general faculty assembly "shall receive prompt notice of action of the University Council [senate] which results in important changes in university policy in which the faculty has a reasonable concern." The assembly must make a recommendation upon such action before the changes are put into effect. At a state university, the general faculty assembly, by a two-thirds majority in a mail ballot, may not only rescind any action of the senate but can also cause the "dissolution" of that body itself. Finally, a rather unusual set of provisions at another state university should be noted:

Upon petition to the President signed by 10% of the members of the General Faculty [assembly] ... any vote of the Senate shall be submitted to the General Faculty at a meeting that shall be called for that purpose within five weeks after the time of the Senate vote .... The faculty member who originates the objecting petition shall act as chairman of a committee of the opposition, and shall select at least two other signers of the petition to form a committee of three or more to prepare and lead the presentation of the case for the opposition. Amendments to the Senate act may be adopted at this meeting; no

final vote on the decision of the Senate or the version of this decision as amended by the General Faculty shall be taken at this meeting, but voting on this referendum shall be conducted by a secret mail ballot. A majority of the legal votes cast shall be conclusive, provided that a majority of the General Faculty participates in the referendum.
If a majority of the General Faculty do not cast valid votes, the Senate action shall stand as voted.

Other kinds of institutional relationships of general faculty assemblies should be mentioned. At one private college, "legislative action" by the assembly is subject to the approval of the president. But, should any measure which has been vetoed by the president be passed again by a two-thirds vote, it may be submitted for official decision to the trustees, who shall serve as a final court of appeal. In case of such an appeal, the general faculty assembly shall have the right "to have ... [its] views laid before the Trustees by a representative or representatives of ... [its] own choosing." At a state university, questions of jurisdiction between the powers of the general faculty assembly (and the senate) on the one hand, and the faculties of the various colleges on the other hand, shall be referred to the president – with appeals from the president's rulings to be decided by the general faculty assembly.

2. Membership

The membership of general faculty assemblies is precisely that, general – meaning usually virtually all the faculty, and also the administration. For example, at one private university the general faculty assembly consists of all full professors upon appointment; all associate professors who have completed one year of service, provided they are eligible to hold tenure; and all assistant professors who have completed three years of service under full-time appointment. Furthermore, it includes the president and vice-presidents, the deans, the librarian, and the director of the summer session. At a state university the general faculty assembly consists of all professors, associate professors, assistant professors, and instructors; also, the president, the vice presidents and deans, the directors of schools, the dean and associate dean of students, the Director of Women's Affairs, and "other employees of the University concerned with policy making" if admitted to membership by the assembly upon nomination by the president and the senate. At another state university, instructors who are candidates for an advanced degree from the institution serve on the general faculty assembly, but are ineligible to sit on graduate examining committees, vote on candidates for advanced degrees, or participate in faculty actions regarding requirements for advanced degrees. At one state university, professors emeriti have the right to vote in the general faculty assembly. At another state university, every faculty member is a member of the assembly, but persons serving under acting, visiting, or clinical appointments, and those of emeritus status, are non-voting.

3. Officers

General faculty assemblies usually have three or four officers: a presiding officer or chairman, a vice-chairman, a secretary, and sometimes a parliamentarian. The president of the university appears to be, much more frequently than not, the chairman of the general faculty assembly; the vice-chairman is at times an elected faculty member, while the secretary (whose main duty is to keep the minutes) and parliamentarian usually are elected faculty members. For example, at one state university the president of the university presides in the general faculty assembly; in his absence, the vice-president or the "senior academic dean" present take over. However, the secretary is elected annually from the voting members of the faculty, as is the parliamentarian. At a private college, the president presides, and in his absence the dean; the secretary is elected by the faculty.

On the other hand, the officers of the general faculty assembly at another state university, including a chairman, a chairman-elect, and a secretary, are elected annually by the assembly and may not hold "administrative positions at the level of Dean or above." Similarly, the officers of the general faculty assembly at a community college must all be faculty members.

According to the description of the secretary's duties at one state university, he not only keeps the minutes and the records, but also administers "the Office of Faculty Committees," maintaining a file of committee rosters and providing the executive committee with lists of potential nominees for committee appointments. Similarly, at a private university, the secretary prepares the minutes and records, keeps the list of members of committees, and conducts all correspondence of the body.

As to the election of officers of the general faculty assembly, one state university's procedure embraces five steps:

a. the President shall annually appoint an election committee of three voting members
b. the committee shall mail to each voting member a nomination ballot during the first week of March
c. each voting member may submit a nomination for each elective office
d. from the result of this ballot the committee shall submit by mail a second ballot containing the names of the three nominees for each office receiving the largest number of votes
e. the candidate receiving the highest number of votes on the second ballot shall be declared elected and the committee shall report the results to the faculty and to the President. In case of a tie, the selection shall be determined by lot.

4. Procedures

The more important topics under this heading pertain to the frequency of regular meetings of the general faculty assembly; the provisions for special meetings; rules for quorum and voting; restrictions on voting.

Most general faculty assemblies meet at least once each semester; the minimum at some universities is once per year, while it is twice per semester at some others. On the other hand, at some institutions, the general faculty assembly meets every month during the academic year. The most appropriate number of meetings may depend on two factors: the existence of a representative senate with regular (monthly) meetings, and the size of the total faculty. A body containing some one thousand members should hardly be called together more than once or twice per year if the institution has a senate. If there is no senate, it may have to meet more often.

Provisions for the calling of special meetings of the general faculty assembly appear to be within easy reach in most institutions. Twenty or twenty-five faculty members are required at a number of larger universities; thirty faculty members, representing two or more colleges, at one state university. As to small colleges, any three faculty members can call a special meeting at one college, and 10 at another one. Other requirements include 5 per cent of the faculty, 10 per cent, and as many as 25 per cent. At least 60 faculty members must call for a special meeting at one private university, and as many as 75 at another one. Of course, even a successfully called special meeting may have problems with a quorum requirement.

Another kind of numbers game relates to the quorum requirements. These vary from "the members present shall constitute a quorum" at one state university to a minimum set at two hundred members at another state university. Rather frequently appear the proportions of 25 per cent, 20 per cent, $33\frac{1}{3}$ per cent, and the minimum requirement of fifty members. A majority of faculty members is required at one university, and as many as $66\frac{2}{3}$ per cent at a small institution. Quorum rules may have to be delicately attuned to the "culture" of the general faculty assembly, which sometimes does not foster attendance. The picture is further complicated by the fact that the total absence of any quorum rule would permit a minute minority to take action for the entire faculty, while a stringent quorum rule (e.g., more than 50 per cent) would tend to stifle the faculty by permitting a rather small minority to make action impossible.[9]

Voting procedures seem to be similar in most general faculty assemblies. Voting is usually by voice or show of hands, except that a secret written ballot can be requested by a very small number of members – for example, one at a state college, two at a private college, and ten at another state college. (A written ballot is always required at one institution if the voting is about persons.) Most votes in general faculty assemblies do not require written ballots; otherwise, traditionally overcrowded agendas could never be completed.

Special voting rules govern some actions by general faculty assemblies. For example, at one private university "faculty legislation" – "barring special circumstances" – requires voting in two consecutive meetings. At another private university a special majority (two-thirds, or a majority of the total membership) is needed whenever actions of the senate are reversed. Most elaborate is one large state university: "action of a legis-

---

[9] According to McConnell's and Mortimer's findings, Berkeley's general faculty assembly (called senate) averaged only about one member attending for every 14 or 15 members during 1966–67, and some meetings had to be adjourned for lack of the quorum of 75 members – except in time of crisis. Since attendance was so poor, those who wanted a particular proposal defeated could usually manage to muster a sufficient number of opponents. For example, "a proposal to reject classified research projects ... motivated the engineering faculty to attend the senate meeting practically en masse. The proposal was defeated." (McConnell and Mortimer, *The Faculty in University Governance*, p. 36.)

lative nature" cannot be taken in the general faculty assembly but may only be recommended by resolution in the senate; recommendations to the board or the president require the presence of at least 50 per cent of the membership; resolutions directed to or affecting persons outside the university require approval by the senate.

A private college tries to assure the confidential nature of assembly proceedings – decisions may be communicated only through channels authorized by the president. However, other institutions generally authorize or even encourage publicity relating to proceedings, sometimes by permitting the attendance of a reporter of the student newspaper.

5. Committees

Much of the business of the general faculty assembly takes place in committees. Because of the unwieldy size of the assembly, a committee provides the needed intimate milieu where real work can be accomplished, which then may be found acceptable by the parent body. A committee can also be an excellent meeting ground for administration and faculty, and students, where the components can forget their public "class" images and reach consensus in the interest of the academic community. (Senates also use committees extensively, as will be seen later, in spite of the more manageable size of the parent bodies.)

The number of committees, and their particular jurisdictions, vary greatly among institutions. Often, accidents of historical growth rather than logic are responsible for specific committee systems. Also, not all committees contribute equally; some are traditionally powerful on a campus, while others hardly meet or perform meaningless routines. The influence of individual committees, for that matter, can change from year to year, depending on the kind of members who are appointed or elected.

The following list of standing committees at a state university is provided as an example – and variety is infinite – of the committees at one institution.

Academic Privilege Committee
Promotions Committee
Student Affairs Committee
Faculty Research Committee

Budget Committee
Instructional Policies Committee
Graduate Council
Teacher Education Committee
Undergraduate Curriculum Committee
Instructional Materials Committee
Sabbatical Leave Committee.

At a much smaller private college, there are sixteen standing committees. Ordinarily, a faculty member is not to serve on more than one of these; while participation in the committee work of the college is encouraged, "it is not obligatory." The president and the dean are members of all the committees. Two of the sixteen standing committees have their faculty members elected by the faculty, the Committee on Professional Standards and the Judicial Committee. The other committees' faculty members are appointed by the president in consultation with the dean. (The more desirable practice of appointment by a faculty-elected committee on committees or direct election is not followed.) The Committee on Professional Standards at this college serves in an advisory capacity to the president and the dean. It is concerned with faculty appointments, promotions, dismissals, tenure, sabbatical leaves, and all matters relating to professional standards and ethics. The committee has five members who must be tenured faculty members; some of these are elected from particular academic areas, and others are elected at large. Nominations are made by a nominating committee consisting of three faculty members of the college's senate – selected by the dean – and the dean. The nominating committee's slate must consist of at least two candidates for each slot, and additional nominations may be made from the floor. The dean serves as chairman of the Committee on Professional Standards. The other elected committee, the Judicial Committee, serves as the body to examine the grounds for dismissal and charges of misconduct concerning an individual faculty member and reports its findings to the president. Three tenured faculty members and two alternates are elected to this committee by the faculty, on nominations made by the Committee on Professional Standards, with nominations from the floor permitted. The committee elects its own chairman. As was mentioned above, the members of the other standing committees at the college are appointed by the president. These committees include a Committee on Academic Advising; a Committee on Academic Standing; a Committee on Admissions, Scholarships and Student Aid; a Committee on Athletics; a College Scholar Committee; a Curriculum Committee (which approves new courses); a Committee on the Continuing Revision of the Curriculum (which is concerned with the oversight of the total curriculum and with the relevance of the curriculum to the students and the needs of society); a Committee on Evening and Summer Studies; a Committee on Honorary Degrees; a Library Committee; a Committee on Research; a Committee on Special Studies, Honors, and Comprehensive Examinations; a Committee on Uses of the Computer Facilities; a Committee on Student Affairs; a Committee on Student Conduct. A number of these committees have one or more student members, "selected in a manner approved by the Dean of Students."

The committee system at one large state university makes a distinction between the so-called Faculty Councils and the Faculty Committees. A Faculty Council is a standing committee of the general faculty assembly; a Faculty Committee is a special or ad hoc committee of the general faculty assembly, or of the senate, or of a Faculty Council. There are six Faculty Councils, consisting of faculty members (nominated by the Executive Committee of the senate and elected by the senate) and ex-officio administration members – the Faculty Councils on Academic Standards, on Community Services, on Faculty Affairs, on Grants and Contract Research, on Student Affairs, and on University Facilities and Services. The Faculty Councils act as principal advisory bodies also to the senate, and are to concern themselves with broad problems of policy relating to aspects of university government. The basic qualifications of the members of Faculty Councils are to include "a broad familiarity with the problems of University government, an understanding of the particular problems of the faculty within the framework of the University, and a familiarity with the substance of the particular areas of Council responsibility." The Faculty Council on Faculty Affairs is responsible for all matters of policy relating to the interests of the faculty, i.e., appointment, tenure, promotion, professional leave, compensation (including salary), academic freedom, standards of academic performance, and professional ethics. The Faculty Council on Student Affairs is responsible for all matters of policy relating to non-academic student affairs, i.e., financial aid, housing, regulation of social affairs, eligibility rules, inter-collegiate athletics, and general student welfare. The Faculty Council on University Facilities and Services has responsibility for building needs, space utilization, supplies and equipment, administrative services, parking and traffic problems.

Another kind of distinction among committees is made at another large state university. Business which is chiefly administrative in character is to be performed by committees appointed by the president; business which is chiefly policy-determining in character is the responsibility of committees to be elected by the faculty. The standing committees at this university, which does not have a senate, are empowered to act for the general faculty assembly, but their decisions may be reviewed by that body. Also, any action taken by a committee – or, for that matter, by the general faculty assembly – can be reviewed by the Board of Regents if a majority of the deans of the several faculties or at least three of the Regents so desire.

An important body at one state university is the Organization Committee, a kind of committee infrequently provided for. The committee's tasks, related to the organization of the general faculty assembly and other bodies of the university, can be grouped as follows:

(1) it administers the elections for the university's senate and for the committees
(2) it ascertains in advance of each election the number of faculty members in each university division for purposes of representation in the senate
(3) it determines rotational procedures for filling committee positions and methods for filling temporary vacancies in the senate and committees
(4) it recommends "continuously ... adjustments, improvement, and refinements in the faculty organizational structure"
(5) within three years after the establishment of the reorganized general faculty assembly, it brings to that body "a report on the quality and effectiveness of the operation" of the body.

The Steering Committee of the general faculty assembly at one private university has three main functions: to arrange the agenda, to represent the general faculty assembly in the senate, and to act as a nominating committee for the other committees. In its agenda role, it has the interesting power "to reject the inclusion of any item on the agenda of the ... [general faculty assembly] which it deems, upon careful consideration, within the particular jurisdiction of any one college or school." Whether this is a satisfactory device to solve the delicate questions of university-wide versus college jurisdiction may be debatable, but it is desirable to have a committee which can rule, at least in first instance, on claims of "states' rights" on the part of divisions of the university – and, for that matter, academic departments. The Steering Committee consists of seven faculty members; five are elected by five divisions of the university, and two at large by the general faculty assembly. The committee selects its own chairman, who shall also preside at meetings of the general faculty assembly in the absence of the president and the academic vice-president.

An increasingly important committee in a time of financial stress, and one being increasingly utilized, is the Budget Committee. One large private university, for example, has a Budget Committee of the general faculty assembly which consists of five administrative officers – the Comptroller, the Business Manager, the Financial Vice-President, the Provost, the Vice-President for Medical Affairs – and two faculty members. The latter are the chairman and the past chairman of the Committee on Financial Policies and Practices. The Budget Committee has the annual duty of formulating the final budget for submission to the president and transmission to the board of trustees. A budget function is also fulfilled by the Committee on Administration of Faculty Personnel at a state college. This faculty committee determines the faculty's salary structure and salary schedules; although only advisory to the president, the committee's recommendations have apparently been followed by the president for some years. At a private college, the Faculty Advisory Committee of the general faculty assembly receives from the president the college's budget for review prior to its transmission to the board of trustees. (This same committee, incidentally, may be used by the president for advice on the performance of administrative officers "in their role as Faculty members.")

Another noteworthy type of committee jurisdiction concerns faculty advice on administrative appointments. In many institutions this is handled by ad hoc committees, selected or preferably elected for particular deanly or presidential vacancies. At one state college, there is a standing Committee on Appointments and Promotions, consisting of elected faculty members, two for each division of the college, who may not be departmental or divisional chairmen. Among the committee's duties is advice to the president on all administrative appointments above the rank of departmental or divisional chairman. The committee shares this role with two other advisory authorities – the departmental and divisional chairmen, and the dean.

Finally, an interesting – if time-consuming – set of extra checks is imposed on the standing committees of the general faculty assembly at one large state university. First of all,

each committee above the departmental level shall survey its functions and composition at the close of each year, and make such recommendations as are necessary to the appropriate authorities concerning:

1. whether its functions could be advantageously transferred in toto to administrative officers
2. whether an ad hoc organization could handle its function with a significant saving in faculty time
3. any of its functions that could as effectively be performed by administrative officers
4. any of its functions that could properly be turned over to a student organization
5. desirable changes in its size, method of selection or composition, with special reference to the inclusion of faculty members of lower rank, administrative personnel, and student representatives.

In the second place,

each standing committee of the University shall examine its functions and present membership and advise
1. whether student representation is permissible and would be desirable
2. if desirable, the number of students to be recommended for membership and the manner of their selection and
3. whether it is feasible to turn over certain functions entirely to student governing boards.

C. The Senate

I. Functions

The descriptions in constitutions of the functions of senates – the agencies which are the representative structures of university-wide government, as contrasted with the participatory town meeting of the general faculty assembly – are as varied as those of the general faculty assemblies, noted above. An extremely brief clause is used at one state university:

The legislative body of the University Faculty is the University Senate. Under the leadership of the President and subject always to the approval of the Board of Trustees, the Senate has legislative jurisdiction in all matters of student government and educational policy.

Or, at a large state university:

The Senate shall have the general legislative authority over educational matters concerning the University as a whole, but not over the internal affairs of a single institute, college, or school of collegiate rank, except where these materially affect the interests of the University as a whole or the interests of other institutes, colleges, or schools. The Senate shall have the power to enact for the government of the students in those relations with the University which affect the University as a whole.

At both of these institutions educational policy as well as student government are specified; as is frequent in larger universities, the latter institution has a "states' rights" clause for the protection of college jurisdictions.

The purpose of the senate at a private university is described in more elaborate terms:

It is to promote and encourage a more intelligent understanding of the problems that are common to the colleges of the University; to bring into closer relationship all the various schools and colleges of the University in order to unify their work and increase their efficiency; to afford each member an opportunity to become acquainted with the problems, plans and programs of the other individual colleges; to foster a spirit of mutual esteem and cooperation among the individual members of the Council; and to function in an advisory capacity, when requested by either the President or Board of Trustees, on matters relating to academic policies and personnel.

At a state college, the senate "is committed to freedom through the democratic process of sharing responsible ideas and actions through due process of governmental law"; the senate means "consensus in action" to make the institution "a competent, progressive, and vital force toward the achievement of higher education in the lives of its students, faculty, administration and alumni." The same point is made, more briefly, at a private college, where the senate is called the legislative body of a community government that provides for legislation and administration of community affairs "on the basis of joint responsibility of faculty, students and administration."

A typical method for describing senate functions is the listing of specific subjects of senate jurisdiction. For example, at one state university the senate is to make recommendations for the promotion of the objectives of the university with respect to: "curricula, credits, admissions, and registration; student counseling, student discipline relating to scholarship and attendance; extra-curricular activities, general student conduct, libraries, examinations and grades; awards and honors; graduation and the granting of degrees, certificates and diplomas; graduate work ... and other legislative matters not enumerated herein concerning the education, research and service programs of the University." At a junior college, the senate is empowered, "but not limited," to making recommendations concerning:

1. matters of general educational policy such as academic requirements, admissions, and certification of students' completion of graduation requirements
2. matters of general faculty interest, such as professional advancement and academic freedom
3. student affairs
4. certain administrative procedures of general college interest, such as expansion of physical plant and the budgetary process.

At a state college, the senate "shall be empowered to act on and establish policy relating to matters dealing with faculty affairs, student affairs, undergraduate academic affairs, graduate academic affairs, budget, and any other matter of general faculty concern." Moreover, the senate may "discuss and express its views" on any matter deemed to be of general college interest.

More elaboration is used at a large state university. Its senate, as "legislative agency" of the faculty, "is charged with the responsibility of formulating rules for the immediate government of the University ...." Specifically, the senate may enact legislation pertaining to (1) the powers and duties of the faculty; (2) the powers and duties delegated to the faculty by the president; (3) resolutions forwarded to it by the general faculty assembly. In the case of matters in the sphere of the colleges and schools, the legislative powers of the senate are limited to policies which affect the general welfare of the university, or which may be referred to it by the president. The following principles govern the senate's exercise of its powers and duties:

A. The primary concern of the Senate is the general welfare of the University.

B. In those instances in which a conflict of opinion develops as to whether proposed action will promote the general welfare of the University, as well as in its more routine general deliberations, the Senate shall consider the views of spokesmen for all positions, including the views of minorities, of the administration, and of colleges, schools or departments whose interests may be affected by any proposed measure. C. The Senate can accomplish its purpose as the legislative arm of the University Faculty only if each Senator keeps constantly in mind his responsibilities as a Senator to the University, to the University Faculty, and to the group which he represents. In brief, he should endeavor to be a statesman.

At another state university, the senate "shall serve as the agency for the formation of educational policy" for the university; moreover, "it shall serve as a forum for the determination of the official opinion of the professional personnel of the University." The senate is empowered by the board of trustees "to make decisions on the following matters of educational policy subject to review and acceptance or rejection of the Board":

1. standards for admission, selection, and retention applicable to all students of the university
2. requirements for granting of degrees applicable to all students of the University
3. curricular requirements
4. instructional standards throughout the University
5. promotion and facilitation of academic and instructional research
6. procedures for faculty participation in the selection and retention of heads or chairmen of Departments and Divisions, and Deans of Colleges
7. standards for public information programs dealing with educational matters
8. standards of academic freedom throughout the University
9. standards for student affairs
10. other educational matters pertaining to the University.

Moreover, on the following matters "of institutional policy" the senate is empowered to advise the board of trustees:

1. appointment, promotion, tenure and dismissal of faculty members
2. selection and removal of the President and principal academic officers having University-wide responsibilities as well as the creation or abolition of such offices
3. expenditures of funds allocated to instruction and academic or instructionally-related research
4. major issues affecting current or projected budget decisions
5. programs of faculty welfare such as salaries, insurance, and special leave.

The senate of a large private university

shall be a policy-making body which may consider all matters of University-wide concern, all matters affecting more than one faculty or school, and all matters pertaining to the implementation and execution of agreements with the other educational institutions that are now or may hereafter become affiliated with the University. Without limitation by enumeration the Senate shall:

(a) develop and review plans and policies to strengthen the educational system of the University

(b) work on the long-range master plan for the physical development of the University; recommend ways in which it can be improved; and keep the same under continuing review

(c) work for the advancement of academic freedom and the protection of Faculty interests

(d) work for the promotion of student welfare and the enhancement of student life

(e) initiate and review policies to govern the University's relations with outside agencies for research instruction and related purposes

(f) foster policies for cooperative and mutually beneficial relations with the neighboring community

(g) review by broad categories the annual budget of the University after its adoption and advise the Trustees as to its general conformity with the goals of the University

(h) consider and recommend policies relating to the awarding of University prizes and honors, and assist the Trustees in the selection of recipients of such prizes and honors

(i) promulgate a code of conduct for Faculty, students and staff and provide for its enforcement.

Among other specific duties of this senate are the rendering of opinions "as to any exercise of power proposed" by a college or school; proposals "to increase the efficiency of University work"; consideration of any question that may arise "as to the conduct or efficiency of any officer of administration or instruction"; the correlation of courses offered by the several colleges and schools; the determination of the conditions upon which degrees shall be conferred and the recommendation of candidates for these degrees, all this "by concurrent action" with the other colleges and schools.

A major problem for all senates is the relationship with other decision-making bodies of the university. Conflicts may arise not only in the "states' rights" sphere of the jurisdiction of the colleges, schools, or departments, but particularly also in the hierarchical claims of supremacy of the president and the board of trustees. At times, university constitutions attempt to provide for such situations of conflict. For example, at one private university the senate is "the supreme academic body of the University, having all legislative powers except concerning those matters reserved to the Board of Trustees, the Office of the President; or the other Ruling Bodies." If there are jurisdictional conflicts between the senate and other "ruling bodies," the issue is to be decided by the president – the general principle being that the senate has jurisdiction where a matter affects more than one college or similar body or "substantially affects" the general interest of the university. If a jurisdictional conflict arises between the senate and the president, it is to be decided by the board of trustees. If any "ruling body" takes actions within the jurisdiction of the senate, these must be referred to the senate and shall not be effective until the senate has approved. The president may not act in the jurisdictional sphere of the senate without the senate's approval, but he may, as was indicated, appeal the senate's actions to the board of trustees. The president may also send back to the senate for reconsideration any senate action of which he disapproves; if the senate then persists in its action, it shall go to the board of trustees for a final decision. (In cases of final appeal to the board, the senate may request a meeting with the appropriate committee of the board.)

The senate of another private university requires the board of trustees' concurrence for those of its acts involving a change in budgetary appropriations, the acquisition or disposition of real property, affecting contractual obligations of the University, "or as required by law." "In all other matters, the action of the University Senate will be final unless the President shall advise the Senate not later than its next regularly scheduled meeting that Trustee concurrence is necessary." Whenever the board of trustees does not concur in an act of the senate, it shall return the measure to the senate with an explanation of the reason for its non-concurrence. The president has the additional power to convene a special meeting of the senate "within 15 class days of any University Senate action, and may request it to reconsider such action."

At one private university, "in case of failure of the President to concur in any decisions of the Senate," the issue is referred to the board of trustees "with provision for representation of the Senate" before that body for the conflict issue. At one state university, a presidential veto of a senate action may be "overriden" by a three-fourths majority of the general faculty assembly. In all cases of recommendations vetoed by the president, *or* in the case of any recommendation which receives a three-fourths majority in the general faculty assembly, "a statement of the proceedings and recommendations shall be forwarded to each member of the Board of Trustees and the President" – presumably for final decision by the board. Similarly, at another state university, the president may veto any action of the senate, and "by a two-thirds vote, the Senate may appeal to the Board of Control any action so vetoed." The same rule applies at a junior college, except that a three-fourth vote in the senate is needed for the appeal to the board.

Another kind of conflict, involving the senate and the faculty at large, is anticipated at one state university. Any action taken by the senate may be returned to the senate for mandatory reconsideration if a petition by at least 75 faculty members so requests. Also, at any meeting of the general faculty assembly a majority of those present can reject an action of the senate, which forces the senate to reconsider its action. If in either of the above two procedures the senate then reaffirms its original action, the issue must be submitted to a mail ballot of the university faculty which shall decide whether the action of the senate is accepted or finally rejected. At another state university, if a legislative proposal does not receive a two-thirds majority in the senate, it may be submitted to the entire faculty, for a vote by mail ballot. At a large state university, in the event of a dispute between the senate and a college or school as to whether a proposed senate action would improperly affect a college's or school's jurisdiction, the president shall schedule a hearing on the matter before the senate's executive committee and "the Board of Deans" at which senate and college or school spokesmen are heard. Then, "and after consultation with and upon the advice of the Senate Executive Committee and the Board of Deans," the president shall decide on the issue.

An entirely different kind of senate function was proposed for the senate of the State University of New York (SUNY) system in 1968 – to revise its constitution in such a fashion that the senate could serve as the collective bargaining agency for the faculty of the entire university, under New York's Taylor Law. This did not come about in SUNY, but at Nassau Community College (New York) the faculty senate has been certified as the collective bargaining agent after a hearing at which the local of the American Federation of Teachers had challenged its eligibility. Also the faculty senate at Macomb County Community College (Michigan) has acquired status as the negotiating agent for that faculty.

2. Membership

Senates, ordinarily, consist of faculty representatives, elected from their respective university divisions by some principle of proportionality, and of administration representatives with (or, sometimes without) vote. The size of most senates is between 35 and 90 members. The faculty-administration ratio may be anywhere between 2:1 and 10:1. Lately, student representatives are becoming more frequent on senates, usually in rather modest numbers. Of course, "pure" (all-faculty) senates still exist in numerous institutions, as will be seen in some of the examples cited below. Most faculty representatives on senates serve three year terms, with reelection for one consecutive term possible.

For example, at a state university the senate is composed of 87 members, including the president and eight administration representatives designated by the president. (At least three of the latter must be involved "in the activities concerned with the administration and welfare of the student body.") The faculty members are apportioned "among the basic school faculty units of the University, according to the number of faculty members attached to that school . . .," with no school, however, having fewer than three elected senators. All members of the faculty "with professorial rank" are eligible for election to the senate.

In another state university's senate, the president is the only administration representative with vote, but he may appoint other administration officers to the senate with the right to speak but without vote. Of the faculty representatives, the chairmen of certain committees are ex-officio members of the senate with vote; the other faculty representatives are elected in conformity with the following principles: (1) they shall be democratically selected "with care that small or minority groups are assured a voice in University affairs," and (2) they shall be elected by groups composed of faculty members "who are most likely to know them personally and are therefore best able to evaluate their qualities." Ordinarily, there is to be one senator for each 15 voting members of the faculty, and at least one senator from each independently organized college or school, except the graduate school. For purposes of electing senators, the colleges, schools, and departments of this university are combined into groups of related departments – in accordance with the second principle above – which serve as faculty constituencies, such as the humanities, the social sciences, the medical sciences, etc. Some of the groups, however, are not so "related"; for example, one includes Dentistry, Home Economics, Nursing, Pharmacy, Physical Education-Men, Physical Education-Women, and Social Work.

The senate of a large private university consists of 115 members, including 22 administration representatives designated by the president, 30 students (14 undergraduate and 16 graduate or professional), and three categories of faculty representatives – 39 faculty members elected for three year terms from constituencies composed of one or more allied academic disciplines; 18 faculty members elected by the general faculty assembly; 6 faculty members selected by the Steering Committee of the senate "from the assistant professors during the first six years of their membership in the faculty." The senate of another state university consists of 15 ex-officio members designated annually by the president, and 45 faculty members elected on a proportional basis from the various colleges. In addition, the president of the Faculty Association serves on this senate, either ex-officio or under one of the two categories just mentioned. At a small private college, the senate consists of 20 members: 15 members elected by the faculty; 3 student representatives elected by the student body; the president and the Dean of the College. Of the 15 faculty members, 6 are elected at large, and the remainder from the three academic divisions of the college, all for three year terms. At another private university, the senate contains approximately 24 faculty representatives elected proportionally from constituency groups of departments or related departments; 6 faculty members elected at large from the entire faculty; 15 students elected from college or related departmental constituency groups; and 10 administration officers who are ex-officio, but non-voting. (The faculty members have three year terms, and the student one year terms; both are eligible for re-election.)

Features characteristic of the current trend in university senates appear in the membership distribution of the new senate of Columbia University. As was mentioned earlier, the total membership is 101 persons, all voting, consisting of 63 faculty members (including 15 non-tenured faculty members and 6 from institutions affiliated with Columbia University), 21 students, 9 administration members, 2 library staff members, 2 research members, 2 administrative staff members, and 2 alumni members. The 9 administration members include the president, the vice-president, 2 academic deans, and 5 members "who shall be appointed by the President from among officers of administration who are part of the central administration and administrators of Faculties." The 21 student members are elected proportionally from the various divisions of the university – either by direct election, or by indirect election through the elected student governing body of a particular university division. A significant innovation at Columbia is the previously mentioned 40% minimum voting requirement: to be validly elected to the senate, "a minimum of 40% of the eligible voters in the electing category must have voted by direct election"; or, "if the indirect option has been chosen [for student senators], then the 40% minimum voting requirement shall apply to the election of the [respective] student governing body ...." If the 40% voting requirement is not satisfied, after one additional attempt in a specially scheduled election, "a vacancy shall exist until the next regularly scheduled election." [10] Every elected senate member at Columbia is subject to a recall election, "upon petition signed by one-fourth of the number of members of the category from which the member was elected." A majority of votes cast for recall shall cause the recall of the member, but the 40% minimum voting requirement applies also to recall elections.

The commentary to the Columbia senate explained these membership provisions. As to the size of the body, it was limited to about one hundred "because experiences with comparable bodies strongly suggests that a larger body cannot function effectively without elaborate rules of procedure." A small body, such as the proposed senate, "will allow for free debate and active participation by all of its members, thereby facilitating close and productive working relationships." The relative numerical predominance of the tenured faculty (42 out of 101 seats) is appropriate "because it is the component of

[10] During the first elections for the Columbia senate, in May 1969, each constituency succeeded in reaching the 40% minimum voting requirement.

the University having both the most enduring connection with its affairs and the largest responsibility for those activities within the University that differentiate it from other institutions." On the other hand, the 15 seats in the senate to be held by representatives elected from among non-tenured teachers will assure that their interests are adequately represented. "Teachers of non-tenured rank, while having a less permanent connection with the University than tenured faculty, should nonetheless have a voice in determining academic and other University policies because they carry so large a portion of the teaching obligations of the institution." The presence of administration members is justified in some detail.

The inclusion in the University Senate of a small but influential delegation of administrators is necessary for a number of reasons. The administration is much more than a mere service organization to carry out policies made by others. To recruit and retain effective and capable officers, they must be given an opportunity to participate in the making of policies they will carry out. The President and his immediate cabinet are high executive officers, whose views on University policies and whose valuable experience need to be made available to the University Senate, and who ought to share in its deliberations and decisions. Moreover, the President of the University and the other members of the Senate who represent the administration will frequently have to serve as the main source of information for the Senate and as the Senate's major link with the day-to-day activities of the University. Effective cooperation between the administration and the Senate can best be accomplished by closely relating their activities.

The commentary, finally, points to the usually neglected role of the library, research, and middle-level administrative staffs, who are given representation in the new senate. Concerning the latter category particularly, it is stated:

Consideration of the situation of middle-level administrative staff in the University leads to the conclusion that they too fulfill a function so essential to the workings of the University as to argue strongly for their participation in the University Senate. The University depends on middle-level staff for much of its smooth operation both in the details of academic administration and in fiscal and personnel management. In a very real sense the staff is the only group in a position to observe the direct effect of many of the University's policies on the day-to-day workings of the institution. Professional staff, observing the impact of these policies, will have insights to share that may well lead to an improvement of the University's functioning.

As was mentioned earlier, an unusual membership distribution was proposed (and rejected) for the senate of one state university. Its 100 members were to include 40 faculty members, 10 non-teaching professional staff, and 50 students (35 undergraduate, 15 graduate). The undergraduate students were to be elected partly from "residential quadrangles" on the campus, partly by the votes of non-residents of the campus, partly at large; the graduate students were to be partly elected from academic divisions, partly at large. Administration members were not guaranteed any senate seats as such, but could be elected in their faculty capacities; also, administrative officers were promised floor privileges. In the commentary to this proposed constitution, its authors – a mixed faculty-student commission – argued that the distribution of senate seats among the various components "embodies a judgment of the relative weight of each group in, and the approximate distance of each from the central concerns of the University." There was to be a "balance of representation capable of assuring security to each constituency," and no constituency would have to fear "for its ultimate existence." The faculty (and the non-teaching professional staff) voted down this proposed senate in April 1969.

The recently adopted constitution at a state university has both a "pure" and a "mixed" senate: the University Council contains twelve voting administration members, twelve elected faculty members, and two students; the Faculty Senate consists exclusively of elected faculty members. The University Council advises the president of the university "on matters of university governance"; it is to review and make recommendations on matters proposed by the Faculty Senate and other bodies, and to refer appropriate matters to the Faculty Senate and other bodies. The Faculty Senate's purpose is "to create an effective faculty organization which can enter into a partnership for shared responsibility and cooperative action between the Faculty, Administration and Students ..."; in this capacity the Faculty Senate participates in the formulation of academic and educational policies which concern the entire university. A University Council-Faculty Senate Interface Committee is to provide additional liaison between the "mixed" and the "pure" senate.

In the remainder of this section, mostly conventional conditions of senate membership will be described in capsule form. The "pure" senate of state university A has 36 representatives, all faculty members elected proportionally for three year terms

from the colleges and divisions of the institution. The senate of
private university B has 45 elected faculty members (three
year terms); the president, the provost, and the deans are ex-
officio members without vote – except that the president can
vote to break a tie. The senate of state university C contains
approximately 12 administration members and 50 faculty
members elected proportionally from departments and colleges. At state university D the president, vice-president, and
deans are ex-officio members of the senate without vote, in
addition to 50 faculty members elected proportionally from
each college (three year terms); the chairmen of senate committees are also voting members. State university E has a huge
senate, containing all the full professors, 50 tenured associate
and assistant professors elected proportionally, and administration members from the Administrative Council.[11] Private
university F's senate has 38 faculty members elected proportionally from the colleges for three year terms, plus 5 or more
administration members without vote. Private university G's
senate contains approximately 30 faculty members elected
proportionally for three year terms from the various divisions
of the university; also 14 members of the administration and
4 students (2 undergraduates, 2 graduate or professional students) – all with voting privileges. At state university H the
("pure") senate has 35 faculty members elected proportionally
from the colleges for three year terms, but no administration
representatives. The near-"pure" senate of private university I
is composed of 51 elected faculty members and the president
and provost; the president or provost only votes to break a tie.
In the senate of state college J there are 23 voting members; 14
faculty members elected proportionally from divisions of the
college, 6 faculty members elected at large, and 3 members
appointed by the administration. The "pure" senate of state
college K has 30 faculty members, including at least 10 full
professors. The senate of state university L has 6 voting administration members (the president and 5 persons appointed
by him) and approximately 56 faculty members elected proportionally from the departments for three year terms. At
state university M there are 75 elected faculty members in the

---

[11] Since this university had 321 full professors during 1968–1969, its senate had
close to 400 members. This body could also have been classified as a general
faculty assembly, although it is representative as far as the associate and assistant
professors are concerned.

senate; also, without vote, 12 or more administration members including two staff members from the library and student welfare. At state university N the senate contains 43 proportionally elected faculty members and the president. The "pure" senate of private university O has no administration members; there are 25 faculty members, 12 elected at large and 13 elected proportionally from the colleges. At private university P there are 25 elected faculty members in the senate and 12 administration members; of the latter, only the president can vote (to break a tie). The senate of state college Q has 75 voting members: the president, the dean, the dean of students, 10 members of the "administrative faculty" elected by that group, 16 faculty members elected at large (including 8 with more than five years service, and 8 with two to five years service at the college), and 46 faculty members elected proportionally from the divisions of the college. The senate of state university R includes 50 faculty, 25 administration, and 18 student members, while the senate at state university S includes the chancellor, 39 faculty and 11 students.

At state university T the voting senate membership includes the president and the deans, the business manager, the chairmen of departments, and one elected faculty representative for each 10 full-time faculty members. The senate of state university U contains the president, the Provost's Council, and four times as many elected faculty members as there are persons on the Provost's Council. All full professors and chairmen of departments sit on the "senate" of state university V, with the president, the deans and directors, and other administrative officers. At state university X all the full professors are in the senate, together with other elected faculty members, one representative for every 20 full-time faculty members; there is one elected representative for every 20 professional staff members from the following administrative units: business affairs, public affairs, student affairs, and such services as curriculum advising; finally, the president, the vice presidents, and the academic deans are also senate members.[12] The senate of church-related university Y is organized so that the number of

[12] During 1968–1969 there were 1035 full professors at university V, all of them members of the senate. Obviously, this body is not really a senate in the sense that the term is used in the present study; yet, it is not a general faculty assembly because the associate and assistant professors are not members. Also university X has a large senate, since during 1968–1969 there were more than one hundred full professors on its faculty.

elected faculty members is equal to the number of administration members in the senate. Finally, a system-senate, that
of an eastern state, has faculty representatives from each unit
of the system, proportional to the number of faculty members
of each unit; the chancellor of the system is also a member,
together with two system-wide administrative officials.

3. Officers

There are usually three principal officers in a senate – the
chairman, the vice-chairman, and the secretary. These officers
are frequently assisted by a parliamentarian and some kind of
assistant secretary. The secretary's duties merit some elaboration. For example, the secretary of the senate at one private
university, who has to be a faculty member elected by the
senate from among its members, "shall prepare minutes of
Senate proceedings and debates, to be distributed throughout
the University community; he shall be assisted by a clerical
staff and appropriate equipment." Moreover, this secretary
presides over the so-called Secretary's Council composed of
himself and four senators elected by the senate (including one
administration representative, and three faculty representatives from three different divisions of the university). The
Secretary's Council

(1) shall prepare the agenda of the Senate in consultation with the
Chairman; (2) shall plan the apportionment, staggering and elections
for the elective senate seats; (3) shall propose for approval by the senate
appropriate methods for determining who qualifies as a full-time faculty
member for the purpose of election . . ., and for that purpose only; and
(4) shall propose for approval by the Senate appropriate methods for
the nomination and election of the student Senators.

One state university has, in fact, two senate secretaries, the
secretary and the undersecretary. Similarly, at a community
college there is a secretary (elected by the senate) and a re-
cording secretary to assist the secretary in keeping and distrib-
uting the minutes (appointed by the chairman of the senate).
At another state university, the secretarial function has been
divided among three persons: a corresponding secretary, a re-
cording secretary, and a treasurer – all elected by the senate.

Unusual senate officers include a sergeant at arms at one
state university; its president is to select a member of the
voting faculty who is not a member of the senate to act as

sergeant at arms for the senate. This officer maintains a record of attendance at all senate meetings, and reports attendance to the Agenda Committee after each meeting. He is also charged with separating faculty visitors from voting members of the senate, and controlling the presence of persons not authorized to attend senate meetings. At a large state university the senate designates one faculty member to represent it in all matters of legislation affecting the university, to attend sessions of the state legislature, and to appear before legislative committees in behalf of the faculty. This legislative representative is an ex-officio member of several crucial bodies and committees of the university. The senate of one private university has the offices of chairman-elect and secretary-elect, who serve, respectively, as vice-chairman and vice-secretary and succeed automatically to the offices of chairman and secretary.

Senate officers are appointed, elected, or obtain their office because of another position held. The latter is particularly true in the case of many chairmen of senates. More than half of all chairmanships, most likely, are held ex-officio by the president of the university. Examples include colleges and universities of all types. On the other hand, the chairman of the senate may also be elected by that body; again, examples for this practice include many types of institutions. A provision at one junior college specifies, rather paradoxically, that as president of the college, the chairman of the senate has the veto power over senate action; but, as chairman of the senate, the president has no vote in the senate except to break a tie. In a state college where the president does not preside in the senate, it is the Vice President for Academic Affairs who "shall be the administrator immediately responsible for the Senate and any matter from this body should be referred to the President via this channel."

Secretaries of senates, unlike chairmen, are probably most frequently elected by the senate from its own members. Sometimes, the secretary of the senate is appointed by the president, while at some other institutions the registrar, ex-officio, acts as the secretary. At one state university the president appoints the secretary (called "clerk") with consent of the senate, but he need not be a member of the senate. Vice-chairmen of senates are frequently elected by the senate; in other institutions, a vice-president, provost, or senior dean may act,

ex officio, as vice-chairman. At one state university there is a
"Co-Chairman" who is elected by the senate, but the vice-
president can also act for the president in presiding. Parlia-
mentarians, apparently, are usually elected by the senate itself, but relatively few constitutions elaborate on this position.

The new constitution of Columbia University makes virtually no mention of senate officers. Under the heading of "Meetings," it is provided that the president of the university shall
preside in the senate or, in his absence, the chairman of the
most important senate committee, the Executive Committee.
In the drafting committee's opinion, the president of the university is the appropriate presiding officer of the senate "in
recognition of his high office as the chief executive of the University" and also because this "accords with prevailing practice
at other universities." The very last provision of the Columbia
senate's constitution furnishes financial assistance to the
senate from the university's budget for staff and other official
expenditures. In this connection, a clause in the constitution
of one state university grants faculty members serving as
chairman and vice-chairman of the senate reductions of at
least one-half and one-third, respectively, "of their normal
duties."

4. Procedures

Senate procedures are discussed here under the following
headings: frequency of regular meetings; special meetings;
quorum rules; voting rules; outsiders' attendance at meetings;
distribution of minutes; agenda provisions; election rules.

It is quite safe to say that in the great majority of senates
regular meetings are scheduled once a month during the academic year. More frequent regular meetings were noted at a
junior college ("at 3:30 P. M., on the 2nd and 4th Thursday of
each month") and at a state university (also twice per month).
At least six regular meetings are scheduled at another state
university, of which one – somewhat surprisingly – must be
during the summer. An unusual kind of regularly scheduled
meeting is foreseen at one private university – in addition to its
ordinary meetings, "the Senate shall meet at least once each
semester in joint session with all of the deans and chairmen of
departments" in order to assure "that the Senate is fully
informed of all matters of current concern to the various

schools, faculties, and departments of the University."

Special meetings of the senate can almost always be called by the chairman of the senate or by some minimum number of either the senate membership or the entire faculty membership. Great variety exists in these minimums: 3 members of the senate; 5 members of the senate; 7 members of the senate; 8 members of the senate; 10 members of the senate; 20 members of the senate; 50 members of the senate; $\frac{1}{4}$ of the senate; the majority of the members of the senate; 25 members or 20% of the members of the senate, whichever is smallest; 10 members of the senate or any 20 faculty members; $\frac{1}{4}$ of the senate or 25 faculty members; $\frac{1}{3}$ of the senate or 10% of the total faculty; 10% of the total faculty.

Quorum rules show somewhat greater uniformity, as most senates seem to set the quorum at the majority of the members. Yet, many quorum requirements are quite different: 19 members at one state college (however, a majority of at least 15 affirmative votes is needed there for any official senate action); 20 members; 60 members; $\frac{1}{3}$ of the members, or 50 members, whichever is smallest; $\frac{1}{2}$ of the members; $\frac{2}{3}$ of the members; even $\frac{3}{4}$ of the members at one state college and a community college. Although most senates are not likely to have problems in producing quorums, unlike many general faculty assemblies, it is interesting to note that at one large state university elected senators are penalized for too many unexcused absences: "an elected senator shall be deemed to have vacated his seat when he has been absent from three Senate meetings in an academic year" – unless he has informed the secretary prior to the meeting of his inability to attend.

The basic voting rules seem fairly uniform. Typically, as at one private university, "voting shall ordinarily be by voice, with the presiding officer calling for the Ayes and Nays and declaring the result; except that any member, elected or ex officio, may call for a division of the Senate; voting in a division of the Senate shall ordinarily be by show of hands . . . ." A secret ballot may be taken if a majority so desires. However, at a state university, any one member of the senate can request a secret ballot – a rule which is perhaps extreme yet preferable to the majority required for secret balloting at the previously mentioned institution.

Numerous senates permit attendance (without voting or floor privileges) to non-members who belong to the campus community. At one private university the senate's meetings are open to members of the university community, campus press and other campus news media, "unless such meetings have been designated closed by the Executive Committee of the Senate and such designation has not been overruled by a majority vote of the members of the Senate present and voting thereon." At a state college, "meetings are open ... to members of the faculty, to accredited representatives of news media and to students who are members of standing committees of the faculty or Senate." In several other institutions any faculty member may attend senate meetings; often, this right is also granted to members of the administration and even to "staff" members. At one state university all members of the faculty may "observe" senate proceedings, but, "normally," only one student representative chosen by the Student Senate. Another state university's senate is open to all the faculty, but specifically not to the press. However, at one private university the only outside observer, as specified in the constitution, is a reporter of the student newspaper, who may be barred if an executive session is voted. One state university's senate, which is open to all faculty members, has the additional, rather unusual provision granting the right to address the senate to any faculty member who so requests "at least 24 hours in advance of a Senate meeting; the time of a non-member shall be limited to 5 minutes except that this time limit may be waived by majority consent of the Senate."

Senate minutes in many institutions are widely distributed to non-members. At one state university, for example, they go to all members of the faculty and the administration, including specifically the professional staffs of the library and the Division of Student Welfare. At a private university, "a copy of the official minutes of the Senate, excluding any identification of candidates for honorary degrees, shall be sent to each member of the faculty, and the Senate may in its discretion send whatever other reports it desires to each member of the faculty." Complete faculty distribution of senate minutes is stipulated at several institutions. At one state university, "extensive minutes of Senate proceedings and debates" are to be distributed "throughout the academic community," including to students. At a church-related college, "majority and minority positions" are to be published in the minutes. The commentary to the new Columbia University senate stipulates that the minutes "shall be widely disseminated and shall be made available to the campus press and other news media"; moreover, copies of the minutes shall be posted in several prominent places on the campus.

Senate agendas tend to follow definite patterns. Approval of the minutes of the previous meeting is usually followed by unfinished business, committee reports, general business, and new business. At one institution, new items may be taken up "only by a suspension of the rules of order." In other senates, however, "new business" is always the final item on the regular agenda before adjournment. At some universities, the detailed agenda of upcoming senate meetings is distributed not only to members of the senate but to all faculty members.

Qualitative distinctions between items on the agenda are sometimes made. At a junior college two readings, in two successive sessions, are required for all "legislative" actions. At one large state university a complex system of "Classes of Senate Actions" is in operation: Class A senate actions, which amend the constitution; Class B senate actions, which legislate; Class C senate actions, which produce routine resolutions, etc. Amendments (Class A) require more than one reading, and the approval of other university components and structures of decision-making. Routine actions (Class C), such as resolutions, appointment of committees, and approval of committee reports, are effective upon adoption by the senate, but must be communicated to each faculty member. Legislative actions (Class B) cannot be finally acted upon at the meeting in which the action is first introduced, unless the measure has been proposed in the agenda or unless consent is given by a $\frac{2}{3}$ vote of those present. Furthermore, legislative actions (Class B) require consideration by the president of the university:

Except as provided below, the President within fourteen days shall note ... his approval or disapproval of the action and notify the chairman and the secretary of his decision. If the action requires additional consideration, the President may extend this time limit, in which case he shall notify the chairman and the secretary of the extension. If the president does not act upon the matter in any of the ways here specified, the action shall be deemed approved. If the President disapproves a Class B action he shall present to the Executive Committee, for the information of the Senate at its next regular meeting, a statement of the reasons for his decision.

Upon the approval of a legislative action (Class B) by the president, each member of the faculty is informed. At that point, such an action can still be suspended if written objection to its substantive nature, signed by at least ten faculty members, is presented to the secretary of the senate within fourteen days.

Persons offering such an objection shall be invited to express their views at the next meeting of the Executive Committee and, if they desire, of the Senate. If the Senate amends the disputed action, it shall be submitted in its revised form to the President and, if approved by him, made subject to review by the faculty in the manner prescribed for original Class B actions. If the Senate reaffirms the disputed action it becomes final unless a referendum poll is requested in writing by 10 per cent or more of the voting members of the faculty within fourteen days following announcement of the Senate's reaffirmation .... The referendum poll shall be completed within twenty-one days after letter-ballots are mailed by the secretary and the result, which is final, announced by the chairman at the next meeting of the Senate.

As to procedures for elections to senate seats, at one state university each school or college establishes its own nomination and election procedure, which can be challenged by any individual faculty member or any department and is then submitted to the senators of the school or college for adjudication. At another institution, a state college, there is a similar provision that each faculty or school "shall determine its own method of nominating and electing members and shall file a copy of a description of its methods with the secretary of the Academic Senate."

As was mentioned previously, the new constitution of the Columbia senate requires a minimum of 40% of the eligible voters to have voted in the election of a senator. Minimum requirements are also stipulated at another private university where in faculty meetings during which senators are elected the quorum is set at 60% of the eligible faculty members. At a private college, at least 50% of the eligible voters must vote in the election of the three student senators.

Virtually all senates require staggered elections, so that only some of the senators each year are new. Since most senators' terms are three years, the following provision is probably standard: "Terms of Senators shall be staggered so that insofar as possible each year one-third of them will complete their terms."

A final procedural matter relates to eligibility of faculty members for voting and for election to senatorial office. Usually, these rights are only held by full-time faculty members, although the definition of full-time status presents problems. At one large private university the concept of "full affiliation" has been applied to determine eligibility.

The term *affiliation* is used to describe the relationship to the University of faculty members of professorial rank and of professionally qualified instructors, associates, lecturers, research investigators and senior research investigators.

Full affiliation defines the relationship of such an individual with the University when the individual makes the University the principal center of his educational and professional effort, and University affairs primarily determine the employment of his time and talents. A fully affiliated member of the University may engage in other professional activities on a limited basis, but his major work is conducted under the auspices of the University ....

Partial affiliation denotes the status of individuals who devote a part of their professional effort to the University. The remainder of their activity may be directed to study at the pre- or post-doctoral level, to professional activity in other institutions or outside agencies, or to the pursuit of their own interests....

5. Committees

All senates have committees, and much of the work is done there. Virtually all "legislation" coming before a senate has been introduced by a committee; frequently, the committee's stamp of approval makes passage in the senate itself a formality. Since committee systems in most senates are rather similar, only a few enumerations of committees in different institutions are provided as examples.[13] In the senate of a large private university the following standing committees are established: Executive Committee; Committee on Educational Policy; Committee on Budget Review; Committee on Physical Development of the University; Committee on Faculty Affairs, Academic Freedom and Tenure; Committee on Student

[13] Mortimer, in his Berkeley case study, devotes one chapter to a detailed description of the formal and informal operations of four "important" committees: the Budget Committee, the Committee on Academic Planning, the Committee on Educational Policy, and the Committee on Courses of Instruction. (Mortimer, *Academic Government at Berkeley*, chapter V.) In the same study is a table on standing committees at Berkeley, classified by issue areas – 8 committees on educational policy; 8 on curriculum; 4 on faculty affairs; 7 on senate affairs; 5 on awards; 3 on student affairs. (*Ibid.*, p. 20.) The monograph by McConnell and Mortimer contains a table describing, comparatively, the standing committee structure of the three senates of the case studies, by issue areas. (McConnell and Mortimer, *The Faculty in University Governance*, p. 16.)

Affairs; Committee on External Relations and Research Policy; Committee on Community Relations; Committee on Rules of University Conduct; Committee on Alumni Relations; Committee on Honors and Prizes; Committee on the Libraries.

At one state college, these are the standing committees: the Executive Committee; the Committee on Faculty Affairs; the Committee on Student Affairs; the Committee on Undergraduate Academic Affairs; the Committee on Graduate Academic Affairs; the Committee on Budget. The short list of six at this institution can be contrasted with the fairly lengthy list of fourteen committees at a state university: Executive Committee; Academic Standards Committee; Admission Policy Committee; Curricular Affairs Committee; Constitution and By-Laws Committee; Faculty Welfare Committee; Honors Program Committee; Liaison Committee on the ROTC Program; Educational Procedures and Facilities Committee; Coordination of Academic Programs with the Division of University Extension Committee; Educational Policy Committee; Salary Committee; University Manual Committee; University Calendar Committee.

Finally, a state-wide system's senate has the following standing committees: Executive Committee; Committee on Personnel Policies; University Planning Committee; Graduate Program Committee; Undergraduate Program Committee; Faculty Research Committee; University Budget Committee; Committee on Faculty Governance; Committee on Student Affairs; Committee on Conferences and Assemblies; University Faculty Programs Committee.

The above lists, of course, do not cover the many *ad hoc* committees which often are created, for shorter or longer periods of service, at all institutions. Moreover, sub-committees of standing committees abound, and often tend to develop an independent status of their own.

The most important senate committee is usually the executive committee, which can be found in many, but not all senates. At one private university, the executive committee consists of five elected faculty members of the senate and the president of the university; it is chaired by one of the five faculty members. Its duties and tasks include the following: to arrange the agenda for senate meetings; to serve as the channel through which any member of the general faculty assembly may introduce matters for the consideration of the senate; to serve as the committee on committees for the senate; to assist in carrying into effect the actions of the general faculty assembly and the senate; to prepare and submit progress reports and reports on the work of the senate; to receive reports prepared by any college, school, or division of the university which may be of concern or interest to any other college, school, or division, or the faculty generally; to act on behalf of the senate in emergencies on matters requiring immediate action when it is not feasible to call a special meeting of the senate (such action to be reported to the senate for confirmation at its next regular meeting). Finally, in the event of any question or dispute as to the jurisdiction of any standing or special committee, the matter shall be referred to the executive committee for resolution.

The executive committee of the senate at a state university has twelve members, all elected by the senate. Of these twelve, three are administration members and nine are faculty members. The president of the university is chairman of the executive committee, ex-officio, but voting. The committee performs the following tasks:

1. it shall propose such standing and special committees of the Senate as may be needed and recommend to the Senate the membership of those committees
2. it shall examine the work of the various Senate committees with the view of evaluating the work of all committees in such a way as to prevent duplication of effort and to insure the carrying out of all committee assignments
3. it shall act as a steering committee to make sure that problems are referred to the proper committees
4. it shall act as a liaison committee to harmonize the work of all committees
5. it shall transact such business as may be referred to it by the Senate
6. it shall act for the Senate on urgent matters and consider current problems of general interest to the University which cannot wait for action by the Senate in regular sessions; such actions of the committee shall be reported to the Senate at its next meeting and shall be subject to ratification by it unless the nature of the action or the terms of the authorization make the action of the committee final.

The general role of the executive committee of the senate of a large state university, consisting mostly of elected faculty members and faculty members who are chairmen of committees, is described in terms which reveal its importance:

The Executive Committee of the Senate is the faculty committee primarily responsible for the participation of the faculty in University government. Its main responsibilities are to assist the Senate in the discharge of its legislative duties and to provide an effective channel of communications and consultation between the President and the University Faculty with respect to their joint and several responsibilities in the immediate government of the University.

The committee's specific duties include constitutional interpretation of the Faculty Code "on matters other than those within the jurisdiction of the Tenure Committee."

Finally, the senate of a large private university has an executive committee consisting of 13 members: 7 tenured faculty, 2 non-tenured faculty, 2 administration, and 2 students. All these are elected by the senate, except the administration members – the president of the university and one administrator chosen by him. The committee's duties, which include those of a committee on committees, are described as follows:

> The Executive Committee shall be the Senate's agenda committee, as well as its committee on committees. The Executive Committee shall have the power to call the Senate into extraordinary session, and shall have such powers, functions and duties as the Senate may delegate to it during periods when the Senate is not in session. The Executive Committee shall also serve as continuing liaison between the University Senate and the central administration. The Executive Committee may create sub-committees and may delegate any of its powers, functions and duties. As agenda committee, the Executive Committee shall prepare the Senate's agenda.
>
> As committee on committees, the Executive Committee shall nominate from the membership of the University Senate and from among other members of the University community the members and the chairmen of the several standing and special committees of the Senate. Nominations made by the Executive Committee shall be submitted to the Senate and shall become effective when confirmed by the majority vote of the members of the Senate voting thereon.
>
> The Executive Committee shall participate ... in the selection of University Professors, senior administrators with University-wide powers, and 6 Trustees. In performing these functions, the Executive Committee or the appropriate subcommittee thereof may act in executive session and in a confidential manner and shall not be required to report its deliberations or actions to the Senate as a whole.

Service on this committee is expected to be time-consuming. Therefore, faculty members are to receive reductions in teaching loads, while students are to be granted "appropriate point credit" for their participation on the executive committee.

One unusual committee might well be mentioned at this

point – the so-called Summer Committee of the senate at a state college. Composed of no fewer than six members of the senate, it "shall be available on an emergency basis during the months of June, July, and August for consultation, calling of special Senate meetings, and handling such duties as may be delegated to it by the Senate." The summer recess presents a decision-making gap of considerable proportion in many institutions, when even executive committees may not be able to muster any kind of quorum; in many institutions a summer moratorium on all action is no longer feasible.

Another general kind of committee in a number of senates provides for special liaison between faculty and president, partly for times of special emergency. The President's Faculty Advisory Committee at one private university consists of six faculty members, elected by the faculty representatives in the senate from their own group. The committee's purpose is "to advise the President of the University upon matters of University policy, particularly when subjects of great urgency or delicacy require immediate consultation." At another private university, the Consultative Committee is charged "with consulting and advising with the Chancellor and his officers on matters of general University concern." This committee consists of elected members of the senate in their final year of office, and the chairman-elect and secretary-elect; "no formal votes shall be taken at such consultations, nor shall the Consultative Committee take any action that might commit the Senate against its will." The Faculty Consultative Committee of the senate at a state university "shall meet with the President at regular times to discuss matters of policy relating to instruction, research, personnel, service functions, and the budget." Its general purpose is to initiate and further communications between the faculty and the president. The committee is composed of seven elected faculty members; only associate professors or full professors may be nominated for membership or may vote for members of this committee. "The committee shall represent the faculty-at-large and not individual institutes, colleges, schools, or departments of the University."

Agenda committees are important in some senates and carry out some of the functions of executive committees. At one large state university, the agenda committee has four areas of jurisdiction: placing of items on the agenda; drafting of legislative proposals; implementation of legislative actions; invitation of non-members to senate meetings. This committee is composed of the secretary and two additional members of the senate. The agenda committee at another state university consists of the chairman, the vice-chairman, the secretary, and six elected members of the senate. Its duties include the establishing of "procedures whereby the policy-forming activities of the Senate and its committees may be expedited."

The committee on committees is another crucial committee (whose functions in some senates are carried out by the executive committee). To cite one example, at a state university the committee on committees has the following responsibilities:

a. to recommend all council and committee appointments to be made by the Senate (except where members are to be elected) with the approval of the President or his representative and the individuals involved
b. to make a continuous study of the distribution of committee assignments to assure equitable distribution among the colleges, administrative units, and academic ranks
c. to recommend the formation or abolition of councils or committees
d. to appoint a committee each year to nominate a slate of Senate Officers
e. to prepare and submit to the Senate an annual evaluative report of the Committees' activities.

This committee on committees consists of senate members, elected by the senate.

The budget committee is now becoming important in many senates. At one state university, the Committee on the Budget is to concern itself "with policies relating to the University budget and budgetary procedure, to consult with the Vice President-Dean of the Faculties and Director of the Budget, to report to the Faculty Council [senate] its recommendations concerning proposed budgets or any revision of current budgets." This budget committee consists of ten elected members. At a state college, the Committee on Budget is to conduct "a continuing study of the College budget; to maintain liaison for suggestions on budgetary affairs from the faculty to the administrative officers responsible for the College budget." This committee consists of at least seven faculty senators, and two administration senators appointed by the president. The Budget Council of the senate of another state university is composed of nine tenured members of the faculty and two administrators, with the Vice-President for Business and Finance as chairman. Its duties are:

1. to assist the President by making budget recommendations for all academic units
2. to review budget requests made by deans of the various colleges
3. to act as an advisory council to the President on matters related to the budget
4. to recommend policy on questions of budgetary concern to the University
5. to recommend solutions for major differences of opinion on budgetary matters.

The Budget Committee of the senate of another state college has as members the business manager and five faculty members "selected on the basis of particular abilities in budgetary matters." This committee "shall act as a review and recommending source reflecting a faculty viewpoint" with respect to:

1. the level of budgetary support required to attain the goals of the educational program
2. the allocation of available budgetary support to the various educational programs of the College
3. the methods and procedures to be employed in the development of annual budgets.

The members of the Educational Policies Council of the senate of one state college are to serve "as designated leaders of the faculty charged with transmitting and explaining to the President and the Board of Trustees the views of the faculty in the making of policy decisions." A specific duty of the Council in this respect is to make recommendations "on the allocation of funds for education" and "on major issues of policy affecting current or projected budget decisions."

The final budget committee to be covered here is the Committee on Budget Review of the new senate of Columbia University. It has seven members, all of whom must be members of the senate – 4 tenured faculty representatives, 1 non-tenured faculty, 1 student representative, and the chairman of the Executive Committee or his designee serving ex-officio. These are the committee's functions:

The Budget Review Committee shall review the annual budget of the University after its adoption to assure its general conformity with short-range and long-range priorities of the University and expressions of policy by the Senate. The chairman of the Budget Committee or his designee may sit with the appropriate committee of the administration when it formulates its budget policy guidelines for the coming year and when categories of the budget are discussed or adopted. The Budget Review Committee shall report its activities to the Senate and shall bring to its attention any instances of noncompliance of the budget with existing priorities or policies and any other allocations which in the Committee's opinion are not in the best interests of the University.

In the commentary to the committee's proposed operations, its natural limitations are acknowledged:

The delegation of functions to the Budget Review Committee accepts the obvious difficulty that neither the University Senate nor any of its committees is capable of participating fully in the minutiae of budgetary development and allocation. The Budget Review Committee is intended to serve as a watchdog committee, not on line-by-line allocations, but on major allocations between departments, faculties, schools and divisions of the University, so as to assure that budgetary decisions accord with outstanding University policies. The presence of the chairman of the Executive Committee or his designee as an ex-officio member of the Budget Committee is intended to assure close collaboration between these two important committees.

Another sphere of rather unusual committee activity relates to planning and development. For example, at one state university there is a Council on Planning and Development which consists of four faculty members, two students, and several administration officials (including the Director of Physical Plant and the University Architect). Among the committee's general responsibilities are recommendations regarding "the orderly development and expansion of the University's physical facilities." At a state college, the Academic Policy and Planning Committee includes six faculty members ("selected on the basis of particular abilities in policy and planning") and several administration officers. Its functions are far-reaching. The committee

shall consider the future development of the College in its broadest scope and shall formulate goals which it believes the College should seek in fulfilling its educational mission; it shall prepare proposals for long-range policy with regard to curriculum development, College administration, faculty government, academic standards, educational philosophy, physical facilities and other appropriate subjects.

Perhaps the most recent of all senate committee jurisdictions is represented by Columbia University's Committee on Community Relations which, of course, reflects the urban university's increasingly delicate relationships with its surroundings.

The Committee on Community Relations shall consist of 19 members apportioned as follows: 9 tenured faculty, 2 non-tenured faculty, 5 students and 3 administration. The Committee shall recommend policies to govern the University's relations with the surrounding community so that they may become and remain harmonious and mutually beneficial. The Committee shall also work with the President and the Board of Trustees in the development of measures to effectuate such policies. In carrying out its responsibilities, the Committee shall take into account the potential impact of the University's development plans on the interests of the surrounding community, and shall work closely with the Committee on Physical Development of the University to minimize conflicts and to create opportunities for the cooperative and mutually advantageous solution of problems.

The subject of university government is not, as yet, the concern of a specific committee at most institutions. It is provided for at one large state university, which has an Advisory Committee on Faculty Code and Regulations. In addition to rendering advisory opinions on interpretations of the instruments of university government, that committee is asked to:

(a) draft proposed additions to or amendments of University regulations at the request of the Senate or of any Faculty Council or of any faculty committee or member of the Senate
(b) be available for consultation upon the meaning of the University regulations or upon the status of existing rules governing any situation
(c) maintain a master copy of University regulations kept up to date by incorporation of new legislation and amendments
(d) edit for publication, when necessary, new editions of University regulations; and
(e) recommend revision or clarification of University regulations.

The committee is assisted by a "committee counsel," appointed by the executive committee, who "shall be a member of the faculty who has either legal training or other training and experience which qualifies him for the drafting of regulations and the interpretation and codification of enacted materials." The counsel, and the committee, are advisory to the executive committee. A somewhat similar committee operates in the system-wide senate of an eastern state. Its Committee on Faculty Governance is to foster "the development of local campus faculty by-laws" and to serve as an advisory body concerning inquiries about faculty rights and responsibilities in the governmental sphere.

Many other areas of senate committee activity cannot be covered here for reasons of limitations of space. Student affairs committees, for example, exist in most universities for problems pertaining to the non-academic sides of student life. Such committees usually consist of students, faculty, and administration; but, increasingly, students tend to dominate. (In the new Columbia senate, the Committee on Student Affairs is composed of eleven members, all students.) Committees on academic freedom, tenure, and responsibilities of faculty are universal, as are committees on student discipline; these committees ordinarily assure the rendering of justice by peer groups, and follow more or less closely the standards set by the AAUP's Committee A on Academic Freedom and Tenure, and more recently, Committee S on Faculty Responsibility for the Academic Freedom of Students.[14] So complex and numerous are the committees in most senates that yet one additional committee, at a private university, seems worthy of attention – a Coordinating Committee whose membership consists of all the committee chairmen. The committee's aim is to promote more effective operation of the senate's committee system, "especially through exchange of information with respect to overlapping and interrelated committee problems." In some universities, the executive committee is specifically charged with coordinating tasks; some executive committees are composed of the chairmen of standing senate committees.

One final question remains to be mentioned in this section: should the members of the senate committees be members of the senate? This is required at some institutions. In most universities, however, such a rule would not be feasible because of the great number of committee positions, and for other reasons. In the senate of one large private university, the chairmen of committees and at least a majority of every committee must be members of the senate, but even this provision is probably not applicable in many senates. To make, nevertheless, for maximum coordination between the committees and the senate, one state university permits all members of a com-

---

[14] The AAUP's Handbook, *Academic Freedom and Tenure*, provides, of course, extensive analyses of these topics. Concerning the status of students, note the 1967 *Joint Statement on Rights and Freedoms of Students*, cited in the 1969 edition of the above Handbook, pp. 66–74; also, the report of the Ad Hoc Committee on the Role of Students in the Government of the University, University of Wisconsin, February 6, 1968. Concerning a new academic institution, the campus ombudsman, see Stanley V. Anderson, *Ombudsman Papers: American Experience and Proposals* (Institute of Governmental Studies: University of California, Berkeley, 1969), pp. 61–71.

mittee to attend those meetings of the senate, with privileges of the floor, at which the committee's business is discussed. In the senate of another state university committee members are given voting privileges at such occasions.

D. *The College Faculty Assembly*

The college, as subdivision of the university, can easily be underestimated in its significance to the whole university. The college certainly lacks the tight, collegial, discipline-related unity of the department; on the other hand, it can be a much more meaningful unit than the university-wide institutions of the faculty. The dean of the college may well be the most academic of administrators. As has been suggested in the previous chapter, the government of the university should be carried out, principally, with the close cooperation of administration and faculty; a meaningful locale for such cooperation is at the college level – between the dean of the college and faculty leaders in the faculty assembly or the committees of the college. The departmental level, the most successful certainly, tends to ignore issues pertaining to the university as a whole. The university-wide levels of the general faculty assembly and the senate may suffer from an unwieldy or depersonalized atmosphere of discussion and decision-making. The college level, in many ways, combines some of the advantages of the department with attention to concerns beyond the department, in a milieu which often still permits individual participation in a reasonably collegial group.

In this sense, the constitution of one large state university quite appropriately calls the college "the largest educational and administrative group," and grants it "the fullest measure of autonomy consistent with the maintenance of general University educational policy and correct academic and administrative relations with other divisions of the University."

1. Functions

The functions of college faculty assemblies include much of the jurisdiction also assigned to the department, but more for coordinating than initiating purposes. For example, the department decides what courses it should teach, but the college (or its curriculum committee) sees to it that departmental offerings do not conflict, or exceed the financial and other limits of the college's capacity. However, when conflicts between a department and the college occur on such issues, the department may turn out to be stronger than the college, because of its greater cohesion and purposefulness. (The college's actions may be "non-actions" due to the effects of departmental courtesy and log-rolling among departments.) Some college functions are not shared by departments – for example, the admission of students at the undergraduate level is not a departmental responsibility.

A brief description of the functions of the college faculty assembly is used at one large private university, where each assembly is given "general legislative power over all matters pertaining to its own meetings, and to the admission requirements, curricular instruction, examinations, grading, and degrees in its own School or Division, and these powers ... shall be exclusive and final." At a state university, college jurisdiction includes admission requirements, requirements for majors, requirements for graduation, and the nature, content, and scheduling of its courses. Another state university describes college functions particularly with reference to university-wide interests.

The several schools and colleges represent organized responsibility for carrying out the following functions:
  to enforce the rules and regulations of the Senate as they apply to the college;
  to set up and administer curriculum and undergraduate degree requirements for its own students;
  to set up admission requirements in line with the purpose and responsibility of the school or college;
  to submit to the President for transmittal to the Board of Trustees the names of students who have completed graduation requirements;
  to plan and execute programs of research and service in line with the general policy of the University and the available staff and facilities;
  to integrate its program with the general program of the University and to foster effective coordination of effort.

At a large state university, college jurisdiction is subject to the university-wide senate if the "general welfare" of the university is affected or for purposes of coordination of the various colleges. Within these limits, the college assembly shall determine its own requirements for admission and graduation, its curriculum and academic programs, the scholastic standards required of its students, and shall exercise the additional powers necessary to provide adequate instruction and supervision of its students.

The faculty of the college, acting through the general faculty assembly of the college (whatever its name may be, if any), is in many institutions still of a size which permits fairly effective participation in decision-making by all. Committees are important and usually numerous in carrying out special functions of the college. Not infrequently an elected (or appointed) executive committee acts as a kind of senate for the routine business of the college – and sometimes also for the other business.

2. Membership, Officers, Procedures, and Committees

The following provision at a state university appears standard for membership qualifications of the general faculty assemblies of colleges: "The faculty of each college, school or division shall consist of the President, the Provost, the Dean and all persons who give instruction in the college, school, or division with the exception of student assistants ... [and teaching assistants]."

The dean heads the college and usually presides in its general faculty assembly. His functions are described at one large state university. An unusual feature, however, is the biennial election of the deans at this institution by the board of trustees. (In virtually all institutions the deans' terms are unlimited, although it has been suggested lately that deans should be limited to five-year or seven-year terms and then return to regular faculty duties.)

The Dean is the chief executive officer of the college, responsible to the President for its administration.

He is the agent of the College Faculty for the execution of College educational policy.

He shall be elected biennially by the Board, on nomination of the President.

On the occasion of each election, the President shall have the advice of the Executive Committee of the faculty concerned.

On the recommendation of the Dean and on the nomination of the President, the Board may appoint biennially associate or assistant deans as required.

The Dean shall call meetings of the Faculty at such times as he or the Executive Committee may deem necessary and shall preside over such meetings.

He shall formulate and present policies to the faculty for its consideration.

He shall serve as the medium of communication for all official business of the college with other University authorities, the students, and the public.

He shall prepare the budget of the College in consultation with the Executive Committee of the College.

He shall recommend the appointment, reappointment, or promotion of the officers and members of the teaching staff.

He shall make his recommendation after consultation with the chairman and Executive Committee . . . of the department concerned.

The following provisions at a state university seem typical enough for procedures used in college faculty assemblies: each college faculty assembly meets at least once a semester at the call of its dean and determines its own procedures, consistent with policies prescribed by the university's senate; the dean shall call a special meeting of a college faculty assembly on the written request of 25% of its members; one half (one third for colleges with more than 200 members) of the membership constitutes a quorum. Considerable diversity may exist among institutions with respect to some of the variables in these procedures – for example, in several colleges considerably fewer faculty members than 25% of the membership can call for special meetings. (However, the prescribed monthly meeting of the college faculty assembly at one state university must be very unusual.)

A typical list of committees in a college of arts and sciences may include the following: Academic Performance, Committees, Curriculum, Executive, General Studies, Honors Programs, Junior Year Abroad, Petitions, Promotions and Tenure, Registration. (Admissions and financial aid committees do not always appear at the college level, since these two functions may be taken care of by university-wide committees.)

Executive committees, usually elective, can be very powerful at the college level. One private university has a representative Legislative Council in its college of arts and sciences, "sufficiently compact" to consider legislation. This body consists of approximately 44 faculty members: the chairmen of all twenty-one departments in the college; an additional representative from each department with five or more faculty members, elected by the department; nine members at large, elected from the three divisions of the college. The dean of the college and certain other administrators are ex-officio members, but without vote. The Legislative Council has three standing committees (Admissions and Scholarships, Academic Policy and Standards, Curriculum), each consisting of nine faculty members and three students.

An unusual set of committees exists at one large state university – the so-called Conference Committees. They are intended to coordinate parallel programs in different colleges, and are composed of elected members from the various colleges concerned. Each Conference Committee reports to the various faculty assemblies involved, but its decisions may also be reviewed at university-wide levels.

3. The Graduate Faculty

The graduate faculty of a university is, in a sense, just another college – but a college quite different from the other colleges of a university. The membership of the graduate faculty generally comes from a number of colleges and divisions, and thus represents a university-wide constituency. Next to the senate, the graduate faculty is often the most significant faculty unit at, in effect, the university-wide level. It is supposed to include the scholarly elite of the university; therefore, it may put much stress on membership qualifications in terms of research and active supervision of graduate students. In most institutions, however, the graduate faculty is only the second "home" of the faculty member, whose primary college-size unit (not just for budget purposes) is a specific college – such as arts and sciences, engineering, or medicine. Thus, the intensity of affiliation to the graduate faculty may be low. Another handicap of the graduate faculty is that academic departments fulfill much more unilaterally some of the functions which in undergraduate colleges may be more evenly shared by the department and college – for example, curriculum and academic performance. Although the graduate faculty is weakened by the effects of traditions of departmental hegemony and autonomy, a variety of functions must be performed at the faculty-wide level – particularly in the spheres of budget allocation and quality control of graduate student performance. Also, while the graduate dean lacks the direct budget powers of other deans, he usually plays an important role in the committee which distributes research grants and similar funds.

The structures of the graduate faculty include a general faculty assembly, but also, usually, a graduate council, which may play the role of an extra-powerful executive committee within the graduate faculty. Other committees exist, but are usually limited in number. A recent graduate faculty constitution – adopted at Tulane University in 1969 – is reproduced as Appendix D to this study.

E. The Department

1. Functions

A characterization of the functions of departments is provided at one large state university, with emphasis on the primacy of the department as an educational unit, its relationship to a specific field of knowledge, and its necessary but limited autonomy within the university.

The department is the primary unit of education and administration within the University. It is established for the purpose of carrying on programs of instruction and research in a particular field of knowledge. The department has the fullest measure of autonomy consistent with the maintenance of general college and University educational policy and correct academic and administrative relations with other divisions of the University. Should a dispute arise between the department and another unit of the University concerning the proper limits of this autonomy, the department may appeal for a ruling directly to the dean and the Executive Committee of the college and, where the President considers it proper, to the President, who shall make a decision after consultation with the Senate Coordinating Council.

More specifically, a state college assigns the department

primary responsibility for initiating and making recommendations on all matters relating to:
a. selection, retention, and promotion of personnel
b. development and improvement of the Departmental curriculum, both graduate and undergraduate
c. budget
d. growth and improvement of the Department in terms of professional development and School, College, and community relationships.

One reason why another state university insists on departments as distinct administrative units is "to insure that the attention of small groups of staff members will be centered on

the problems of teaching, planning, research, and service...."
Thus, although departments are in many respects interrelated,
they should remain separate along the lines of their subject
matter areas. In other words, one might add, if scholarly disciplines had not developed in great number, some other device
would have to be found to keep the primary administrative
unit of the university small and accessible. Of course, many
departments are neither small nor accessible to their members.
An oligarchy of full professors may dominate – or, perhaps, an
oligarchy of younger scholars who are up-to-date with respect
to the latest national trends in the discipline. No device, unfortunately, has been invented to take the place of a department which has grown beyond "accessible" size. One solution
may be to divide departments into parallel sub-departments,
with more or less separate units, for example, for graduate,
undergraduate male, and undergraduate female students.

2. Membership and Officers

A basic rule of departmental equity is the universality and
equality of membership provisions. As is stated at one state
university, all persons "engaged in the teaching of courses
offered by the department" are members of the department,
and "all members of the department shall have equal voting
rights." Some limitations on this basic principle do exist. For
example, departments at a large private university invite only
persons above the rank of instructor, or even only those holding tenure appointments, to departmental meetings. At another state university all members with the rank of instructor
or higher are invited, but not "temporary appointees." At a
state college, all full-time faculty "with tenure or appointed
with the expectancy of tenure" are invited and vote at departmental meetings. In any case, teaching assistants or teaching fellows – usually Ph.D. or M.A. candidates in the department – are ordinarily not granted full membership.

The most crucial officer of the department is, of course, the
chairman, whose role has been discussed already in the previous chapter. Nowadays, chairmen tend to be appointed for
limited terms, after some process of consultation or election
involving the departmental faculty – in accordance with practices noted with approval by the AAUP. At a state university,
for example, the deans of the colleges are responsible for recom-

mending the appointment of the department chairmen to the Provost. "Faculty members may discuss freely the recommendations with the Provost before final action is taken." Chairmen at this institution are appointed annually and are usually reappointed for no more than five consecutive years. At one large private university, a chairman

is appointed annually by the President, upon recommendation by the Provost or Vice-President, who in turn makes his nomination after receiving a recommendation from the dean of the faculty concerned. The dean, in his turn, is supposed to have consulted with and to transmit the views of his faculty members, both those within and those without the department concerned. The consultation prescribed between dean and department members may vary from informal conversations with some or a few members, to presentation of the matter to a full department meeting. Usually a chairman holds office for a succession of years, being reappointed annually. Although there is a tradition in some departments that the chairmanship is to rotate from year to year among the senior professors, this is quite exceptional.

At a Roman Catholic university, chairmen are appointed for a stated term, usually three years, and may be reappointed. When a chairman of a department is to be appointed, the dean of the college consults formally with all professors and associate professors of the department and then with the dean of the graduate school.

In a number of institutions, chairmen of departments are called "heads," without any particular reason for the difference in title except tradition of the institution. It is sometimes argued, however, that a head is more powerful than a chairman, and this may be true in certain universities. (Still another title, Executive Officer of the department, may indicate a rather weak and junior "chairman.") At one state university, both chairmen and heads exist side by side, and there the chairman is intended to be the weaker of the two. The chairman is appointed biennially by the board on nomination by the president and after consultation with the dean and the executive committee of the department; the head, on the other hand, is appointed without specified term, after similar procedures of nomination and consultation. Moreover, in the chairman's department an elected executive committee plays an important role; in the head's department, there is merely an advisory committee with considerably less power than an executive committee.

At one private college, the chairman is elected by his faculty colleagues, and such an election "shall take place at least once in three years." Similarly, at another private college, "the chairman shall be elected by the department ... from the group of professors, associate professors, and assistant professors of the department for the term of three years and shall be eligible for re-election." At a state college, each department is to develop its own policy for nominating a chairman; however, "he must have achieved the rank of assistant professor... and served a minimum of four years of full-time college teaching in his field." His term of office "shall be no less than three and no more than five years."

Chairmen's functions or duties are frequently described in constitutions. At a private college, the (elected) chairman presides at meetings of the department and its main committees, and "shall execute the will of the majority"; he may participate in discussions and has the right to vote; he appoints such subcommittees as the work of the department may require; he represents the department on public occasions and before the trustees, the president, and the students; he is responsible for the guidance of inexperienced instructors; finally, he acts in cases of emergency, e.g., in the summer when the department is scattered.

The chairmen at one state university are elaborately instructed as to their tasks, which include hierarchical and pedagogical leadership roles. The chairman "is responsible to his dean for the educational and administrative affairs of his department; in administrative matters, a department chairman is the representative through his dean of the President and also of the department faculty, and is responsible for observance of the policies of the University by the department." In his leadership role, "he should be cognizant of the aims and purposes of the department, and through his leadership provide an atmosphere in which integrity and inquiry become characteristic of the faculty and students of the department." He shall prepare and transmit to his dean "his own and his department's recommendations upon matters of personnel, budget, and curriculum; shall evaluate the educational activities of the department, formulate plans for its future development, and transmit these evaluations and plans to his dean for appropriate action." Moreover, "he shall keep his dean informed of all departmental matters of concern to the college or school, and he shall circulate full and accurate minutes of department meetings to members of the department as soon as possible after each meeting." Finally, "he shall assume or delegate to a specific faculty member responsibility for orientation of new and/or inexperienced faculty members in the philosophy and procedure of the department and in appropriate pedagogical methods." At a large state university, on the other hand, the description of chairmanly duties is more modest, but with a formal arbitration task added. He is, *inter alia*, "to be the channel of official communications for all matters affecting the department as a whole," and "to act as a source of arbitration, when necessary, either between students and any member of the department, or between different members in the department." [15]

More interesting than the enumeration of functions of chairmen is the attempt, in some constitutions, to distinguish between the powers reserved to the chairman and those reserved to the departmental faculty. At a state university, the chairman shall make decisions on such matters as:

1. setting the time and frequency of staff meetings, except that staffs shall meet at least once each month
2. approving class schedules for the department
3. fixing policies for expenditures from the departmental budget
4. selecting representatives to attend professional meetings at University expense, within the limits of the out-of-state travel allowance established for the department by the President.

The departmental faculty, "acting as a group," shall decide such matters as:

1. recommending appointments of new staff members
2. recommending tenure of faculty
3. recommending policies and procedures as to teaching methods, curricula, coordination with other departments, and, in general, matters of policy concerning the work of the department.

At another state university, the "Departmental Committee" (consisting of all the members of professorial rank) – rather than the chairman – is put in charge of "the immediate government" of the department and "shall have jurisdiction over all the interests of the department with power to determine all

---

[15] It should still be mentioned that in larger or medium-sized departments some of the functions of the chairman are frequently delegated to other departmental officers – such as assistant chairmen, graduate studies directors, and freshman program directors.

questions of educational and administrative policy pertaining thereto." Departmental recommendations regarding "the annual budget, appointments, dismissals, promotions and salaries" are to be made by the full and associate professors of the department. At a private college, the departmental meeting, rather than the chairman, makes recommendations as to courses of study, "arrangement of course sections and hours," departmental committees, and "the budget exclusive of salaries." At one state university, a departmental action is effective only if it is passed by a majority of all voting members of the department; if a chairman does not agree with a departmental majority, he may submit his individual views, together with the departmental action, to the dean. Each member of a department "is entitled to information concerning salary scales, teaching schedules, salary and operations budget requests, appropriations, allotments, disbursements and similar data pertaining to his department."

3. Procedures and Committees

At one large private university some departments have meetings at regular intervals while other departments call meetings only when the need arises – a lack of uniformity which probably prevails in many institutions. A state university imposes a rather rigid rule on departments: meetings must be held "once during each full month of term time, on the first Thursday of each month." In addition, special meetings may be called at any time by the chairman or "on the written request by any two members of the department." The agenda must be in the hands of all members not less than two days preceding the meeting; as is the case in most departments, minutes are to be kept.

As to departmental voting, at the large private university just mentioned decisions are sometimes reached by unwritten consensus, sometimes by majority vote recorded in departmental minutes; "they are binding upon the conscience of the chairman in his presentation of his department's views to the dean, but he remains free to present his own views if they differ from those of his department." At another private university, special majorities are required for certain decisions in at least one department. For promotions, the departmental promotions committee is to make every effort to obtain unanimity;

if this fails, at least $\frac{2}{3}$ of the committee are required to approve. New appointments must be approved by the departmental faculty with at least a $\frac{2}{3}$ majority of those present and voting. Tenure is granted by a $\frac{2}{3}$ vote of the tenured members of the department present and voting, provided a quorum of half of the tenured members plus one is present. Other special voting requirements pertain to Ph.D. examinations. Finally, a $\frac{2}{3}$ vote of those present and voting is required for amendments to the departmental constitution. At one large state university, the departments may determine their own form of organization – but "such organization of the departments shall not prejudice the rights of professors and instructors to vote on substantial questions"; furthermore, the president must approve all departmental constitutions.

Departments, as a rule, use committees. For example, at one private university, "a department usually has an executive committee, more or less formally constituted, consisting sometimes of the full professors, sometimes of a small group of senior members personally selected by the chairman, sometimes a body explicitly elected by the department ...." The chairmen consult these committees particularly regarding appointments and promotions, and sometimes also regarding increases in salaries. At one state university, as was mentioned previously, a department organized with a chairman has to have an executive committee elected annually by the members of the department from the ranks of assistant professor or above; or, if a department has a head, there is an advisory committee which is also elected by the departmental faculty. All departments at a Roman Catholic university must have a Committee on Appointments and Promotions. At a state university each department, normally, is to have a so-called Committee A, consisting of the chairman and two elected faculty members. Its functions include formal recommendations on such matters as budget allotment requests, increases in salary, and promotions in rank. A so-called Department Committee must be instituted in all departments of one private college. It is to consist of all members of the department who serve on the senate of the institution and of other departmental members elected by them. This committee elects the departmental chairman and makes the major policy decisions. Departments in this college must also have a so-called Small Committee, consisting of the chairman, full and associate professors who have served at least three years on the senate, and other associate professors elected by them. This committee makes recommendations on appointments, most promotions, dismissals, reappointments, and courses of instruction (after consultation with all the members of the department).

The most obvious departmental functions which may require standing committees relate to graduate curriculum, undergraduate curriculum, budget, personnel (appointment, tenure, and promotion), supervision of graduate teaching assistants, selection of new graduate students, academic performance of graduate students, organization of departmental "core" courses (for freshmen and incoming graduate students), library acquisitions, and allotment of computer time. (Of course, several of these functions can be assigned to one committee.)

As was emphasized previously, the department should be the primary locale for student participation. More and more elected student representatives, graduate and undergraduate, at present participate in departmental meetings or serve on departmental committees, especially those concerned with curriculum and general academic requirements. For example, the constitution of the graduate school at Tulane University requires graduate departments to elect graduate student representatives, who are to "work" with the departmental faculty "in order to facilitate discussion of problems concerning students." [16]

F. Constitutional Documents

1. Adoption

A method requiring only simple majority votes by the faculty and administration, and approval by the trustees, was used for the adoption of a new constitution at one state college. Similarly, the constitution of a state university became operative "upon ratification by a majority of the University Council [senate], the faculty, and approval by the President and the

---

[16] There is no discussion in this chapter of the divisional units which are not uncommon particularly in liberal arts colleges. Divisions of natural sciences, social sciences, and the humanities, for example, may provide a convenient level between the college and the department where the college has become too large, or where the departments are too small.

Board of Trustees . . . ." At another state college there was one additional requirement: "this constitution shall be adopted by a favorable vote of the majority of the Faculty of the College who vote . . ., but shall not be adopted if less than 200 favorable ballots are cast."

In other institutions, however, more than simple majorities were specified for adoption of a new constitutional document. At a private university, "this constitution shall be declared ratified and in force by concurrent vote of $\frac{2}{3}$ of the entire membership of the Faculty Senate." At another private university, "the Constitution will come into effect when ratified in a mail ballot by the members of the Faculty Assembly, provided approval is expressed by at least $\frac{2}{3}$ of those voting." Similar $\frac{2}{3}$ requirements were set at a state college and a private college. An even more stringent adoption rule prevailed at a community college, where $\frac{3}{4}$ of the faculty had to approve the constitution before it was sent on to the trustees. At a junior college, an affirmative vote by $\frac{2}{3}$ of the senate and $\frac{3}{4}$ of the total faculty was needed. The minimum was set even higher – 80% of the representatives in the old Faculty Assembly – at a state university.

Finally, two recent constitutional innovations – at a private university and at a state university – required majority approval by each of the components, including the students.

2. Amendment

Provisions for amendment of constitutional documents reveal a great variety of different formal requirements – with respect to the proposal stage, the adoption stage, and the participation of the various bodies and components.

At one private university, amendments to the constitution may be proposed either by the president, or by the senate, or by 15% of the members of the general faculty assembly, or by a special committee of the faculty established to review the constitution. An amendment is adopted by a favorable vote of either $\frac{2}{3}$ of those voting or a majority of the voting members of the general faculty assembly. Finally, approval by the board is needed before an amendment is effective.

At a state university, an amendment to the constitution may be proposed by a $\frac{2}{3}$ vote of the membership of the senate; it is adopted by a simple majority of those voting among the members of the faculty, but requires approval of the board to become effective.

At another private university, an amendment may be proposed by the senate or by any of the general faculty assemblies of the several colleges or schools. It is adopted by a $\frac{2}{3}$ vote of those present and voting at a meeting of the general faculty assembly, provided that at least one month before such meeting the members of the assembly have been notified in writing of the proposed amendment.

At a state college, proposals for amendments must be supported by petitions of 10% of the total faculty. Adoption of amendments requires a majority vote of the total voting faculty at a faculty meeting or by "mailbox ballot." (If a "mailbox ballot" is used, it must be preceded by an announced open hearing with discussion of the amendments, and a report of this hearing shall be distributed to the voting faculty prior to the voting.)

At a church-related college, proposals to amend the constitution require a $\frac{2}{3}$ vote of the senate; ratification must be by $\frac{2}{3}$ of the student body, $\frac{2}{3}$ of the faculty, the administration, and the board.

At a large state university, amendments must first be approved by a $\frac{2}{3}$ vote of all members of the senate, and are then submitted in writing to all the members of the faculty who are entitled to vote for members of the senate. An amendment is adopted unless it is disapproved by at least $\frac{1}{3}$ of the members of the faculty by written vote, but requires final approval of the board.

At a community college, amendments are proposed by the senate or by a petition signed by $\frac{1}{3}$ of the members of the general faculty assembly. An amendment is adopted when approved by a $\frac{2}{3}$ majority of the entire general faculty assembly, and by the board. (No amendment shall be voted on until there has been "opportunity for discussion.")

At a private university, amendments shall be made by the passage, by a majority of the whole senate, of a motion to amend the constitution in two regular meetings of the senate. Between these meetings the various schools and colleges must have had a reasonable opportunity to discuss the amendments and report thereon. All amendments require approval by the board.

At a state university, amendments may be proposed by 25%

of the total faculty or by a majority of the senate. To be effective, they require adoption by a majority of the senate, and by a majority of the total faculty, and also by the president and the board. If a majority of the senate cannot be found for an amendment, it can still be ratified by a favorable vote of 75% of the total faculty, if the president and board approve.

At a private college, an amendment originating from the faculty or the board must first be submitted to a special committee for its consideration and recommendation. The amendment is adopted by an affirmative vote of $\frac{2}{3}$ of all members of the faculty, if the board approves. If the faculty does not approve an amendment, or if the president is opposed, the amendment must be considered at two consecutive regular meetings of the board. In the case of faculty opposition to an amendment, final approval requires a $\frac{2}{3}$ vote of all the members of the board.

Additional complexity develops when system-wide constitutions have to be amended. For example, the charter of the university system of a large metropolitan area may be amended if $\frac{2}{3}$ of the system-wide senate or $\frac{1}{3}$ of the senates of the constituent units so propose; ratification requires passage by the system-wide senate, and the amendment becomes valid if one-half of the senates of the constituent units have accepted it. The constitution of the university system of an eastern state can be amended if a majority vote in the system-wide senate so proposes, and if ratification is voted by the faculties of $\frac{3}{4}$ of the component units. Of course, in both of these systems, amendments must also be approved by the appropriate boards.

CHAPTER 3

SUGGESTED CONSTITUTIONAL PROVISIONS

The first chapter of this handbook has provided principles as culled from the literature and related to the 1966 *Statement on Government of Colleges and Universities*. In the second chapter a not so random sample of recent constitutional documents has been surveyed, which reflect, to some extent at least and perhaps only on "paper," these same principles. In the present chapter model constitutional provisions are suggested as they have occurred to the present writer on the basis of his experiences with principle and practice. These model provisions are subjective in style as well as content; they may not be suitable at all for a particular campus – nor, perhaps, for any campus when the evidence of empirical work has been gathered.

The models face a perennial problem of academic constitutions, "ideal" or real: a university's constitutional document does not, and probably should not, depict all the actual relationships among the components. Numerous boards of trustees no longer insist on exercising their "final" or "legal" powers; many presidents leave academic decisions to faculty organs. Yet, trustees' and presidents' powers are usually surrendered only informally or *de facto*; a kind of academic natural law of inter-component relationships has indeed developed, but its contents are not supposed to be codified – and may, in fact, survive only if not put in writing. Since the models are intended to be applicable in real colleges and universities, their language may not violate these tabus of inter-component relationships; nevertheless, an attempt has been made to reflect the unwritten academic law as closely as feasible in the written constitutional texts proposed here. As was discussed in the first chapter, the relations among the four components should be based on a "co-sovereign" power structure without hierarchical overtones and without a "supreme" or "final" decision-maker. It is this kind of structure, undoubtedly existing *de facto* in many academic institutions, which may not be depicted in entirely clear constitutional language even in model codes.

Another problem of constitutional model-building will become abundantly obvious to the reader of the following pages: precise numerical suggestions – for example, membership distribution in a university senate – can hardly satisfy all the requirements of the great variety of institutions. Yet, numerical suggestions are put forward here to convey the author's best guess about the needs of a particular situation. While there is obviously nothing sacrosanct about these numbers, it may be useful to provide one person's estimate of the most appropriate ratios and percentages in various situations of academic government.

Certain major questions pertaining to constitutional arrangements will not be resolved in the present chapter – particularly not the debate between those favoring a "mixed" or all-component senate and those preferring a "pure" or faculty-only senate. The two types of senates will be presented as possible alternatives, with references to appropriate discussion and materials in the previous chapters. Also, the emphasis here on "centralist" university-wide senates should not necessarily be taken as reflecting the present author's lack of appreciation for the intermediate levels of academic governance, the liberal arts colleges and professional schools within universities. While the autonomy of the departments appears today as secure as ever, the recent trend has indeed been the establishment of central, representative senates. Yet, many institutions may prefer more decentralized forms of governance than are suggested here, with much greater emphasis on the autonomy and jurisdictions of the colleges and schools. Finally, the suggestions pertaining to student participation are not very specific on such points as student voting rights or modes and proportions of student representation; in fact, several of the provisions for students, as presented below, resemble a delineation of principles rather than working provisions. No attempt is made to incorporate into the governmental structure of the university adaptions to inputs of physical force on the part of "student power" activists.

1. The Board of Trustees: Delegation of Authority to Administration, Faculty, and Students

a. State University

For the proper use of the funds appropriated by the legislature and for the proper administration and government of the university, the board of trustees is responsible to the people of this state. In exercising its jurisdiction over the university and believing that the attainment of the highest academic objectives requires mutual trust and joint effort of the four components of the university, the board shall delegate authority to the president and the other administrative officers, to the faculty, and the students. Thus, when acting on matters having to do with educational policy and organization of the university, the board shall rely upon the advice of bodies of the faculty, and, when acting on matters concerning administrative policy and organization, the board shall act on the advice of the president and other administrative officers. Or, for both educational and administrative policy, the board shall accept the advice of the senate and other bodies representing the administration, faculty, and students.

The powers of review or final decision lodged in the board will be exercised adversely to received recommendations only in exceptional circumstances, and for reasons communicated in some detail to the persons or body where the advice originated. Before rejecting a faculty recommendation, the board will refer the matter back to the faculty for further consideration, with a statement of its objections.

b. Private University

The board is the legal repository of authority yet it is prepared to undertake appropriate self-limitation, believing that the attainment of the highest academic objectives requires mutual trust and joint effort of the four components of the university. Thus, the board shall entrust the conduct of administration to the president and the deans, and the conduct of teaching and research to the faculty, or all of these tasks to bodies representing the administration, faculty, and students. The board's responsibility for long-range planning shall be carried out together with the administration and the faculty.

The powers of review or final decision lodged in the board will be exercised adversely to received recommendations only in exceptional circumstances, and for reasons communicated in some detail to the person or body where the policy or action originated. Before rejecting a faculty recommendation, the board will refer the matter back to the faculty for further consideration, with a statement of its objections.

2. *Special Devices of Communication Between the Board of Trustees and the Faculty and Students*

a. Mixed Committees

Mixed committees shall be established in the areas of educational policy, faculty affairs, and student affairs. Each of the mixed committees shall consist of trustees, the president and other officers of administration, elected faculty members, and elected student members. The mixed committees shall advise the board or any other body of the university on matters brought forward by any of the components of the university.

b. Special Selection of Board Members

A certain proportion of board members (e.g., 25%) shall be selected jointly by the board and the executive committee of the senate or any other such body representing the administration, the faculty, and the students. The terms of these board members shall be limited (e.g., to six years).

c. Special Board Membership of Faculty and Students

Some elected faculty members (e.g., three) and students (e.g., two) shall participate as non-voting (or voting) members in meetings of the board. (*Or*, some prominent faculty members from neighboring institutions shall serve as [non-voting] members of the board.)

3. *The President: Cooperation with the Faculty*

The president shall rely on the faculty for formulating, in part or in whole, the policy for the academic government of the institution. In carrying out his duties, the president shall consult with the faculty at an early stage in policy formulation and shall communicate to the board all the recommendations of the faculty which concern the welfare of the university.

4. *Selection of Administration Officers*

Major academic officers of the institution shall be appointed only after joint approval by the administration and agencies representing the faculty and students.

5. Description of Faculty Authority

The faculty is granted primary responsibility for decisions in the areas of curriculum, degree requirements, subject matter and methods of instruction, research, faculty status, and those aspects of student life which relate to the educational process. The board and president will concur with faculty judgment in these areas except in exceptional circumstances and for compelling reasons which will be stated in detail. In other areas – particularly in the determination of policies and procedures governing salary, long-range planning, physical plant, and general allocation of resources – the faculty shall act with the administration through agencies for faculty participation to be established at all levels of decision-making.

6. Faculty Authority at the System-Level

The system-senate is the voice of the faculties of the system's institutions in matters of system-wide concern – such as general educational policy and curricular matters; general requirements for admission and degrees; allocation of system-wide educational resources; establishment and location of new units; advice to the chancellor on system-wide and local administrative appointments. The system-senate shall also provide a forum for the interchange of ideas concerning all matters of mutual interest to the faculties of the system's institutions.

Actions of the system-senate may be challenged by a call for a referendum by the senates of at least one-third of the system's institutions, or by 40% of the votes in the system-senate. Approval of the actions so challenged shall require a majority of the votes cast by the faculty members in the system.

The system-senate shall have jurisdiction, subject to the above provision for referendum, concerning only those matters which substantially affect more than one institution of the system. In the development of the necessary system-wide policies the diversity and autonomy of the separate institutions shall be preserved. The system-senate shall have no jurisdiction over matters delegated to the individual institutions; the senates of these institutions are authorized to originate and take final action on matters substantially affecting only the institution, and their right to communicate directly with the chancellor and trustees of the system is guaranteed.

7. *Coordinating Mechanisms at the System Level*

a. Mixed Committees

An executive committee shall be instituted consisting of members of the system's board of trustees, the system's chancellor and the presidents of the system's units, and as many proportionally elected faculty members as there are trustees and administrators on this committee. This committee shall serve in an advisory capacity concerning matters substantially affecting the system and its institutions.

A budget committee shall be authorized to confer with the system's chancellor on general policy concerning the system's budget and to review and advise on the standards and policies applied by the budget committees of the individual institutions in the system. The committee shall consist of representatives of the system's trustees and administration and of elected faculty members.

A coordinating committee on graduate programs shall advise on basic policies and procedures for coordinating the work of the various graduate faculties, such as the introduction of new M.A. and Ph.D. programs, minimum standards of admission for new students, and support of research. The committee shall consist of representatives of the system's chancellor, the deans of the system's graduate faculties, and elected faculty members.

b. Joint Departmental Conference Committees

Conference committees – one for each department or groups of related departments at each campus of the system – shall serve in an advisory capacity to the various departments on each campus of the system on major matters of policy and standards affecting the entire system, so as to provide for parallel development and mutually beneficial coordination of the activities of departments of the same or related disciplines at each campus.

8. *Role of the General Faculty Assembly*

The general faculty assembly is charged with the fundamental responsibility for the formulation, revision, and continuous review of educational policy, a responsibility which may be delegated in part to the senate. The trustees or the administration shall make no alterations in the educational policy of the institution without a prior and full review by the general faculty assembly or its delegate, the senate.

Subject to the authority of the board of trustees and in consultation with the president, the general faculty assembly shall have the general power and responsibility to adopt policies, regulations, and procedures intended to achieve the educational objectives of the university and the general welfare of those involved in these educational processes.

9. Review of Senate Actions by the General Faculty Assembly

Except where the senate has been granted final authority by delegation from the general faculty assembly, the general faculty assembly has the right of review over senate actions. Matters considered by the senate shall be reported to the membership of the general faculty assembly. They may be reviewed, overruled, or otherwise considered by the general faculty assembly in one of two ways: first, through submission to the general faculty assembly for its consideration (by a majority vote of the senate), or, secondly, through a petition for a meeting of the general faculty assembly signed by at least 15% of the members. This petition shall explicitly state the matter(s) to be the subject of the petitioned meeting.

10. Veto of General Faculty Assembly Actions by the President

If an action of the general faculty assembly is vetoed by the president, and if this action is then passed again by a $\frac{2}{3}$ vote in the general faculty assembly, the issue may be taken to the board of trustees for a consultative session at which the president and elected representatives from the assembly shall be heard.

11. The General Faculty Assembly: Membership

The membership of the general faculty assembly shall consist of all professors and instructors; the professors emeriti and visiting professors; the president, vice-presidents, the provost, academic deans, directors of schools, the dean of students; and other persons concerned with policy making in the university, but only if admitted to membership by the general faculty assembly, upon individual nomination by the senate.

Instructors (but not teaching assistants or teaching fellows) who are candidates for advanced degrees in the university shall be members of the general faculty assembly, but shall be ineligible to participate in actions regarding requirements for advanced degrees.

Military officers in R.O.T.C. departments shall be nonvoting members of the general faculty assembly.

12. The General Faculty Assembly: Officers

Chairman – the president of the institution
Vice-chairman – an elected faculty member
Secretary – an elected faculty member (assisted by appropriate secretarial staff)
Parliamentarian – an elected faculty member
The officers who are faculty members shall be elected by the general faculty assembly. The vice-chairman shall preside when the chairman is absent or when the chairman desires to participate actively in the debate on the floor.

13. The General Faculty Assembly: Procedures

a. Regular Meetings
If a general faculty assembly has more than 400 members, and the institution has a senate: at least once per academic year;

if a general faculty assembly has from 100–400 members and the institution has a senate: at least twice per academic year;

if a general faculty assembly has from 100–400 members and the institution does not have a senate: at least four times per year;

if a general faculty assembly has fewer than 100 members: at least six times per academic year. (No senate is needed in such institutions.)

b. Special Meetings
Special meetings of the general faculty assembly may be called by the president, or if 10% of the membership so desires, or if 10% of the membership of the senate so desires.

c. Quorum Rule
If the general faculty assembly has more than 200 members:
15% of the membership;
if the general faculty assembly has fewer than 200 members;
25% of the membership.

d. Voting Rules
normally by voice vote
division vote (show of hands or standing) – if one member so requests
secret vote (written ballot) – if 10% of the members present so request.

e. Reporting at Meetings
Reporters of the campus news media may attend meetings of the general faculty assembly; they may be barred from a particular meeting or portion thereof if a majority of the members present and voting desire to go into executive session.

14. Role of the Senate

a. General Principles
The senate shall have general legislative authority over educational matters concerning the university as a whole, as delegated to it by the general faculty assembly and other components of the university. This authority shall not extend over the internal affairs of a single institute, college, or school of collegiate rank, except where these affect the interests of the university as a whole or the interests of other institutes, colleges, or schools.

b. Subjects of Primary Senate Jurisdiction–Educational Policy
(1) standards for admission, selection, and retention applicable to all students of the university
(2) requirements for granting of degrees applicable to all students of the university
(3) curricular requirements
(4) instructional standards throughout the university
(5) promotion and facilitation of academic and instructional research
(6) procedures for faculty participation in the selection and retention of chairmen of departments and divisions, deans of colleges and schools, vice-presidents, the provost, and the president

(7) standards for public information programs dealing with educational matters
(8) standards of academic freedom and faculty status throughout the university
(9) appointment, promotion, tenure, and dismissal of faculty members
(10) standards of due process for student affairs.

c. Subjects of Joint Senate Jurisdiction (Shared with Other Bodies) – Institutional Policy
  (1) selection and removal of the president and principal academic officers having university-wide responsibilities as well as the creation or abolition of such offices
  (2) expenditures of funds allocated to instruction and academic or instructionally-related research
  (3) major issues affecting current or projected budget decisions
  (4) programs of faculty welfare such as salaries, insurance, and special leave
  (5) long-range master plans for the physical development of the university
  (6) policies to govern the university's relations with outside agencies for research, instruction, and related purposes
  (7) policies for cooperative and mutually beneficial relations with the neighboring community.

15. Senate – Role of Board of Trustees

The board of trustees' concurrence is necessary for those of the senate's acts which, directly or indirectly, involve a change in budgetary allocations, or the acquisition or disposition of real property, or which affect contractual obligations of the university.

The board will concur with decisions of the senate in the area of educational policy, except in exceptional circumstances and for compelling reasons. In the other areas of senate jurisdiction the board will consult with the senate and attempt to reach consensus before reaching a decision different from that of the senate. Whenever the board finds it necessary to disagree with the senate, it will provide a detailed statement of its position. Before rejecting a senate recommendation, the board will refer the matter back to the senate for further consideration, with a statement of its objections.

16. Senate – Role of the President

Whenever the president does not concur with an action of the senate, he may ask the senate to reconsider its action at the next regular meeting. If the senate maintains its original position, the issue may be taken to the board of trustees for a consultative session at which the president and elected representatives from the senate shall be heard.

17. Senate – Review by the General Faculty Assembly

(See #9 above).

18. Senate – Conflict with Colleges, Schools, and Departments

In the event of a dispute between the senate and a college, school, or department as to whether a proposed senate action would improperly affect one of these bodies' jurisdiction, the president shall make a ruling on the disputed issue after consultation with the Committee on University Government and the senate's Executive Committee.

19. Senate Membership Distribution ("Mixed" or University Senate) [1]

a. Small College
   15 faculty members elected by the faculty:
      6 at large
      9 from the academic divisions
   5 student members elected by the student body
   3 administration members.

b. Medium-Size or Large University
   Total membership: 50–80
   Faculty: 60% of members (including 10–15% non-tenured)
   Students: 18% (including undergraduates, graduate students, and professional students)
   Administration: 18%

---

[1] Note the discussion in Chapter 1 (pp. 73–75) on the advantages of "mixed" senates. Examples of institutions with "mixed" senates are cited in Chapter 2 (pp. 135–142).

Staff: 4% (including library, research, and administrative staff).

20. Senate Membership Distribution ("Pure" or Faculty Senate)[2]

The membership of the faculty senate shall consist of elected faculty members. The president, vice-presidents, and deans (including associate and assistant deans) who hold professorial rank are ineligible even if their administration appointment is on a part-time basis only.

In small colleges the senate shall consist of 20 faculty members, with up to 50% of the members elected at large and the remainder elected from the academic divisions, while one or two seats shall be reserved for non-tenured faculty members. In medium-size or large universities the faculty senate's optimum size is 50–60 faculty members, 10% of whom shall be non-tenured.

21. Senate Members' Constituencies

a. Faculty

Faculty senators shall be elected by constituencies composed of faculty members who are most likely to know them personally, i.e. groups of departments and schools. There shall be at least one senator from each college or school, and as many as are approximately proportional to the number of faculty members in the school or college. In small colleges, some of the faculty senators shall be elected at large.

b. Students

Graduate students: to be elected from their departments or groups of departments

Professional students: to be elected from their schools

Undergraduates: one-half to be elected from their departments or groups of departments; one-half from residential units on the campus. (Or, to be elected from the undergraduate organs of student government by the members of these organs.)

c. 40% Rule

A minimum of 40% of the eligible voters must have voted in a constituency during the election for a particular senate seat.

---

[2] Note the discussion in Chapter 1 (pp. 73–75) on the disadvantages of "pure" senates. Examples of institutions with "pure" senates are cited in Chapter 2 (pp. 135–142).

If fewer than 40% of the eligible voters voted, the seat shall remain vacant until another election can be held.

d. Terms of Senate Members

Faculty members of the senate shall be elected for a three-year term, with re-election possible for one consecutive term; if a division has more than one representative, terms shall be staggered. Student members shall be elected for a one-year term, with re-election possible for one consecutive term.

e. Full Affiliation Rule

To be eligible for voting for senators or for being elected a senator, a faculty member or student must be in full-time status at the institution. The concept of "full affiliation" may be used to determine the full-time status of a faculty member.

Full affiliation defines the relationship of an individual with the university when the individual makes the university the principal center of his educational and professional effort, and university affairs primarily determine the employment of his time and talents. A fully affiliated member of the university may engage in other professional activities on a limited basis, but his major work is conducted under the auspices of the university.

Partial affiliation denotes the status of individuals who devote a part of their professional effort to the university. The remainder of their activity may be directed to study at the pre- or post-doctoral level, to professional activity in other institutions or outside agencies, or to the pursuit of non-university interests.

22. Senate Officers

Chairman: the president of the institution (in the "pure" senate: an elected faculty member)
Vice-chairman: an elected faculty member
Secretary: an elected faculty member
Parliamentarian: an elected faculty member

The officers who are faculty members shall be elected by the senate from among its own members. The vice-chairman shall preside whenever the chairman is absent or when the chairman desires to participate actively in the debate on the floor.

23. *Secretary's Council* ("Mixed" Senate)

The secretary, as the most important faculty officer of the senate, shall chair the Secretary's Council, composed of himself and five senators elected by the senate (including one administration representative, one student, and three faculty representatives from three different divisions of the university). The Secretary's Council

(1) shall prepare the agenda of the senate in consultation with the chairman

(2) shall plan the apportionment, staggering, and elections for the elective senate seats

(3) shall propose for approval by the senate appropriate methods for determining who qualifies as a full-time faculty member for the purpose of election, and for that purpose only

(4) shall propose for approval by the senate appropriate methods for the nomination and election of student senators, after due consultation with the relevant organs of student government

(5) shall maintain a master copy of the constitution and other rules of the senate kept up to date by incorporation of new legislation and amendments, and edit these for distribution to the university community.

24. *Senate Procedures*

a. Regular Meetings

On fixed day, once per month during the academic year, for at least three hours.

b. Special Meetings

When requested by 25% of the senate, or 10% of the total faculty, or 10% of the student body, or by the president, or by the Secretary's Council.

c. Quorum: 50% of the members plus one.

d. Voting Rules

normally by voice vote

division vote (show of hands or standing) – if one member so requests

secret vote (written ballot) – if 10% of the members present so request roll call vote (recorded by name) – if a majority of the members present so request.

e. Non-Members' Presence at Meetings

Senate meetings shall be open only to members and those invited by the chairman or the secretary for a particular meeting. Reporters of campus news media may attend unless a majority of the members present desire to go into executive session for the entire session or a portion thereof.[3]

f. Distribution of Minutes

Detailed minutes of the proceedings and content of the debates shall be distributed by the secretary's staff, preferably to all students and faculty.

25. List of Senate Committees [4]

Committee on Committees
Executive Committee
Committee on Educational Policy
Committee on Budget Review
Committee on Physical Development of the University
Committees on Faculty Status (Committee on Professional Standards and Academic Freedom; Judicial Committee; Grievance Committee)
Committee on Student Affairs
Committee on External Relations and Research Policy
Committee on Community Relations
Committee on Rules of University Conduct
Committee on University Facilities and Services
Committee on the Libraries
President's Advisory Committee

---

[3] Note the examples in Chapter 2 of senates with restrictions on attendance by non-members – and the more numerous examples of senates with more or less "open-door" policies for visitors from the university community (pp.145–146). The present author believes that the intimacy of the club-like "closed" senate will make for greater legislative effectiveness – although the "open" senate may have advantages in the sphere of public relations and may also produce greater knowledge of university government. In any case, the presence of the student press should be encouraged, since representation of the component with by far the largest number of bodies on the campus is likely to remain minimal in senates. Also, invitations for persons with a great interest in a particular senate meeting should be obtainable through the chairman or the secretary.

[4] This list of committees would be appropriate also for a general faculty assembly.

Committee on University Government (advisory to Executive Committee)

Secretary's Council (see #23, above).

26. Committee on Committees

The Committee on Committees shall have the following responsibilities:

(1) to recommend appropriate persons for all committee appointments to be made by the senate

(2) to make a continuous study of the distribution of committee assignments to assure equitable distribution among the colleges, other academic units, and academic ranks

(3) to recommend the formation or abolition of committees

(4) to appoint a committee each year to nominate a slate of senate officers.

27. Executive Committee

a. General Functions

The Executive Committee of the senate shall be the committee primarily responsible for the participation of the faculty and students in university government. Its main responsibilities shall be to assist the senate in the discharge of its legislative duties and to provide an effective channel of communications and consultation between the president and the faculty and students with respect to their joint and several responsibilities in the government of the university.

b. Specific Functions

The Executive Committee:

(1) shall make recommendations to the senate concerning proposed legislative actions

(2) may request such reports from the committees as it deems appropriate

(3) shall transmit to the senate all committee reports as received and shall recommend appropriate action

(4) may transmit to the senate for its consideration and action any resolution relating to the general welfare of the university and its faculty

(5) shall interpret, after consultation with the Committee on University Government, the provisions of the constitution on matters other than those within the jurisdiction of the Committees of Faculty Status

(6) shall act for the senate during the period from the last senate meeting in the spring until the first meeting in the autumn, and shall report such actions at the first senate meeting in autumn. (Unless a Summer Committee is appointed; see below, #28.)

c. Composition
11 members (6 faculty senators, 2 administration members, 2 student senators, and the president).

28. Summer Committee

Composed of no fewer than six elected members of the senate, if possible all from the executive committee, the Summer Committee shall be available on an emergency basis during the months of June, July, and August for consultation, calling of special senate meetings, and handling of such duties as may be delegated to it by the senate.

29. Committee on Budget Review

a. Function
The Committee on Budget Review shall review the annual budget of the university to assure its general conformity with short-range and long-range priorities of the university and expressions of policy by the senate. The chairman of the Committee or his designee shall sit with the appropriate committee of the administration when it formulates its budget policy guidelines for the coming year and when categories of the budget are discussed or adopted. The Committee shall report its activities to the senate and shall bring to its attention any instances of noncompliance of the budget with existing priorities or policies and any other allocations which in the Committee's opinion are not in the best interests of the university.

b. Composition
8 members (3 administration members, 4 faculty senators, 1 student senator).

30. Committees on Faculty Status

a. General Policy
The *Committee on Professional Standards and Academic Freedom* shall be concerned with general policy on appoint-

ments, promotions, dismissals, tenure, sabbatical leaves, and all policy matters relating to professional standards and ethics. The Committee shall have seven members who must be tenured faculty members; some of these shall be elected from particular academic areas, and others at large.

b. Hearing Committee

The *Judicial Committee* shall hold hearings on charges in dismissal proceedings and on charges of misconduct concerning an individual faculty member. The findings and judgment of the Committee will be reversed by the president or the board only in exceptional circumstances, and for compelling reasons communicated to the Committee in some detail. Seven tenured faculty members and two such alternates shall be elected to this Committee by the faculty, on nominations made by the Committee on Professional Standards and Academic Freedom. The members shall serve five year terms on a staggered basis, and may not be members of the Committee on Professional Standards and Academic Freedom. The Committee shall elect its own chairman and secretary.

c. Grievance Committee

The *Grievance Committee* shall receive a petition from any faculty member who feels that he has cause for grievance in any matter other than dismissal proceedings – such matters as salaries, assignment of teaching duties, assignment of space or other facilities, and propriety of conduct. The petition shall set forth in detail the nature of the grievance, shall state against whom the grievance is directed, and shall contain any factual or other data which the petitioner deems pertinent to his case. The Committee will have the right to decide whether or not the facts merit a detailed investigation. Submission of a petition will not automatically entail investigation or detailed consideration thereof. The Committee may seek to bring about a settlement of the issue satisfactory to the parties. If in the opinion of the Committee such a settlement is not possible or is not appropriate, the Committee will report its findings and recommendations to the petitioner and to the appropriate administrative officer and faculty body, and the petitioner will, at his request, be provided an opportunity to present his case to them. Seven tenured faculty members and two such alternates shall be elected to this Committee by the faculty, on nominations made by the Committee on Professional Standards and Academic Freedom.

31. Committee on Student Affairs

"Pure": 11 students, elected from departmental and residential constituencies;
  or, "mixed": 6 faculty, 7 students, 3 administration.

32. President's Faculty Advisory Committee

The President's Faculty Advisory Committee shall consist of six faculty members, elected by the faculty representatives in the senate from their own group. The Committee's purpose is to advise the president of the university upon matters of university policy, particularly when subjects of great urgency or delicacy require immediate consultation. No formal votes shall be taken at such consultations, nor shall the Committee take any action that might commit the general faculty assembly, the senate, or any of their committees.

33. Committee on University Government

In addition to rendering advisory opinions for the Executive Committee on interpretations of the instruments of university government, the Committee on University Government shall perform the following functions:
(1) draft proposed additions to or amendments of university regulations at the request of the senate or the general faculty assembly or of any committee or member of the senate
(2) be available for consultation upon the meaning of the university regulations or upon the status of existing rules governing any situation
(3) recommend revision or clarification of university regulations.

34. College Autonomy

A college within a university has the fullest measure of autonomy consistent with the maintenance of general university educational policy and correct academic and administrative relations with other divisions of the university. In questions of doubt concerning the proper limits of this autonomy between the college and the senate or the general faculty assembly, the college shall be entitled to appeal for a ruling to the president, who shall make his decision after consultation with the Committee on University Government and the senate's Executive Committee.

35. College Functions

College jurisdiction is subject to the senate or the general faculty assembly if the general welfare of the university is affected or for purposes of coordination of the various colleges. Within these limits, the faculty assembly of the college shall, with respect to academic matters,
(1) determine its requirements for admission and graduation
(2) determine its curriculum and academic programs
(3) determine the scholastic standards required of its students
(4) recommend to the board of trustees those of its students who qualify for university degrees
(5) exercise the additional powers necessary to provide adequate instruction and supervision of its students.

36. Procedures of the Faculty Assembly of the College

a. Regular Meetings: 3 to 4 times per academic year
b. Special Meetings: if 10% of the members so request
c. Quorum: $\frac{1}{3}$ of the members.

37. College Committees

Academic Performance Committee
Admissions Committee
Committee on Committees
Curriculum Committee
Executive Committee
Financial Aid Committee
Honors Programs Committee
Petitions Committee
Promotions and Tenure Committee
Registration Committee.

38. Department – Functions

The department is the primary unit of education and administration within the university. It is established for the purpose of carrying on programs of instruction and research in a particular field of knowledge. The department has the fullest measure of autonomy consistent with the maintenance of general college and university educational policy and correct academic and administrative relations with other divisions of the university. Should a dispute arise between the department and another unit of the university concerning the proper limits of this autonomy, the department may appeal for a ruling directly to the dean and the executive committee of the college and, in final instance, to the president, who shall make a decision after consultation with the Committee on University Government.

The department has primary responsibility for initiating and making recommendations on all matters relating to:

(1) selection, retention, and promotion of personnel
(2) development and improvement of the departmental curriculum, both graduate and undergraduate
(3) budget of the department
(4) growth and standards of the department in teaching and research.

39. Department – Membership

a. Voting

All full-time faculty with tenure, or those appointed with expectancy of tenure.

b. Non-voting

All other teachers in the department, including temporary instructors but not teaching assistants.

40. Department – Appointment of the Chairman

The chairman of a department, who serves as the chief representative of his department within an institution, shall be selected either by departmental election or by appointment following consultation with members of the department and of related departments; appointments shall normally be in conformity with department members' judgment. The chairman or department head shall not have tenure in his office; his tenure as a faculty member is a matter of separate right. He shall serve for a stated term but without prejudice to re-election or to reappointment by procedures which involve appropriate faculty consultation. Board, administration, and faculty will all bear in mind that the department chairman has a special obligation to build a department strong in scholarship and teaching capacity.

41. Department – Restrictions on the Powers of the Chairman

The departmental faculty, acting as a group, shall decide such matters as:
(1) recommending appointments of new staff members
(2) recommending tenure of faculty
(3) recommending policies and procedures as to promotions and salary increases, teaching loads, curricula, coordination with other departments, and, in general, matters of policy concerning the work of the department.

42. Department – Committees

Promotions and Tenure
Budget and Faculty
Graduate Studies
Undergraduate Studies
Multi-Sectional Courses
(The last three committees shall have student members).

43. Department – Student Participation

Each department shall hold annual elections among the graduate students and majors, respectively, to elect graduate student representatives and undergraduate representatives who shall meet regularly with the respective committees for graduate or undergraduate studies, and at times with other committees. The graduate student representatives shall also attend the major portions of departmental meetings – those at which individual members of the faculty or matters pertaining to individual students are not discussed.

44. Student Participation – Regulation of Personal Lives

Students shall have primary responsibility for the formulation of clear and readily available regulations pertaining to their personal lives, subject only to such restrictions as may be imposed by law. These regulations may be overruled only in exceptional circumstances and for compelling reasons stated in detail.

45. *Student Participation – Extracurricular Activities*

Students shall have primary responsibility for activities sponsored by the student body. Appropriate persons and groups from the other components shall be consulted with respect to these activities, but student action in this sphere may be overruled only in exceptional circumstances and for compelling reasons stated in detail. Among these activities are cultural programs, political programs, and student publications.

46. *Student Participation – Student Discipline*

Students shall have the opportunity to participate actively in establishing standards and procedures which govern student discipline, and take part prominently in the actual disciplinary process. Disciplinary proceedings shall be in accordance with the provisions of the *Joint Statement on Rights and Freedoms of Students*.

47. *Student Participation – The Academic Experience*

a. Courses and Staff

Students shall have the opportunity, through established institutional mechanisms, to assess the value of a course to them, and to make suggestions as to its direction. Students shall also be able to express their views on the form and conduct of a class which they have taken, for example through an evaluative questionnaire prepared by joint faculty-student effort, and their opinions shall be weighed in faculty decisions affecting faculty status. (The faculty member, of course, shall be duly protected from capricious and uninformed judgment by students, just as he shall be from such judgment by anyone else.)

b. Evaluation of Students

The method by which students are evaluated is properly of concern to them. Accordingly, students shall be heard with respect to the grading system at an institution. They shall also have clearly established means of recourse against prejudiced or capricious grading.

c. Academic Arrangements and Services

The scheduling of courses, class size, distribution of night and day classes, calendar arrangements, library policy and development, and similar academic arrangements and services affect the ability of students to do academic work. They shall share in the formation of policies on these matters.

48. Student Participation – The Academic Environment

a. Admissions

Since students are directly affected by the size, composition, and quality of the student body, they shall have the opportunity to present their views on admissions.

b. Academic Programs

Students shall be consulted in decisions regarding the development of existing programs and the establishment of new programs. They shall have the opportunity to present their views with respect to course load and degree requirements.

c. Other Institutional Concerns

Students shall have the opportunity to present their views on questions involving the institution's budget, its physical resources, and its relationship with groups or agencies external to the campus.

49. Constitution – Adoption

A new constitution shall be adopted through procedures which reflect the approval of the student body, the faculty, the administration, and the board.

50. Constitution – Amendment

Amendments to the constitution shall be approved by a two-thirds majority vote in the senate, at a regular or special meeting, provided the proposed amendment has been submitted in writing to each member of the senate and to each faculty member and student entitled to vote for members of the senate at least 20 days prior to the date of the vote on the approval of the proposed amendment. After the approval in the senate such amendments shall be submitted in writing to those faculty members and students entitled to vote for members of the senate and, unless disapproved by at least one-third of such members within 30 days by written vote, shall be submitted to the board of trustees for final approval.

STATEMENT ON GOVERNMENT OF
COLLEGES AND UNIVERSITIES
(as published in the *AAUP Bulletin*, Winter 1966)

Editorial Note. The Statement which follows is directed to governing board members, administrators, faculty members students and other persons in the belief that the colleges and universities of the United States have reached a stage calling for appropriately shared responsibility and cooperative action among the components of the academic institution. The Statement is intended to foster constructive joint thought and action, both within the institutional structure and in protection of its integrity against improper intrusions.

It is not intended that the Statement serve as a blueprint for government on a specific campus or as a manual for the regulation of controversy among the components of an academic institution, although it is to be hoped that the principles asserted will lead to the correction of existing weaknesses and assist in the establishment of sound structure and procedures. The Statement does not attempt to cover relations with those outside agencies which increasingly are controlling the resources and influencing the patterns of education in our institutions of higher learning; e.g., the United States Government, the state legislatures, state commissions, interstate associations or compacts and other institutional arrangements. However it is hoped that the Statement will be helpful to these agencies in their consideration of educational matters.

Students are referred to in this Statement as an institutional component coordinate in importance with trustees, administrators and faculty. There is, however, no main section on students. The omission has two causes: (1) the changes now occurring in the status of American students have plainly outdistanced the analysis by the educational community, and an attempt to define the situation without thorough study might prove unfair to student interests,[1] and (2) students do not in fact presently have a significant

---

[1] Note: 1950, the formulation of the *Student Bill of Rights* by the United States National Student Association; 1956, the first appearance of *Academic Freedom and Civil Liberties of Students*, published by the American Civil Liberties Union;

voice in the government of colleges and universities; it would be unseemly to obscure, by superficial equality of length of statement, what may be a serious lag entitled to separate and full confrontation. The concern for student status felt by the organizations issuing this Statement is embodied in a note "On Student Status" intended to stimulate the educational community to turn its attention to an important need.

This Statement, in preparation since 1964, is jointly formulated by the American Association of University Professors, the American Council on Education, and the Association of Governing Boards of Universities and Colleges. On October 12, 1966, the Board of Directors of the ACE took action by which the Council "recognizes the Statement as a significant step forward in the clarification of the respective roles of governing boards, faculties, and administrations," and "commends it to the institutions which are members of the Council." On October 29, 1966, the Council of the AAUP approved the Statement, recommended approval by the Fifty-Third Annual Meeting in April, 1967,[2] and recognized that "continuing joint effort is desirable, in view of the areas left open in the jointly formulated Statement, and the dynamic changes occurring in higher education." On November 18, 1966, the Executive Committee of the AGB took action by which that organization also "recognizes the Statement as a significant step forward in the clarification of the respective roles of governing boards, faculties and administrations," and "commends it to the governing boards which are members of the Association."

I. INTRODUCTION

This Statement is a call to mutual understanding regarding the government of colleges and universities. Understanding, based on community of interest, and producing joint effort, is essential for at least three reasons. First, the academic institution, public or private, often has become less autonomous; buildings, research, and student tuition are supported by funds over which the college or university exercises a diminishing control. Legislative and executive governmental authority, at all levels, plays a part in the making of important decisions in academic

1961, the decision in *Dixon v. Alabama State Board of Education,* currently the leading case on due process for students; 1965, the publication of a tentative *Statement on the Academic Freedom of Students,* by the American Association of University Professors.

[2] Approval took place.

policy. If these voices and forces are to be successfully heard and integrated, the academic institution must be in a position to meet them with its own generally unified view. Second, regard for the welfare of the institution remains important despite the mobility and interchange of scholars. Third, a college or university in which all the components are aware of their interdependence, of the usefulness of communication among themselves, and of the force of joint action will enjoy increased capacity to solve educational problems.

II. THE ACADEMIC INSTITUTION: JOINT EFFORT

A. Preliminary Considerations

The variety and complexity of the tasks performed by institutions of higher education produce an inescapable interdependence among governing board, administration, faculty, students and others. The relationship calls for adequate communication among these components, and full opportunity for appropriate joint planning and effort.

Joint effort in an academic institution will take a variety of forms appropriate to the kinds of situations encountered. In some instances, an initial exploration or recommendation will be made by the president with consideration by the faculty at a later stage; in other instances, a first and essentially definitive recommendation will be made by the faculty, subject to the endorsement of the president and the governing board. In still others, a substantive contribution can be made when student leaders are responsibly involved in the process. Although the variety of such approaches may be wide, at least two general conclusions regarding joint effort seem clearly warranted: (1) important areas of action involve at one time or another the initiating capacity and decision-making participation of all the institutional components, and (2) differences in the weight of each voice, from one point to the next, should be determined by reference to the responsibility of each component for the particular matter at hand, as developed hereinafter.

B. Determination of General Educational Policy

The general educational policy, i.e., the objectives of an institution and the nature, range, and pace of its efforts, is shaped by the institutional charter or by law, by tradition and historical development, by the present needs of the community of the institution, and by the professional aspirations and standards of those directly involved in its work. Every board will wish to go beyond its formal trustee obligation to conserve the accomplishment of the past and to engage seriously with the future; every faculty will seek to conduct an operation worthy of scholarly standards of learning; every administrative officer will strive to meet his charge and to attain the goals of the institution. The interests of all are coordinate and related, and unilateral effort can lead to confusion or conflict. Essential to a solution is a reasonably explicit statement on general educational policy. Operating responsibility and authority, and procedures for continuing review, should be clearly defined in official regulations.

When an educational goal has been established, it becomes the responsibility of the faculty to determine appropriate curriculum and procedures of student instruction.

Special considerations may require particular accommodations: (1) a publicly supported institution may be regulated by statutory provisions, and (2) a church-controlled institution may be limited by its charter or bylaws. When such external requirements influence course content and manner of instruction or research, they impair the educational effectiveness of the institution.

Such matters as major changes in the size or composition of the student body and the relative emphasis to be given to the various elements of the educational and research program should involve participation of governing board, administration and faculty prior to final decision.

C. Internal Operations of the Institution

The framing and execution of long-range plans, one of the most important aspects of institutional responsibility, should be a central and continuing concern in the academic community.

Effective planning demands that the broadest possible exchange of information and opinion should be the rule for communication among the components of a college or university. The channels of communication should be established and maintained by joint endeavor. Distinction should be observed between the institutional system of communication and the system of responsibility for the making of decisions.

A second area calling for joint effort in internal operations is that of decisions regarding existing or prospective physical resources. The board, president and faculty should all seek agreement on basic decisions regarding buildings and other facilities to be used in the educational work of the institution.

A third area is budgeting. The allocation of resources among competing demands is central in the formal responsibility of the governing board, in the administrative authority of the president, and in the educational function of the faculty. Each component should therefore have a voice in the determination of short and long-range priorities, and each should receive appropriate analyses of past budgetary experience, reports on current budgets and expenditures, and short and long-range budgetary projections. The function of each component in budgetary matters should be understood by all; the allocation of authority will determine the flow of information and the scope of participation in decisions.

Joint effort of a most critical kind must be taken when an institution chooses a new president. The selection of a chief administrative officer should follow upon cooperative search by the governing board and the faculty, taking into consideration the opinions of others who are appropriately interested. The president should be equally qualified to serve both as the executive officer of the governing board and as the chief academic officer of the institution and the faculty. His dual role requires that he be able to interpret to board and faculty the educational views and concepts of institutional government of the other. He should have the confidence of the board and the faculty.

The selection of academic deans and other chief academic officers should be the responsibility of the president with the advice of and in consultation with the appropriate faculty.

Determinations of faculty status, normally based on the recommendations of the faculty groups involved, are discussed in Part V of this Statement; but it should here be noted that the building of a strong faculty requires careful joint effort in such actions as staff selection and promotion and the granting of tenure. Joint action should also govern dismissals; the applicable principles and procedures in these matters are well established.[3]

_____

[3] See the 1940 *Statement of Principles on Academic Freedom and Tenure* and the 1958 *Statement on Procedural Standards in Faculty Dismissal Proceedings*. These

D. *External Relations of the Institution*

Anyone – a member of the governing board, the president or other member of the administration, a member of the faculty, or a member of the student body or the alumni – affects the institution when he speaks of it in public. An individual who speaks unofficially should so indicate. An official spokesman for the institution, the board, the administration, the faculty, or the student body should be guided by established policy.

It should be noted that only the board speaks legally for the whole institution, although it may delegate responsibility to an agent.

The right of a board member, an administrative officer, a faculty member, or a student to speak on general educational questions or about the administration and operations of his own institution is a part of his right as a citizen and should not be abridged by the institution.[4] There exist, of course, legal bounds relating to defamation of character, and there are questions of propriety.

III. THE ACADEMIC INSTITUTION: THE GOVERNING BOARD

The governing board has a special obligation to assure that the history of the college or university shall serve as a prelude and inspiration to the future. The board helps relate the institution to its chief community: e.g., the community college to serve the educational needs of a defined population area or

statements have been jointly approved or adopted by the Association of American Colleges and the American Association of University Professors; the 1940 Statement has been endorsed by numerous learned and scientific societies and educational associations.

[4] With respect to faculty members, the 1940 *Statement of Principles on Academic Freedom and Tenure* reads: "The college or university teacher is a citizen, a member of a learned profession, and an officer of an educational institution. When he speaks or writes as a citizen, he should be free from institutional censorship or discipline, but his special position in the community imposes special obligations. As a man of learning and an educational officer, he should remember that the public may judge his profession and his institution by his utterances. Hence he should at all times be accurate, should exercise appropriate restraint, should show respect for the opinion of others, and should make every effort to indicate that he is not an institutional spokesman."

group, the church-controlled college to be cognizant of the announced position of its denomination, and the comprehensive university to discharge the many duties and to accept the appropriate new challenges which are its concern at the several levels of higher education.

The governing board of an institution of higher education in the United States operates, with few exceptions, as the final institutional authority. Private institutions are established by charters; public institutions are established by constitutional or statutory provisions. In private institutions the board is frequently self-perpetuating; in public colleges and universities the present membership of a board may be asked to suggest candidates for appointment. As a whole and individually when the governing board confronts the problem of succession, serious attention should be given to obtaining properly qualified persons. Where public law calls for election of governing board members, means should be found to insure the nomination of fully suited persons, and the electorate should be informed of the relevant criteria for board membership.

Since the membership of the board may embrace both individual and collective competence of recognized weight, its advice or help may be sought through established channels by other components of the academic community. The governing board of an institution of higher education, while maintaining a general overview, entrusts the conduct of administration to the administrative officers, the president and the deans, and the conduct of teaching and research to the faculty. The board should undertake appropriate self-limitation.

One of the governing board's important tasks is to ensure the publication of codified statements that define the over-all policies and procedures of the institution under its jurisdiction.

The board plays a central role in relating the likely needs of the future to predictable resources; it has the responsibility for husbanding the endowment; it is responsible for obtaining needed capital and operating funds; and in the broadest sense of the term it should pay attention to personnel policy. In order to fulfill these duties, the board should be aided by, and may insist upon, the development of long-range planning by the administration and faculty.

When ignorance or ill-will threatens the institution or any part of it, the governing board must be available for support. In grave crises it will be expected to serve as a champion.

Although the action to be taken by it will usually be on behalf of the president, the faculty, or the student body, the board should make clear that the protection it offers to an individual or a group is, in fact, a fundamental defense of the vested interests of society in the educational institution.

IV. THE ACADEMIC INSTITUTION: THE PRESIDENT

The president, as the chief executive officer of an institution of higher education, is measured largely by his capacity for institutional leadership. He shares responsibility for the definition and attainment of goals, for administrative action, and for operating the communications system which links the components of the academic community. He represents his institution to its many publics. His leadership role is supported by delegated authority from the board and faculty.

As the chief planning officer of an institution, the president has a special obligation to innovate and initiate. The degree to which a president can envision new horizons for his institution, and can persuade others to see them and to work toward them, will often constitute the chief measure of his administration.

The president must at times, with or without support, infuse new life into a department; relatedly, he may at times be required, working within the concept of tenure, to solve problems of obsolescence. The president will necessarily utilize the judgments of the faculty, but in the interest of academic standards he may also seek outside evaluations by scholars of acknowledged competence.

It is the duty of the president to see to it that the standards and procedures in operational use within the college or university conform to the policy established by the governing board and to the standards of sound academic practice. It is also incumbent on the president to insure that faculty views, including dissenting views, are presented to the board in those areas and on those issues where responsibilities are shared. Similarly the faculty should be informed of the views of the board and the administration on like issues.

The president is largely responsible for the maintenance of existing institutional resources and the creation of new resources; he has ultimate managerial responsibility for a large area of nonacademic activities, he is responsible for public understanding, and by the nature of his office is the chief spokesman of his institution. In these and other areas his work is to plan, to organize, to direct, and to represent. The presidential function should receive the general support of board and faculty.

V. THE ACADEMIC INSTITUTION: THE FACULTY

The faculty has primary responsibility for such fundamental areas as curriculum, subject matter and methods of instruction, research, faculty status, and those aspects of student life which relate to the educational process. On these matters the power of review or final decision lodged in the governing board or delegated by it to the president should be exercised adversely only in exceptional circumstances, and for reasons communicated to the faculty. It is desirable that the faculty should, following such communication, have opportunity for further consideration and further transmittal of its views to the president or board. Budgets, manpower limitations, the time element and the policies of other groups, bodies and agencies having jurisdiction over the institution may set limits to realization of faculty advice.

The faculty sets the requirements for the degrees offered in course, determines when the requirements have been met, and authorizes the president and board to grant the degrees thus achieved.

Faculty status and related matters are primarily a faculty responsibility; this area includes appointments, reappointments, decisions not to reappoint, promotions, the granting of tenure, and dismissal. The primary responsibility of the faculty for such matters is based upon the fact that its judgment is central to general educational policy. Furthermore, scholars in a particular field or activity have the chief competence for judging the work of their colleagues; in such competence it is implicit that responsibility exists for both adverse and favorable judgments. Likewise there is the more general competence of experienced faculty personnel committees having a broader charge. Determinations in these matters should first be by faculty action through established procedures, reviewed by the chief academic officers with the concurrence of the board. The governing board and president should, on questions of faculty status, as in other matters where the faculty has primary responsibility, concur with the faculty judgment except in rare instances and for compelling reasons which should be stated in detail.

The faculty should actively participate in the determination of policies and procedures governing salary increases.

The chairman or head of a department, who serves as the chief representative of his department within an institution, should be selected either by departmental election or by appointment following consultation with members of the department and of related departments; appointments should normally be in conformity with department members' judgment. The chairman or department head should not have tenure in his office; his tenure as a faculty member is a matter of separate right. He should serve for a stated term but without prejudice to re-election or to reappointment by procedures which involve appropriate faculty consultation. Board, administration, and faculty should all bear in mind that the department chairman has a special obligation to build a department strong in scholarship and teaching capacity.

Agencies for faculty participation in the government of the college or university should be established at each level where faculty responsibility is present. An agency should exist for the presentation of the views of the whole faculty. The structure and procedures for faculty participation should be designed, approved and established by joint action of the components of the institution. Faculty representatives should be selected by the faculty according to procedures determined by the faculty.

The agencies may consist of meetings of all faculty members of a department, school, college, division or university system, or may take the form of faculty-elected executive committees in departments and schools and a faculty-elected senate or council for larger divisions or the institution as a whole.

Among the means of communication among the faculty, administration, and governing board now in use are: (1) circulation of memoranda and reports by board committees, the administration, and faculty committees, (2) joint *ad hoc* committees, (3) standing liaison committees, (4) membership of faculty members on administrative bodies, and (5) membership of faculty members on governing boards. Whatever the channels of communication, they should be clearly understood and observed.

ON STUDENT STATUS

When students in American colleges and universities desire to participate responsibly in the government of the institution they attend, their wish should be recognized as a claim to opportunity both for educational experience and for involvement in the affairs of their college or university. Ways should be found to permit significant student participation within the limits of attainable effectiveness. The obstacles to such participation are large and should not be minimized: inexperience, untested capacity, a transitory status which means that present action does not carry with it subsequent responsibility, and the inescapable fact that the other components of the institution are in a position of judgment over the students. It is important to recognize that student needs are strongly related to educational experience, both formal and informal. Students expect, and have a right to expect, that the educational process will be structured, that they will be stimulated by it to become independent adults, and that they will have effectively transmitted to them the cultural heritage of the larger society. If institutional support is to have its fullest possible meaning it should incorporate the strength, freshness of view and idealism of the student body.

The respect of students for their college or university can be enhanced if they are given at least these opportunities: (1) to be listened to in the classroom without fear of institutional reprisal for the substance of their views, (2) freedom to discuss questions of institutional policy and operation, (3) the right to academic due process when charged with serious violations of institutional regulations, and (4) the same right to hear speakers of their own choice as is enjoyed by other components of the institution.

TABLE 1, REPORT OF THE SURVEY SUBCOMMITTEE OF COMMITTEE T

(as published in the *AAUP Bulletin*, Spring 1971, p. 69)[1]

Decisions Relative to	Forms of Faculty Participation				
	Determination	Joint Action	Consultation	Discussion	None
1 Appointments	4.3	25.1	28.1	29.5	13.1
2 Reappointments or Nonrenewal	4.3	20.9	29.8	25.5	19.6
3 Promotions	4.9	26.4	30.8	18.9	19.1
4 Tenure	5.4	29.0	29.1	16.4	20.1
5 Dismissal for Cause	4.9	29.5	32.3	12.4	20.8
6 Curriculum	41.1	38.7	12.9	6.0	1.3
7 Degree Requirements	43.4	35.1	11.9	6.2	3.5
8 Academic Performance of Students	85.9	8.7	2.9	1.8	0.7
9 Types of Degrees Offered	18.6	49.5	15.7	8.0	8.2
10 Establish . . . New Educational . . . Programs	14.2	51.4	18.2	10.9	5.4
11 Admission Requirements	14.7	27.5	18.0	16.0	23.8
12 Relative Staff Sizes of . . . Disciplines	1.3	9.5	19.7	30.2	39.3
13 Programs for Buildings . . . Facilities	0.4	7.3	28.4	38.3	25.6
14 President	0.4	9.2	36.7	20.4	33.3
15 Academic Deans	0.5	12.2	32.4	24.0	31.0
16 Department Chairmen	6.8	15.7	26.6	24.9	25.9
17 Faculty Salary Scales	0.4	10.4	24.0	18.8	46.4
18 Individual Faculty Salaries	1.0	8.4	14.9	25.7	50.0
19 Short Range Budgetary Planning (1-3 Yr.)	0.6	4.7	22.8	29.2	42.8
20 Long Range Budgetary Planning	0.3	2.6	16.4	25.8	54.9
21 Average Teaching Loads	4.1	21.2	22.3	29.6	22.8
22 Teaching Assignments	13.9	49.6	14.2	17.0	5.2
23 Specification . . . Department Committees	41.0	24.8	12.2	10.9	11.0
24 Membership Departmental Committees	47.1	21.2	9.8	10.9	11.1
25 Authority of Faculty in Government	9.8	36.9	27.5	7.2	18.6
26 Specification . . . Senate Committees	21.0	35.5	17.8	10.1	15.6
27 Membership . . . Senate Committees	32.2	28.2	14.1	9.3	16.2
28 Academic Discipline	26.0	35.9	17.4	10.5	10.3
29 Specification Student Extracurricular Rules	5.0	25.0	22.3	20.4	27.3
30 Extracurricular Behavior	3.9	25.6	21.4	18.1	31.0
31 Student Role in Institutional Government	15.2	32.8	21.6	15.5	14.8

[1] Table 1 shows the average reply at each level of participation for each question. This is an institutional average rather than a weighted faculty average, each institution having been weighted equally. Where there were two replies from a given institution, chapter and administration, each was given a weight of one half. On the average, the median response to each question, shown by the moving line in Table 1, is slightly below the level of CONSULTATION, but with considerable variation from question to question.

DRAFT STATEMENT ON STUDENT PARTICIPATION IN COLLEGE AND UNIVERSITY GOVERNMENT

(as published in the *AAUP Bulletin*, March 1970)

The 1966 Statement on Government of Colleges and Universities [1] *refers to students as "an institutional component coordinate in importance with trustees, administrators, and faculty," notes that "students do not in fact presently have a significant voice in the government of colleges and universities," and expresses the hope that the educational community will "turn its attention to an important need."*

The Statement which appears below has been prepared by Committee T on College and University Government, and has been approved by the Committee and the Association's Council for publication in the AAUP Bulletin. *The Association elicits reactions from its members, chapters, and conferences, as well as other interested parties, for this version is only a provisional approach to a complex subject.*

Comments should be directed to the Association's Washington office. At an early date, it is hoped, joint discussion of the topic will be undertaken with representatives of other educational organizations.

INTRODUCTION

The purpose of this Statement is to define the principles and identify several appropriate areas of student participation in

---

[1] Jointly formulated by the American Association of University Professors, the American Council on Education, and the Association of Governing Boards of Universities and Colleges. The AAUP approved the Statement at its Fifty-third Annual Meeting in April, 1967; the ACE and AGB have commended it to their member institutions and boards.

Other statements deal with the protections due the individual student or faculty member: the 1940 *Statement of Principles on Academic Freedom and Tenure,* the 1958 *Statement on Procedural Standards in Faculty Dismissal Proceedings* (the basic policy statements, formulated and adopted by the American Association of University Professors and the Association of American Colleges, relating to academic freedom, tenure, and academic due process); the 1968 *Joint Statement on Rights and Freedoms of Students,* approved by the American Association of University Professors, U.S. National Student Association, Association of American Colleges, National Association of Student Personnel Administrators, and National Association of Women Deans and Counselors.

the government of colleges and universities. The Statement itself is based on the premise that students as members of the academic community, in addition to their rights as set forth in the *Joint Statement on Rights and Freedoms of Students,* have a distinctive role which, in respects stated below, qualifies them to share in the exercise of responsible authority on campus; the exercise of that authority is part of their education. Furthermore, there is a greater likelihood of responsible student involvement when students participate in institutional decisions through orderly processes and to the degree appropriate in particular circumstances.

Most importantly, joint effort among all groups in the institution – students, faculty, administration, and governing board – is a prerequisite of sound academic government. A further prerequisite is that all must see themselves as custodians of academic freedom. Like any other group, students should have a voice, sometimes the predominant voice, in decisions which affect them, and their opinions should be regularly solicited even in those areas in which they hold a secondary interest. But academic government depends on more than the accommodation of diverse interests. Joint effort, to be effective, must be rooted in the concept of shared authority. The exercise of shared authority in college and university government, like the protection of academic freedom, requires tolerance, respect, and a sense of community which arises from participation in a common enterprise. The exact mode and extent of student participation depend on conditions which vary from one institution to another, but whatever the area of participation or the form it assumes, the need for cooperation among all groups is inescapable.

STUDENT PARTICIPATION IN ACADEMIC AFFAIRS

The rights of students to free inquiry and expression in the classroom and in conference is asserted in the *Joint Statement on Rights and Freedoms of Students.* Students also have a stake in the quality of their formal education, which must take into account their needs and desires. The categories which follow are those in which student involvement is commonly found; they are not intended to exclude other areas of involvement, which might be developed where there is sufficient student interest. It is for the particular institution to determine the mode and extent of student involvement and the criteria of eligibility for that involvement.

A. Admissions

Students have a stake in the size, composition, and quality of the student body, and should have their views on admissions heard along with those of faculty and administration. Similarly, graduate students should be able to participate constructively in decisions regarding the admissions policy of their respective departments.

B. Academic Programs

Students should be consulted in decisions regarding the development of already-existing programs and the establishment of new programs. As members of the academic community they should have the opportunity for similar involvement with respect to course load and degree requirements. For example, they may submit reports to the administration or the appropriate faculty or departmental committees through their own curriculum committees, or through membership in joint curriculum committees. When provision is made for an experimental student-operated curriculum, students should have primary responsibility for decision-making.[2] When provision is made for student participation in curricular decisions, criteria for eligibility should be devised jointly by faculty and students.

C. Academic Courses and Staff

Students should have the opportunity, through established institutional mechanisms, to assess the value of a course to them, and to make suggestions as to its direction. Students should also be able to express their views on the form and conduct of a class which they have taken, for example through an evaluative questionnaire prepared by joint faculty-student effort, and their opinions should be weighed in faculty decisions affecting faculty status. The faculty member, of course,

---

[2] By "primary responsibility" is meant the ability to take action which has the force of legislation and can be overruled only in rare instances and for compelling reasons stated in detail.

should be duly protected from capricious and uninformed judgment by students, just as he should be from such judgment by anyone else.

D. Academic Evaluation

The method by which students are evaluated is properly of concern to them. Accordingly, students should be heard with respect to the grading system at an institution. They should also have clearly established means of recourse against prejudiced or capricious grading.

E. Academic Environment

The scheduling of courses, class size, distribution of night and day classes, calendar arrangements, library policy and development, and similar academic arrangements and services affect the ability of students to do academic work. They should share in the formation of policies on these matters.

STUDENT PARTICIPATION IN OTHER INSTITUTIONAL AFFAIRS

A. Extracurricular Activities

Students should have primary responsibility for activities sponsored by the student body. Other appropriate persons and groups should be able to discuss such activities and be consulted with respect to them. Among these activities are cultural programs sponsored by the student body, student political affairs, and student publications; the intellectual vitality and academic freedom of the student body will be insured in such activities by adequate representation of student taste and opinion.

B. Student Regulations

Students should have primary responsibility for the formulation of clear and readily available regulations pertaining to their personal lives, subject only to such restrictions as may be imposed by law.

C. Student Discipline

Students should have the opportunity to participate in establishing standards and procedures which govern student discipline, and take part also in the actual disciplinary process. Disciplinary proceedings should be in accordance with the provisions of the *Joint Statement on Rights and Freedoms of Students*.

D. Other Institutional Concerns

Students have a right to be heard, through formal means, on questions involving an institution's budget, its physical resources, and its relationship with groups or agencies external to the campus. Provisions should exist for the transmission of student views on such matters to the faculty, president, and governing board.

IMPLEMENTATION

The implementation of the above principles is properly subject to innumerable local variations. On students themselves falls the difficult task of assuring that the diversity of student interests and opinions is adequately represented. All individuals and groups at an institution should support the development of appropriate forms of student participation by assuring that organizations purporting to represent student interests possess a mandate from a clearly defined electorate, are accountable to that electorate, and function through orderly procedures agreed upon through joint action by students and the other members of the academic community. Student representatives, like other representatives in any area of university government, should be free to vote according to their best judgment. At all times, students should enjoy protection from the exercise of tyranny by a majority or a minority, the right to petition for and be granted an open hearing on a question of student rights or student participation, and the right of access – both to information on institutional government and to grievance procedures for complaints relating to their life in and out of the classroom.

Limits on participation by students may be dictated in some instances, such as those in which a violation of law or of confidentiality might result. Where any limitation exists, the student should have the right to challenge it in a manner consistent with legality and the principles of academic freedom. All forms of participation in the government of the institution should be so devised as to preserve the academic freedom to which all groups are equally entitled.

Student involvement in institutional government may include membership – voting and nonvoting – on departmental committees, on college or division councils and committees, or on the university senate or any other principal legislative body and its committees. Where they do not hold membership on these bodies, students should be able to place matters for action on their agendas and to receive a prompt report on the disposition of those matters. Student opinion should also be consulted, where feasible, in the selection of presidents, chief academic and nonacademic administrative officers including the dean of students, and faculty. Sometimes separate and parallel student structures are desired in place of or in addition to mixed bodies. Where this is the case, care should be taken to guarantee that the student bodies not function merely as subordinate entities subject to arbitrary veto by faculty or administrative groups, and that all groups enjoy meaningful channels of appeal. The procedure for election or appointment of students to duly constituted instruments of student participation should be developed in consultation with all directly concerned persons and groups. It should be made available as information to the entire campus community, and be reviewed periodically.

Meaningful participation in college and university government is not guaranteed merely by the presence of students on committees; in some cases, indeed, this may inhibit free student expression. Such expression may well play an important role in institutional affairs through the campus newspaper, published evaluations of courses, or discussion programs on the state of the institutions which bring different constituencies together. In any case, the informal exchange of opinion, like the formal participation in the processes of institutional government, should involve students, faculty, administration, and governing board in a continuing joint effort.

CONSTITUTION AND BY-LAWS FOR THE
FACULTY OF THE GRADUATE SCHOOL
(Tulane University, 1969)

Article I. Membership

The members of the Faculty of the Graduate School shall be: The President, the Vice-Presidents, the Provost, and the Director of Libraries of the University; the Dean of the Graduate School and the Deans of those Schools or Colleges of the University that participate in programs offered through the Graduate School; and those members of the faculties of such Schools or Colleges who are elected according to the By-laws.

Article II. Meetings

1. There shall be two regular meetings each year, one in the Fall semester and one in May.
2. Special meetings shall be called by the Dean on his own initiative or on the request of the Graduate Council or on petition signed by at least 20 members of the Faculty of the Graduate School.
3. One week's notice of every meeting shall be sent to each member of the Faculty of the Graduate School.
4. The Dean or his appointee shall preside at meetings of the Faculty of the Graduate School.

Article III. Functions

The Faculty of the Graduate School may consider any question germane to the organization, conduct or policies of the Graduate School provided that before final action is taken such question shall be referred to the Graduate Council for its recommendation, but a negative opinion or failure to respond on the part of the Graduate Council shall not preclude Faculty action. By a two-thirds majority of members present and voting at a meeting of the Faculty of the Graduate School at which a quorum is present, the Faculty may take action without referral to the Graduate Council.

Specifically, the Faculty of the Graduate School shall:

1. Make recommendations for adding or dropping of degree programs offered through the Graduate School;
2. Formulate policies for the admission and retention of graduate students; and for residence, credit, and other academic requirements for degrees awarded by the Graduate School;
3. Approve the list of candidates to be recommended for degrees awarded by the Graduate School at any University Commencement, provided that this authority may be delegated to the Graduate Council at specific times;
4. Elect representatives to the University Senate, to the Senate Committee on Academic Freedom, Tenure, and Responsibilities, and to other bodies requiring representation of the Faculty of the Graduate School;
5. Take action on such other matters as are germane to the organization, conduct or policies of the Graduate School.

Article IV. Graduate Council

1. Members of the Graduate Council shall be the Dean of the Graduate School, and nine members elected by the Faculty of the Graduate School for terms of three years. Six members shall be elected from subject-matter areas and three shall be elected at-large. The subject-matter areas shall be: Biological Sciences, Engineering, Humanities, Medical Sciences, Physical Sciences, and Social Studies. Two members from subject-matter areas shall be elected each year. Of the three Council members-at-large, each shall be elected to be the Chairman of one of the three Standing Committees of the Council provided for in this Constitution. One member-at-large shall be elected each year.
2. The Graduate Council shall:
   a. Advise the Dean and the Faculty of the Graduate School concerning all major policy questions affecting the Graduate School;
   b. Serve as an Executive Committee to advise and assist the Dean in the administration of the Graduate School;
   c. Elect members to the Faculty of the Graduate School in accordance with this Constitution and By-Laws;

d. Act as a nominating committee in accordance with these By-laws;

e. Approve the list of candidates to be recommended for degrees awarded by the Graduate School when so authorized by the Faculty of the Graduate School.

3. The elected members of the Graduate Council shall represent the Faculty of the Graduate School in advising the President of the University upon the appointment of a Dean of the Graduate School when a vacancy occurs.

4. The Graduate Council shall report to the Faculty of the Graduate School annually on its major activities.

5. There shall be a regular meeting of the Graduate Council each month of the academic year, and such special meetings as may be called by the Dean or by any four Council members.

6. There shall be the following Standing Committees of the Graduate Council:

a. Admission and Financial Aid. This Committee shall make recommendations to the Graduate Council concerning the adoption and change of policies of admission, of granting financial aid to students, and of the conditions under which Departments use graduate students as teaching assistants.

b. Academic Performance. This Committee shall make recommendation concerning the grading system; it shall recommend policy on separation of students from the Graduate School and on the readmission of former students; it shall recommend to the Graduate Council the admission of candidates for degrees; it shall consider appeals from decisions concerning separation or readmission; and it shall review Departmental petitions for relief of individual students from the language requirements.

c. Curriculum. This Committee shall make recommendations concerning programs of study and requirements for degrees; it shall approve new courses to be offered in the Graduate School; and it shall have authority to require justification of retention of courses offered in the Graduate School.

7. The Chairman of each Standing Committee shall be that member-at-large of the Graduate Council elected to be Chairman. The members of each Standing Committee

shall be appointed by the Graduate Council from the Faculty, but there shall be at least one member from each of the subject-matter areas on each Committee.

8. Standing Committees shall meet at the call of their Chairman or at the call of the Graduate Council.
9. Special Committees may be appointed by the Graduate Council.
10. All Standing Committees and Special Committees appointed by the Graduate Council shall be responsible to the Council.

Article V. Student Participation

1. The graduate student body of each department or program offering courses leading to a degree through the Graduate School shall elect from its full-time membership at least one and as many as three representatives to serve in the capacities described below. If as many as three students are elected, one of the three representatives shall be a first-year graduate student. These student representatives shall work with the department's or program's faculty in order to facilitate discussion of problems concerning students. The student representatives shall also meet with the student representatives of the other departments or programs in their subject-matter field, under the chairmanship of the subject-matter field's faculty member of the Graduate Council, to discuss matters of common interest.

2. a. Six students serve as non-voting associates of the Graduate Faculty, one from each subject-matter field of the Graduate Faculty.
   b. The student member from each subject-matter field shall be elected annually by the departmental or program student representatives of the subject-matter field from among their own group, meeting for the purposes of the election under the chairmanship of the subject-matter field's faculty member on the Graduate Council.
   c. Each student member shall serve a one-year term as a non-voting associate of the Graduate Faculty, but may be reelected for one consecutive term.

Article VI. Amendments

This Constitution may be amended by two-thirds of those members present and voting at a meeting of the Faculty of the Graduate School at which a quorum is present, provided that at a previous meeting the proposed amendment has been approved by a majority vote and referred to the Graduate Council for its consideration.

BY-LAWS FOR THE FACULTY OF THE
GRADUATE SCHOOL

By-law I. Meetings

1. One-fourth of the membership of the Faculty of the Graduate School shall constitute a quorum for the conduct of business at all regular or special meetings of the Faculty.
2. Seven members of the Graduate Council shall constitute a quorum for the conduct of business at all regular or special meetings of the Council. The Dean of the Graduate School or a member of the Graduate Council whom he shall appoint shall preside at meetings of the Council.
3. Meetings of the Faculty of the Graduate School shall be conducted according to Robert's Rules of Order Revised except when provided otherwise in this Constitution or By-laws.

By-law II. Membership of Faculty

1. Members of the constituent faculties shall be elected to the Faculty of the Graduate School by the Graduate Council subject to the following conditions:
   a. The candidate for membership should regularly teach yearly at least one one-semester course yielding credit toward a degree granted by the Graduate School or should participate substantially in the Graduate program in his Department.
   b. He should have had some experience as a member of thesis, project or dissertation committees.
   c. He must give evidence of research competence (or of artistic creativity in suitable Departments). The evidence adduced may be publications, papers delivered

before learned societies, works of art or other scholarly or artistic accomplishment.

d. He shall be nominated by the members of the Faculty of the Graduate School in his Department, and the nomination approved by the Dean of the School or College of his major appointment.

e. He shall hold the same rank in the Faculty of the Graduate School as he holds in his major appointment.

2. If a person who is not a member of the Faculty of the Graduate School teaches a course yielding credit toward a degree granted by the Graduate School for at least one semester per year for two consecutive years, he shall be considered by the Graduate Council for membership in the Faculty of the Graduate School without nomination. If he is not elected to membership at that time, the Curriculum Committee, after consultation with the Dean and the Department Chairman involved, may consider and make a recommendation to the Graduate Council concerning the suitability of continuing the course he teaches.

By-law III. Membership of Council

1. Nominees for the Graduate Council from subject-matter fields

   a. Shall be nominated by a committee appointed by the Dean for that purpose from the faculty of the subject-matter field and chaired by the retiring Council member from that field.

   b. Two names shall be put in nomination for each election, and each nomination shall be accompanied by a brief *curriculum vitae* describing qualifications for election.

   c. Council members from subject-matter fields shall be elected by written ballot by the graduate faculty of the subject-matter field before the first Fall meeting of the Faculty of the Graduate School. The election shall be conducted by the Nominating Committee from the subject-matter field.

   d. A place must be provided on the ballot for write-in candidates.

2. Nominees at-large for the Graduate Council

   a. Shall be nominated by a committee of three members

chosen by the Dean from a list of five names submitted to him by the Graduate Council for that purpose.

   b. Two names shall be put in nomination for each election, and each nomination shall be accompanied by a brief *curriculum vitae* describing qualifications for election.
   c. Additional nominations may be made from the floor.
   d. Council members at-large shall be elected at the May meeting of the Faculty.

3. No person shall be eligible immediately to succeed himself on the Council.
4. If the place of a member of the Graduate Council becomes vacant before the end of the term for which he was elected, and if the unexpired portion of the term is less than one year, the Council shall make an appointment to fill the unexpired portion of the term; but if the unexpired portion of the term is one year or more, the Faculty shall elect a member to fill the term.

By-law IV. Graduate School Representatives

1. The Faculty of the Graduate School shall elect at its May meeting a representative to the University Senate as the term of the previous representative expires.
   a. The Council shall nominate two persons for each election and each nomination shall be accompanied by a brief *curriculum vitae* describing qualifications for election.
   b. Additional nominations may be made from the floor.
   c. If a vacancy occurs before the end of a term, and the unexpired portion of the term is less than one year, the Council shall make an appointment to fill the unexpired portion of the term; but if the unexpired portion of the term is one year or more, the Faculty shall elect a member to fill the term.
2. The Faculty of the Graduate School shall elect at its May meeting a member of the Senate Committee on Freedom, Tenure, and Responsibilities as the term of the previous member expires.
   a. The Council shall nominate two persons for each election and each nomination shall be accompanied by a brief *curriculum vitae* describing qualifications for election.

b. Additional nominations may be made from the floor.

c. If a vacancy occurs before the end of a term, and the unexpired portion of the term is less than one year, the Council shall make an appointment to fill the unexpired portion of the term; but if the unexpired portion of the term is one year or more, the Faculty shall elect a member to fill the term.

By-law V. Amendments

These By-laws may be amended by a majority vote of those members present and voting at a meeting of the Faculty of the Graduate School at which a quorum is present, provided that at a previous meeting the proposed amendment has been approved by a majority vote and referred to the Graduate Council for its consideration.

BIBLIOGRAPHICAL REFERENCES*

Richard P. Adams, "Faculty Participation in College and University Administration." (Address, Florida Association of Colleges and Universities, April 1968.)

—, "Tulane University: Faculty Participation in the Government of the University," *AAUP Bulletin*, Autumn 1963.

AAUP, *Academic Freedom and Tenure*, Madison, Wisconsin, 1969.

—, "Draft Statement on Student Participation in College and University Government," *AAUP Bulletin*, March 1970.

—, "Joint Statement of Rights and Freedoms of Students," *AAUP Bulletin*, Summer 1968.

—, "Policy on Representation of Economic and Professional Interests," *AAUP Bulletin*, Winter 1969.

—, *Statement on Government of Colleges and Universities*, American Association of University Professors: Washington, D.C., 1966.

W. Donald Bowles, "Student Participation in Academic Governance," *Educational Record*, September 1968.

Ralph S. Brown, "Collective Bargaining in Higher Education," *Michigan Law Review*, March 1969.

—, "Rights and Responsibilities of Faculty," *AAUP Bulletin*, Summer 1966.

McGeorge Bundy, "Faculty Power," *The Atlantic*, September 1968.

John H. Bunzel, "Some Reflections on Student Participation and Representation," *PS*, Spring 1970.

Gerald P. Burns, ed., *Administrators in Higher Education*, New York, 1962.

Theodore Caplow and Reece J. McGee, *The Academic Marketplace*, New York, 1961.

Burton R. Clark, "Faculty Authority," *AAUP Bulletin*, Winter 1961.

—, "The New University," *American Behavioral Scientist*, May-June 1968.

John J. Corson, *Governance of Colleges and Universities*, New York, 1960.

W. B. Cunningham, "Within or Without? – The Location of the Faculty Association," *C.A.U.T. Bulletin*, December 1968.

* Two recent symposia on restructuring university governance came to my attention after completion of the present manuscript. One, as published in the *Journal of Higher Education* of June 1971, featured papers by Stanley T. Ikenberry, John Corson, T. R. McConnell, Kenneth Mortimer, Talcott Parsons, Burton Clark, and Marvin Peterson; the other was edited by H. L. Hodgkinson and L. R. Meeth – *Power and Authority: Transformation of Campus Governance* (San Francisco, 1971). Note also the following symposia on vaious generals campus problems and crises: "Rights and Responsibilities: Ther University' Dilemma," *Daedalus*, Summer 1970; "The Embattled University," *Daedalus*, Winter 1970; G. Kerry Smith, ed., *Agony and Promise* (San Francisco, 1969).

James M. Darlington, "Faculty–Administration Relationships," *AAUP Bulletin*, Autumn 1960.

W. L. Deegan, T. R. McConnell, K. P. Mortimer, and H. Stull, *Joint Participation in Decision Making: A Study of Faculty Government and Faculty-Administrative Consultation at Fresno State College*, Center for Research and Development in Higher Education, University of California: Berkeley, 1970.

— and K. P. Mortimer, *Faculty in Governance at the University of Minnesota*, Center for Research and Development in Higher Education, University of California: Berkeley, 1970.

Nicholas J. Demerath, Richard W. Stephens, and R. Robb Taylor, *Power, Presidents, and Professors*, New York, 1967.

Philip Denenfeld, "Western Michigan University – Faculty Participation in the Government of the University: The Faculty Senate," *AAUP Bulletin*, Winter 1966.

Harold W. Dodds, *The Academic President – Educator or Caretaker?*, New York, 1962.

Paul L. Dressel, F. Craig Johnson, and Philip M. Marcus, *The Confidence Crisis*, San Francisco, 1970.

James Duff and Robert O. Berdahl, *University Government in Canada*, Toronto, 1966.

Troy Duster, "Student Interests, Student Power, and the Swedish Experience," *American Behavioral Scientist*, May-June 1968.

Archie R. Dykes, *Faculty Participation in Academic Decision Making*, American Council on Education: Washington, D.C., 1968.

H. Eulau and H. Quinley, *State Officials and Higher Education*, New York, 1970.

"Faculty – Administration Relationships: The School of Medicine at The University of Miami (Florida)," *AAUP Bulletin*, Spring 1961.

Faculty Participation in Academic Governance, American Association for Higher Education: Washington, D.C., 1967.

Matthew W. Finkin, "Collective Bargaining and University Government," *AAUP Bulletin*, Summer 1971.

Caleb Foote and Henry Mayer, *The Culture of the University: Governance and Education*, San Francisco, 1968.

Julian F.S. Foster, "A Political Model for the University," *Educational Record*, Fall 1968.

Edward Gross, "Universities as Organizations: A Research Approach," *American Sociological Review*, August 1968.

— and Paul V. Grambsch, *University Goals and Academic Power*, American Council on Education: Washington, D.C., 1968.

J. Habermas, *Protestbewegung und Hochschulreform*, Frankfurt am Main: Suhrkamp Verlag, 1969.

Dexter L. Hanley, S.J., "Issues and Models for Collective Bargaining in Higher Education," *Liberal Education*, March 1971.

Joseph G. Herzberg, "Goheen Suggests Dual Leadership," *The New York Times*, December 26, 1968.

C. Addison Hickman, "Faculty Participation in Academic Governance," *Proceedings*, 2nd Minnesota Intercollegiate Faculty Conference, March 1968.

Winston W. Hill and Wendell L. French, "Perceptions of the Power of

Department Chairmen by Professors," *Administrative Science Quarterly*, March 1967.

Mark H. Ingraham, *The Mirror of Brass*, Madison, Wisconsin, 1968.

Christopher Jencks and David Riesman, *The Academic Revolution*, New York, 1968.

Louis Joughin, "The Role of the Student in College and University Government." (Address, California State College at Los Angeles, May 1968.)

Sanford H. Kadish, "The Strike and the Professoriate," *AAUP Bulletin*, Summer 1968.

Gladys M. Kammerer, "The State University as a Political System," *Journal of Politics*, May 1969.

Morris Keeton, *Shared Authority on Campus*, American Association for Higher Education: Washington, D.C., 1971.

Clark Kerr, *The Uses of the University*, Cambridge, Mass., 1964.

Frederick S. Lane, *A Study in Role Conflict: The Department Chairman in Decisions on Academic Tenure*, University of Florida, Studies in Public Administration No. 29, 1967.

Paul F. Lazarsfeld and Wagner Thielens, Jr., *The Academic Mind*, Glencoe, Ill., 1958.

Terry F. Lunsford, "Authority and Ideology in the Administered University," *American Behavioral Scientist*, May-June 1968.

T. R. McConnell and Kenneth P. Mortimer, *The Faculty in University Governance*, Center for Research and Development in Higher Education, University of California: Berkeley, 1971.

Robert M. MacIver, *Academic Freedom in Our Time*, New York, 1955.

John D. Millett, *The Academic Community: An Essay on Organization*, New York, 1962.

Glenn R. Morrow, "The University of Pennsylvania – Faculty Participation in the Government of the University," *AAUP Bulletin*, Winter 1962.

Kenneth P. Mortimer, *Academic Government at Berkeley: The Academic Senate*, Center for Research and Development in Higher Education, University of California: Berkeley, 1970.

E. Nolte, *Deutsche Universitäten 1969*, Marburg, 1970.

Walter Oberer, "Faculty Participation in Academic Decision Making," in S. Elam and M. H. Moskow, eds., *Employment Relations in Higher Education*, Bloomington, 1969.

Morton A. Rauh, "The Trustees of Higher Education," *AGB Reports*, January 1968.

Francis E. Rourke and Glenn E. Brooks, *The Managerial Revolution in Higher Education*, Baltimore, 1966.

Richard H. Shryock, ed., *The Status of University Teachers*, Ghent, 1961.

Martin Trow, "Conceptions of the University: The Case of Berkeley," *American Behavioral Scientist*, May-June 1968.

Logan Wilson, *The Academic Man*, New York, 1964.

—, "Changing University Governance," *Educational Record*, Fall 1969.

INDEX OF NAMES

Adams, Richard P., 55, 57, 68, 69
Anderson, Stanley V., 158
Barber, B., 46
Berdahl, Robert O., 26, 27, 29, 30, 31, 63, 64, 67, 68, 69, 70, 71, 72, 73, 74, 75, 76, 77, 78, 80
Bowles, W. Donald, 87
Brewster, Kingman, Jr., 64
Brooks, Glenn E., 35, 42, 44, 45, 51, 52, 66, 67, 82
Brown, Ralph, Jr., 15, 22, 23, 55
Bundy, McGeorge, 25, 27, 82
Bunzel, John H., 89
Burns, Gerald P., 3
Campbell, Ralph N., 19, 48
Caplow, Theodore, 18, 19, 59, 79, 81
Clark, Burton R., 1, 2, 4, 5, 6, 15, 16, 17, 34, 35, 49, 50, 60, 77, 89
Corson, John, 1, 2, 4, 14, 17, 25, 26, 28, 36, 37, 38, 41, 43, 49, 59, 60, 64, 78, 79, 80, 81, 88
Cunningham, W. B., 68
Darlington, James M., 47, 56, 60
Deegan, W. L., XI, 36, 42, 43, 71
Demerath, Nicholas J., 3, 5, 6, 10, 11, 38, 39, 46, 47, 48, 68, 78
Denenfeld, Philip, 58, 73
Dodds, Harold W., 55, 56, 59, 60, 61, 65
Dressel, Paul L., 17, 51, 62, 80, 81, 87
Duff, James, 26, 27, 29, 30, 31, 63, 64, 67, 68, 69, 70, 71, 72, 73, 74, 75, 76, 77, 78, 80
Duster, Troy, 16, 55, 88
Dykes, Archie R., 7, 45, 46, 59, 61, 65, 66, 78
Elam, S., 23
Enarson, Harold, 3
Eulau, H., 67
Finkin, Matthew, 21, 22, 23, 90
Foote, Caleb, 9

French, Wendell L., 80
Goheen, Robert F., 40
Grambsch, Paul V., 45
Gross, Edward, 45
Habermas, J., IX
Hanley, Dexter L., S.J., 23
Herzberg, Joseph G., 40
Hickman, C. Addison, 34, 67, 82
Hill, Winston L., 80
Ingraham, Mark, 40, 88
Jencks, Christopher, 19
Johnson, F. Craig, 17
Joughin, Louis, XII, 83, 84, 89
Kadish, Sanford, XIII, 44, 56
Kammerer, Gladys, X, XI
Keeton, Morris, 17, 89
Kerr, Clark, 9, 10, 12, 13, 15, 41, 90
Kimpton, Lawrence A., 42
Lane, Frederick S., 80
Lazarsfeld, Paul F., 15, 46, 48
Lunsford, Terry F., 16, 52, 53, 54, 70, 71
MacIver, Robert, 30, 31
Marcus, Philip M., 17
Mayer, Henry, 9
McConnell, T. R., XI, 16, 31, 36, 41, 50, 51, 52, 61, 62, 75, 109, 122, 149
McGee, Reece J., 18, 19, 59, 79, 81
Meyerson, Martin, 75
Michels, R., 62
Millett, John D., XII, 2, 3, 4, 5, 6, 11, 12, 25, 33, 34, 86
Morrow, Glenn, 27, 57
Mortimer, Kenneth P., XI, 16, 31, 36, 41, 50, 51, 52, 61, 62, 65, 75, 109, 122, 149
Moskow, M. H., 23
Nolte, E., IX
Oberer, Walter, 22, 23
Patridge, P. H., 34, 35
Quinley, H., 67

Rauh, Morton A., 30
Riesman, David, 19
Rourke, Francis E., 35, 42, 44, 45, 51, 52, 66, 67, 82
Shryock, Richard H., 48, 57
Singer, J. David, 33
Stephens, Richard W., 3

Stull, H., XI
Taylor, R. Robb, 3
Thielens, Wagner, Jr., 15, 48
Trow, Martin, 16, 45, 50, 77, 82, 88, 89
Wilson, Logan, XI, 3, 60, 61

INDEX OF SUBJECTS

AAUP, attitude on collective bargaining, 23–5; roles for local chapter, 68–70; Statement on Government of Colleges and Universities, *see* Statement on Government of Colleges and Universities

Adelphi University, 24

Administration, "bloc-voting" on senates, 74; conflicts of jurisdiction with faculty, 104–5; faculty participation in selection of, 97, 127–8, 178; functions, 33–4, 97–9; importance of senate membership, 73–5, 138; irritants to faculty, 47–8, 51; isolation and frustrations, 53–5; "persuade or perish," 35–6, 64; structure, 6, 41–2, 95–6

American Council on Education (ACE), XII

American Federation of Teachers (AFT), 24, 135

Association of Governing Boards of Universities and Colleges (AGB), XII

Berkeley Study Commission on University Governance (Foote-Mayer Commission), 8–9, 11, 15–6, 18, 58–9, 76–8, 81, 83–8

Board of trustees, committees, 93; composition and selection, 29–32, 91–2, 178; faculty representation, 30–2, 93–4, 178; financial controls, 28–9; functions and limits of powers, 25–8, 94–5, 176–7; joint committees with other components, 32, 178; models of board behavior, 28; representative of outside world, 26, 29; review of general faculty assembly actions, 119; review of senate actions, 132–4, 184; student representation, 93–4, 178

Boston State College, 21

Brock University (Canada), 7, 32, 36, 40, 43

Bryant College of Business Administration (Rhode Island), 21

Budget questions, *see* Financial questions

Bureaucratic authority, principle of academic authority, 5

California, University of, 67

California, University of (Berkeley), XI, 8–9, 12, 15–6, 41, 62, 65, 75, 82, 122, 149, 158

Cambridge University (England), 26

Central Michigan University, 21

Chairman, and "head," 166; as faculty member, 79–80; functions, 80, 167–8; limited term, 80, 165–7; limits of power, 168–9, 196; selection, 79–80, 165–7, 195–6

Chicago, University of, 42

City University of New York (CUNY), 21–2, 24

Colleague authority, principle of academic authority, 5

Collective bargaining, and faculty participation in university government, IX, 20–3; and professional status of faculty, 19–20; attitude of AAUP, 23–5; attitude of National Labor Relations Board, 24–5; composition of bargaining unit, 22; examples in colleges and universities, 21; position of departmental chairman, 22; rival faculty organizations, 24; senates as agents, 134–5

College, committees, 162–3, 194; faculty assembly, 161–2, 194;functions and jurisdiction, 159–161, 193–4

Collegialization, principle of academic decision-making, 5–6, 46–7

Columbia University, 15, 32, 72, 91–2, 106–8, 137, 144, 146, 148, 155–6, 158

Committees, *see* College, Department, General faculty assembly, or Senate

Conflict-reducing mechanisms, *see* Shared authority

Constitutional documents, adoption, 171–2, 198; amendment, 172–4, 198–9; written and unwritten, 175

Consultation, definition and importance, 13, 52, 70–1, 104

Culture of the university, and governance, 8–9

Dean (academic), crucial role, 42–3; functions, 161–2; limited term, 43, 161

Dean of students, status, 88

Decentralization, of decision-making, 2, 15–6, 76–7

Department, as academic decision-making unit, 78, 164–5; chairman, *see* Chairman; committees, 170–1, 196; effective size, 78–9, 99; functions and jurisdiction, 164–5, 168–9, 194–5; importance for student participation, 87, 171, 196; importance to faculty member, 77–8, 81; internal conflict, 81; meetings, 169; membership, 165, 195; voting procedures, 169–70

Divisional units, 171

Duke University Commission on University Governance, 28–9, 31–2, 40, 42–3, 93

East Carolina University, 109

Eastern Michigan University, 24

Faculty, conflicts of jurisdiction with administration, 104–5; conservative-liberal paradox, 9–10; definition of faculty authority, 101–6, 179; definition of faculty status, 99; Faculty Association, 67–8, 100–1; general faculty assembly, *see* General faculty assembly; irritants to administration, 48–9, 61; need for faculty's "civil service," 66; non-tenured faculty representation, 72; oligarchs' role, 50, 61–2; participation in selection of administration, 97, 127–8, 178; "party" divisions, 10–11, 36, 69; reasons for participation in governance, 2, 55–6; reluctance to participate in governance, 57–61; representation on board of trustees, 93–4, 178; representation on system-wide level, 110–13, 179–80; structures for faculty participation, 99–101

Faculty meeting, *see* General faculty assembly

Financial questions, budget committee, 127, 154–6, 191; budget debate in senate, 75–6; interrelatedness with academic questions, 7, 32

Florida, University of, 80

Foote-Mayer Commission, *see* Berkeley Study Commission on University Governance

Fordham University, 24

Fresno State College, XI, 36

General faculty assembly, committees, 123–8; functions and jurisdiction, 115–7, 180–1; meetings, 121–2, 182; membership, 119–20,

181–2; officers, 120–1, 182; publicness, 123, 183; quorum, 122, 183; review by president and board of trustees, 119, 181; review of senate actions, 117–9, 134, 181; secretary, 120–1; 182, voting procedures, 122–3, 183

Governance (academic), and political science, X–XI; complexity, 17; dependence on quality of educational effort, 8; inappropriateness of outside political analogies, 18

Graduate faculty, 163–4, 218–225

Hierarchical organization, inappropriateness in university, 1; quasi-hierarchical features in university, 2–4

Interest group politics, inappropriateness in university, 11

Kerr, Clark, exercise of presidential leadership, 41

Long Island University Brooklyn Center, 21

Macomb County Community College (Michigan), 135

Miami (Florida), University of, 57

Michigan, University of, 33

Minnesota, University of, XI

Monmouth College (New Jersey), 21

Nassau Community College (New York), 134

National Education Association (NEA), 24

National Labor Relations Board, position on collective bargaining in universities, 24–5

Newark College of Engineering, 21

New Haven, University of, 24

New Jersey State Colleges, 21

New York Institute of Technology, 21

North Carolina, University of (Chapel Hill), 11, 68, 78

Oakland University (Michigan), 21, 24

Oligarchs, see Faculty

Ombudsman, in universities, 158

One-tier system, 7, 32–3, 93

Oxford University (England), 26

Pennsylvania, University of, 27, 57

Planning (academic), 2, 63

Policy on Representation of Economic and Professional Interests (AAUP), 23–25

Polytechnic Institute of Brooklyn, 21

Pratt Institute, 21

President, as chairman of general faculty assembly, 120, 182; as chairman of senate, 143–4, 187; Clark Kerr's example of leadership, 41; division of task with chancellor, 40; frustations, 38–40; functions, 37–8, 178; review of general faculty assembly, 119, 181; review of senate, 132–4, 185

Princeton University, 40, 109

Professional school, 81

Proportional representation, in senate, 72

Public trust, principle of academic authority, 4

Representative bodies, see Senate

Rutgers University, 21, 24

Saint John's University (New York), 21, 23–4

San Francisco State College, 89

Scranton, University of, 23

Senate, administration "bloc-voting," 74; agenda, 147–8; as collective bargaining agent, 134–5; attendance by non-members and publicity, 145–7, 189; budget committee, 154–6, 191; budget debate, 75–6; committees, 149–59, 189–93; committee membership qualifications, 125, 158–9; conflicts with colleges and departments, 132–4, 185; decentralization, 76–7; effective size, 71–2; eligibility rules and constituencies, 72, 148–9, 186–7; executive committee, 150–2, 190–1; functions and jurisdiction, 128–35, 183–4; importance of administration membership, 73–5, 138; meetings, 72, 144–5, 188; membership, 135–42, 185–6; "mixed," 73–4, 139, 186; officers, 142–4, 187–8; preference for town meeting, 65; primary decision-making unit, 70; proportional representation, 72; "pure," 73–4, 139, 185; quorum, 145, 188; representation for non-tenured faculty, 72; review by board of trustees, 132–4, 184; review by general faculty assembly, 117–9, 134, 181; review by president, 132–4, 185; secretary, 142–3, 187–8; term of faculty senators, 72; voting procedures, 145, 188–9; weaknesses, 75–6

Shared authority, basic concept, 44, 63; conflict-reducing mechanisms (faculty-administration), 49–50, 105; faculty-administration continuum, 46–7, 52, 63–4; irritants faculty- administration, 47–9, 51–2; pancake analogy, 13; shared growth for administration and faculty, 44–6

Singer, J. David, proposal for university government reform, 33

Southeastern Massachusetts University, 21

State University of New York (SUNY) system, 21, 24, 134

State-wide level, see System-wide level

Statement on Government of Colleges and Universities (AAUP), XII–XIII, 12–13, 25, 27, 41, 44, 63, 65, 80, 102, 107, 200–10 (text)

Student participation, and faculty collective bargaining, 90; "consumer" status, 82; Draft Statement on Student Participation in College and University Government (AAUP), 90, 212–17 (text); 40% rule, 108–9; importance of departmental level, 87, 171, 196; Joint Statement of Rights and Freedoms of Students, 83; numerical strength of representation, 89, 107–9; "omnibus" student affairs committees, 87–8; position of dean of students, 88; "proletarian" status, 82; reasons for, 81–2, 108; relationship to educational process, 83, 85; representation on board of trustees, 93–4, 178; restrictions, 84–6; scope of involvement, 83–4, 196–8; student government and university government, 86–7; "student power," IX, X, 85; student sub-cultures, 89–90; tokenism, 14, 89; voting in committees and senates, 89, 107–9, 136–7, 139

Survey Subcommittee of Committee T (AAUP), 64–5, 211

System-wide level, bureaucratic problems, 67; coordinating mechanisms, 114–15, 180; faculty representation, 66–7, 110–13, 179–80; jurisdiction, 111–13; structures, 109–13

Taylor law (New York), 134

Term, of chairman, 80; of dean, 43; of faculty senators, 72

Tulane University, VII, VIII, 55, 57, 164, 171, 218

Types of academic institutions, 15

Unionization of faculty, see Collective bargaining

United States Merchant Marine Academy, 21

Wayne State University, 24
Western Michigan University, 58, 73
Wisconsin, University of, 158